Thomas Mortimer

The British Plutarch

Vol. II

Thomas Mortimer

The British Plutarch
Vol. II

ISBN/EAN: 9783743401976

Manufactured in Europe, USA, Canada, Australia, Japa

Cover: Foto ©ninafisch / pixelio.de

Manufactured and distributed by brebook publishing software (www.brebook.com)

Thomas Mortimer

The British Plutarch

CONTENTS

OF THE

SECOND VOLUME.

THE Life of Roger Afcham — Page 1
The Life of John Jewel, Bifhop of Salifbury 9
The Life of John Knox — — 18
Matthew Parker, Archbifhop of Canterbury, including Memoirs of George Browne, and of Hugh Corwin, Archbifhops of Dublin — 39
The Life of Sir Thomas Grefham, Merchant and Citizen of London — — — 59
The Life of Robert Dudley, Earl of Leicefter, including Memoirs of Sir Philip Sydney, and Sir Robert Dudley — — — 79
The Life of Sir Francis Walfingham, Secretary of State to Queen Elizabeth — — 115
The Life of Sir John Perrot — — 123
The Life of Sir Francis Drake — — 143
The Life of Sir John Hawkins, including Memoirs of Sir Richard Hawkins, his Son, and of Sir Martin Frobifher — — — 159
The Life of William Cecil, Lord Burleigh, including Memoirs of Sir Nicholas Bacon, Sir Nicholas Throgmorton, and Thomas Howard, Duke of Norfolk — — — 180
The Life of Robert Devereux, Earl of Effex 202

The

CONTENTS.

The Life of Charles Howard, Earl of Nottingham, and Lord High Admiral of England, including an Account of the laſt Illneſs and Death of Queen Elizabeth — — — 234
The Life of George Buchanan — — 252
The Life of Edmund Spenſer — — 262
The Life of William Shakeſpeare — 277
The Life of William Camden, including Memoirs of Sir Thomas Bodley, Founder of the Bodleian Library — — — — 298

Being the moſt eminent perſons, who flouriſhed in the reign of Queen Elizabeth.

THE BRITISH PLUTARCH.

The LIFE of ROGER ASCHAM.

[A. D. 1515, to 1568.]

WE are now entering upon the brightest period of the British history, in any time preceding our own.

A princess endowed with every talent requisite for the art of government, ascended the throne in 1558; and happily found herself surrounded by men of distinguished eminence, equally qualified to serve their country, in every public department of the church and state.

The seeds of true piety, of sound learning, and of civil liberty, which had been sown at the reformation, and had escaped the cruel ravages of popish bigotry during the turbulent reign of Mary, now produced a plentiful harvest of illustrious Englishmen, many of whom were wandering in exile, and suffering all the inconveniences of obscurity and indigence, till this happy revolution restored them to their country and their friends.

Of these, as they contributed to lay the foundation of Elizabeth's future glory, concise memoirs must be given, before we bring upon the carpet, a general review of the important national transactions of this long and prosperous reign; not less celebrated by foreign, than by British historians.

And the first on the list, who merits our grateful remembrance, for the principal share he had in forming the mind, and improving the understanding of our renowned queen, is Roger Ascham, the son of John Ascham, steward to the antient and noble family of Scroop: he was born at Kirkby-Wiske, near Northallerton in Yorkshire, about the year 1515; and in his early youth, was taken into the family of the Wingfields, by Sir Anthony Wingfield, who became his patron, and finding in him an apt disposition for literary attainments, he sent him in the year 1530, to St. John's college, Cambridge, at the critical juncture when the Greek language began to be taught without opposition, in our universities. The doctrines of Luther, promulgated and circulated through all parts of Europe, by means of the rapid progress of the art of printing, had diffused a general inclination throughout the republic of letters, to study the points in controversy between the Romish church, and the celebrated reformer, which could only be done by attaining a competent knowledge of Greek and our young student being one of those

whose

whose mind was fired with generous emulation, applied himself so assiduously to this branch of learning, that he soon became so great a proficient, as to be able to read lectures, and to teach other youth, who were desirous of instruction. " To teach, or to learn, was at this æra the business and the pleasure of the academical life," and young Ascham had the happiness to associate with men of uncommon genius, and of similar dispositions with himself. Sir John Cheeke, who was preceptor to Edward VI. and died in the reign of Mary, of grief, at having recanted his profession, of the reformed religion, was his rival and friend: this gentleman, in conjunction with Sir Thomas Smith, secretary of state in the reigns of Edward VI. and Elizabeth, had introduced a new pronunciation of the Greek tongue, which Mr. Ascham at first opposed, till being convinced they were in the right, he finally adopted and recommended it in his public lectures: a circumstance which served to strengthen the social intimacy that had subsisted between the three students. Mr. Ascham likewise gained the approbation of Dr. Metcalf, the master of his college, who, having the interest of learning greatly at heart, recommended him to a fellowship in 1534, when he was but eighteen years of age. At the same time, Pember, a person of great eminence in the university, and a zealous promoter of the study of the Greek language, took him under his protection, and increased his reputation, not only by applauding his public lectures, but by recommending the young gentlemen of his acquaintance, to attend Mr. Ascham at his chambers, to hear the Greek authors read and explained by him. By the advice of this gentleman, Mr. Ascham, as a relaxation from study, learned to play on musical instruments, and to write a very fine hand, an accomplishment then growing into repute; and he excelled in it, which contributed not a little to his future success in life.

In 1536 he took the degree of master of arts, and soon after, he was appointed by the university, teacher of the Greek language in the public schools, for which he had a genteel salary: he likewise commenced tutor, and had several young students of rank under his care for other branches of education; some of whom proved eminent scholars, particularly William Grindal, recommended by Sir John Cheeke, to be master of languages to the princess Elizabeth.

The reputation of Mr. Ascham, as a man of extensive learning, was so firmly established in the university, that he was elected to the honourable office of public orator, and all the university letters were composed by him: his skill in the Latin language, and his fine writings which he used to embellish with drawings, having recommended him to these employments. But in all ages, and in every country, conspicuous merit, while it meets with its due reward from the liberal mind, will always be exposed to the hatred of the selfish and envious; no wonder therefore, Mr. Ascham should find himself attacked by his enemies, for indulging himself in a manly exercise at his leisure hours. He was particularly fond of archery, and this being an amusement better suited to the soldier than the scholar, he was freely censured for bestowing his time upon it, which gave birth to a vindication of himself, in an excellent little treatise, intitled TOXOPHILUS, or, *the schole or partitions* of shooting, in which he not only commends the art, but lays down rules for teaching in better English than is to be found in any of the writers of that æra: he dedicated this tract to Henry VIII. who was so well pleased with it, that he allowed him an annual pension of ten pounds, a sum equal to one hundred pounds at present. With this pension, and his other appointments in the university, it appears he had a very comfortable income, besides gratuities for teaching persons of the first distinction to write, particularly prince Edward, the princess Elizabeth, and the two brothers, Henry and Charles Brandons, dukes of Suffolk.

Upon the accession of Edward VI. Mr. Ascham's pension was renewed, and he was desired to continue at Cambridge to promote the cause of the reformation, in conjunction with his learned friend Bucer, the celebrated German divine, who had been invited over by the university, to fill the chair of divinity professor. But the death of Grindal brought him to court, to attend the princess Elizabeth, whose studies he directed for two years, by her own appointment; and in this time, she acquired a perfect knowledge of the best Greek and Latin authors, by reading them familiarly with Mr. Ascham. This pleasing task performed, he returned to his former station at the university; and in 1550, being upon a visit in Yorkshire, he received intelligence that he was appointed secretary to Sir Richard Morisine, who was preparing to set out on an embassy to Charles V. emperor of Germany; this promotion obliged him to proceed directly to London, but in his journey he visited Lady Jane Grey, at her father's house at Broadgate in Leicestershire, whom he found reading the Phœdo of Plato in Greek, and he discovered such an uncommon share of learning and good sense in her conversation, that he mentions her in his works, as the wonder of her sex.

Mr. Ascham attended the ambassador to Germany, and remained with him three years, during which time, he cultivated the friendship of the learned

learned in that country, and applied himself to the study of politics, which made him very useful to Sir Richard, whom he assisted in his private studies, and in the public business of his embassy. Yet neither the concerns of his station, nor his assiduity in reading the Greek authors with the ambassador, prevented his keeping up a correspondence with his friends at Cambridge, to whom he wrote several letters, which are still preserved with his other works, and shew him to have been an accurate observer of men and manners; but his abilities as a political writer, likewise appeared, in a curious treatise which he wrote, while he was on an excursion to Italy, it is intitled " A report and discourse of the affairs and state of Germany," and is addressed in the form of a letter to his friend, Mr. John Astley, to whom he gives the clearest account of any writer of those times, of the motives which induced the emperor to resign his crown to his son, and retire from the world: it contains also, a great number of historical and political anecdotes and reflections of a very interesting nature.

While he was thus agreeably employed, his friends at home procured him the post of Latin secretary to the king, but before he could return to take possession of his new dignity, he received the melancholy news of the death of his royal master, by which fatal event he not only lost his place and his pension, but seemed to have lost every prospect of future preferment: however, contrary to his expectations, being protected by lord Paget, he was raised to the same post under queen Mary, and such was his diligence and dispatch, that it is said, he composed and transcribed, in three days, no less than forty seven Latin letters to princes and other foreigners of distinction, particularly to the cardinals, on the
subject

subject of electing cardinal Pole, by whom he was greatly caressed on account of his universal learning; and though a good scholar himself, he gave the preference to Mr. Ascham's style in Latin, employing him to translate into Latin, the speech he made to the parliament when he reconciled the kingdom to the see of Rome, and our author's translation was sent to Rome, where it was greatly admired, for the purity of the diction.

In 1554, Mr. Ascham resigned his fellowship, and married Mrs. Margaret Howe, a young lady of good family, with whom he had a considerable fortune, and this acquisition enabled him to live in a great measure independent of the court, during the remainder of queen Mary's reign; and it is to be presumed, that he must have put in practice some of his political tenets to have enabled him to remain unmolested, and even unquestioned on the subject of his religious principles in the time of the persecution, when his fellow student and old companion Sir John Cheeke, fell a victim to his forced recantation.

Upon the accession of Elizabeth, his royal pupil, he was sent for to court, continued in his station of Latin secretary, and allowed the same salary as in the late reign, which was only twenty pounds *per annum*; and though he was admitted to a degree of familiarity with the queen, sometimes assisting her in her private studies, and at others partaking of her diversions, she never made any addition to his fortune, except a prebendary in the cathedral of York, which was bestowed on him in 1559. This inconsiderable preferment was so inadequate to his services, and to the rank he held at court in the reign of Edward VI. that it cannot be accounted for on any principle, but that of his extreme modesty, which prevented him from asking any favours, and Elizabeth loved to be courted, and even to be flattered to excefs, to which foible it is highly probable our author did not make a proper facrifice; however, one refpectable writer, Camden, afferts, that he grew diffipated towards the clofe of his life, and confequently negligent of his intereft, fpending much of his time at dice and cock-fighting. In 1563, he compofed an efteemed treatife, intitled The SCHOOL-MASTER, which he undertook at the requeft of Sir Richard Saville, on account of a warm conteft amongft the nobility and gentry, concerning the beft method of teaching youth the Latin language, but this work was not publifhed till after his death.

From this time, to the year 1568, we have no account of any exertion of his literary talents, and it appears, that his bad ftate of health obliged him to forbear all intenfe application to ftudy. Yet, as a laft effort, he attempted to compofe a poem this year, to be prefented to the queen on the anniverfary of her acceffion, but his diftemper, which was a confumption, growing worfe by this attempt, and depriving him of reft, he was obliged to decline it, and prepare to meet his approaching end, which he did with pious fortitude and refignation. He died on the 30th of December 1568, and was interred in St. Sepulchre's church London, in the moft private manner, agreeable to his own direction. Being only in the *fifty third* year of his age, his death was greatly lamented by the queen, and by all his cotemporaries in the literary world, who juftly confidered it as a public lofs, efteeming him the moft learned man of the age, and the greateft improver of his native language.

⁎ *Authorities.* Grant's life of Afcham, Oxford edit. 1703. Wood's Fafti, Oxon. vol. I. Bennet's edit. of Afcham's works, London 1761.

The

The LIFE of
JOHN JEWEL,
BISHOP of SALISBURY.

[A. D. 1522, to 1571.]

THIS eminent divine, and zealous champion for the proteſtant cauſe, was a deſcendant of an antient family in Devonſhire, and was born at the village of Buden in 1522. He ſtood indebted for the firſt rudiments of grammar learning, to the inſtructions of his maternal uncle Mr. John Bellamy, rector of Hamton, by whom it is moſt probable, for we have no account of his parents, he was ſent to Oxford, about the year 1536, to be under the tuition of Peter Burrey of Merton college, but his friends diſcovering that this man was no friend to the reformation, and but a ſlender ſcholar, he was placed ſoon after, under the care of Mr. John Parkhurſt of the ſame college, a man of extenſive learning, and firmly attached to the proteſtant intereſt. Under this preceptor, who was afterwards biſhop of Norwich, young Jewel was initiated in the principles of the reformed religion, and made a conſiderable progreſs in his academical ſtudies.

In 1539, he removed to Corpus Christi college, of which he was elected a scholar, and the following year, he was admitted to the degree of batchelor of arts, after which, he applied himself with uncommon assiduity to theological learning; accustoming himself to rise at four in the morning, and to continue at his books till ten at night, so that it was absolutely necessary to remind him of the hours of refreshment. By this indefatigable industry, he acquired an amazing fund of knowledge, but at the expence of his health, for in consequence of a cold, he contracted a lameness which became incurable.

Thus qualified, Mr. Jewel commenced tutor, and greatly contributed to promote the reformation, by educating his pupils privately in the doctrines of the protestant religion. He was likewise chosen professor of rhetoric in his college, which office he held with distinguished honour seven years, and his lectures were so much admired, and followed, that the fame of them brought his old preceptor Mr. Parkhust from his country retirement to attend them, who was so highly pleased, that he not only bestowed the greatest encomiums on his abilities, but took upon himself the charge of his commencement as master of arts. In his moral character, he was the example of his college, insomuch that the dean, who was a rigid papist, used to say to him, " I should love thee Jewel, if thou wert not a Zuinglian. In thy faith, I hold thee to be an heretic, but surely, in thy life, thou art an angel."

On the accession of Edward VI. Mr. Jewel threw off the veil of secrecy; made a public declaration of his religious opinions; entered into a close friendship with Peter Martyr, the divinity professor of the university, and took all opportunities

tunities to defend the new established form of worship. In 1550, he took the degree of batchelor in divinity, and upon this occasion he preached an excellent Latin sermon. About this time, he was presented to the Rectory of Sunningwell, in Berkshire, the income of which was but small, but though his lameness made walking painful to him, he never neglected the duty, but went to his church on foot every other Sunday to preach and to catechise.

The result of Mr. Jewel's indefatigable zeal in supporting the rites and ceremonies of the church of England, as by law established, during the reign of Edward, was a virulent prosecution instantly set on foot against him by the Romanists, when Mary came to the crown. The fellows of his own college began it, by expelling him for heresy, before the queen was well seated on the throne, or any public orders issued for restoring the old religion. But the university at the same time, having the highest opinion of his literary abilities, employed him to compose their congratulatory address upon the queen's accession, and appointed him their orator. It is surmised, however, that this distinguished honour was intended to ensnare him, by rendering him odious to his own party if he accepted it, or by provoking the Roman catholics if he refused it: Admitting that such was the design of his enemies, they must have been greatly mortified, for the address met with the approbation of Tresham the vice-chancellor, and the heads of the colleges, and was favourably received by the queen.

Mr. Jewel did not quit the university when he was expelled his own college, but withdrew to Broad-gate-hall, now Pembroke college, where he continued his lectures, and attended his pupils as usual. But being required soon after, upon the

the re-establishment of popery, to subscribe to the popish tenets, his life being threatened if he refused, he outwardly complied, but as it was well known that his signature was compulsive, Dr. Martial, dean of Christ-church, alledged, probably with truth on his side, that his subscription was insincere, and therefore, he resolved to secure him, that he might be closely examined by Bonner the grand inquisitor. Mr. Jewel receiving private intelligence of his design, left Oxford the very night that Martial sent for him, and took a bye road for London. He pursued his journey on foot, till he was quite exhausted, and obliged to lay down upon the ground; in this deplorable situation, totally incapable of proceeding any further, he was providentially found by Augustin Bernher, a Swifs, who had been in the service of Bishop Latimer, and was now a divine. This gentleman procured him a horse, and conducted him to the house of lady Anne Warcup, by whom he was hospitably entertained for some time, and then privately accompanied in safety to the capital: here he was obliged to use the greatest precaution, for his flight alone was a conviction of heresy, and incredible pains were taken to discover him by Bonner's emissaries, which obliged him to change his lodgings frequently in the night; at length his escape from England was happily effected, by the care of Sir Nicholas Throgmorton, his particular friend, who provided him a vessel, and gave him money for his support; and of Giles Lawrence, a fellow collegian, who lived near the Tower, and conveyed him on board.

As soon as he landed upon the continent, he proceeded directly to Frankfort, where he arrived in 1554, and immediately made a public protestation of his sincere contrition, for the subscription he had made to the Romish faith. Peter Martyr
had

had left England upon the first notice of the death of Edward VI. and now resided at Strasburgh; Mr. Jewel, therefore, accepted the invitation of his old friend, and went to reside with him. Peter Martyr had converted his house into a kind of college for learned men, and he made Mr. Jewel his deputy, he likewise assisted him in composing his theological lectures, and accompanied him to Zurich; and it was probably from this place that Mr. Jewel made an excursion to Padua, where he commenced a friendship with Signior Scipio, a noble Venetian, to whom he afterwards addressed his epistle relative to the council of Trent.

When the joyful news of queen Elizabeth's peaceful accession, rendered his return to England not only safe, but eligible, he joined several other protestant exiles, who were all equally anxious to be restored to their native country, and embarked for London the beginning of the year 1559. The fortunate exiles, for such they may be called who escaped the horrors of the last reign, were all graciously received by our protestant queen, and those who were most eminent for their piety and learning, among the clergy, were soon provided for in the church. Mr. Jewel in particular, was put into the lists of the sixteen divines, who were appointed to hold a public disputation against the papists in Westminster Abbey, on the 31st of March 1559. In July of the same year, he was constituted one of the visitors of the dioceses in the west of England, who were enjoined to purge them of popery, and in January 1560, he was promoted to the see of Salisbury.

Certain ecclesiastical habits were enjoined by authority, about this time, to be worn by the different orders of the clergy of the church of England, which occasioned a warm controversy, and it appears that our new prelate, though he
thought

thought proper to comply with the orders issued by his sovereign, by no means approved of these vestments, for he complained of them in his letters to his friends upon the continent, as the relicks of popish superstition; he likewise objected to the crucifix being retained in the queen's chapel, considering it in the light of worldly policy. Yet certainly, these matters were so trifling, in comparison of the essentials of religion, that he acted the part of a pious divine to accept a bishopric, in which station, he knew he could be singularly useful to the new establishment, and perhaps be able in time, to root out every remaining absurd ceremony. Accordingly, we find him very soon after his consecration giving a public challenge, in a sermon preached at St. Paul's Cross, to all Roman catholics, whether natives or foreigners, to produce a single evidence, either from the fathers, or from any other writers who flourished in the six first centuries of the christian æra, in favour of any one of the articles of the church of Rome, and two years after, when he found no convincing answer was likely to be made to this open appeal to the public, he published his famous apology for, or rather defence of the church of England.

The advocates for the old religion, however, were not idle, either at home or abroad, the deprived dean of St. Paul's, Dr. Cole, commenced an epistolary controversy with our prelate, upon the subject of his sermon, but railing instead of argument was Cole's talent, which the reader will recollect in his conduct to archbishop Cranmer. The bishop's challenge was published at London in 1560; and four years afterwards, John Rastal a Jesuit, published at Antwerp, what he styled, " A confutation of Jewel's sermon." The same year Thomas Dorman published at the same place, " A proof of certain articles of religion

ligion denied by Mr. Jewel." Rastall was answered by William Fulke, and Dorman by Alexander Nowell, a brother exile with Jewel, who had been rewarded for his merit and sufferings with the deanry of St. Paul's. But the only opponent, whose work out-lived the controversy, was Thomas Harding of Louvain; this author published an answer to Mr. Jewel's challenge in 1564, a quarto volume, a full refutation of which was published by the bishop in folio, in 1566. It is intitled, " A reply to Mr. Harding's answer." His antagonist printed two rejoinders, and thus ended the controversy. By the perusal of the bishop's work, in which all the arguments in Harding's answer are candidly stated, the unbiassed reader will be able to determine with whom the victory manifestly remains.

Our prelate's apology for the church of England, and his reply to Harding, were translated into all the modern languages of Europe, and into Greek, so that his works converted many thousands to the protestant religion, who could not have the benefit of his personal instructions. In reward for these eminent services, the university of Oxford gave him an honorary degree of doctor in divinity, in 1565, justly considering, that it would be an affront to require the presence, and examination of a divine, who had given such evident proofs of his theological abilities. The following year, bishop Jewel presided at the divinity disputations held at this university, in presence of the queen.

His public conduct in his diocese, likewise procured him the veneration and esteem of all good men; and reflected honour on the whole bench of bishops, most of whom followed his example. By paying a particular attention to the proceedings of his chancellor and archdeacons, by presiding
frequently

frequently in his confistory court, and by infpecting the lives of the private clergy, he produced a perfect reformation, and delivered the people from the fhameful extortions of the ftewards, and the inferior officers of the ecclefiaftical court; his humane concern for the welfare of the poor, was extended alfo to the civil jurifdiction, for as he was in the commiffion of the peace, he frequently fat on the bench with the juftices, and corrected many abufes in the exercife of that office; and acting in the fame capacity at his epifcopal feat (for bifhops at that time refided on their diocefes, except they were fummoned to court, or to attend the parliament) he compofed the petty quarrels arifing among neighbours, and prevented vexatious law fuits.

But his conftant unwearied application to fo many pious and important concerns, added to his fondnefs for ftudy, and the little inclination he had for any recreative amufements, deftroyed his health, yet no intreaties or perfuafions of his friends could induce him to alter his ufual hours, or to remit his inceffant labour. He ftill continued his practice, of rifing about four in the morning, at five, he called his family to prayers, at fix, he attended public worfhip in his cathedral, the remainder of the morning was paffed in his ftudy; the afternoon was taken up in public audiences: about nine, in the evening, he called his fervants to an account, examining how they had paffed their time; and then went to prayers with his family: from this time till midnight he withdrew to his ftudy, and then, he went to bed, but generally one of his chaplains read to him till he fell afleep. A life fo watchful and laborious, could not fail of bringing on a decline, but when a vifible alteration was obferved, all the anfwer he gave to the friendly hints thrown out upon this melancholy melancholly subject was, "A bishop should die preaching." And his words were very nearly fulfilled to the letter: for a short time before his death, having promised to preach at some church in Wiltshire, he was met on the road by a gentleman, who perceiving by his looks that he was very ill, advised him to return home, telling him, that the people had better lose one sermon, than be totally deprived of such a preacher. But the bishop continued his journey, and preached his last sermon, but with great difficulty, for upon his return he grew worse, and died in a few days, in September 1571, at Monkton Farley, in his diocese. He was buried in the choir of Salisbury cathedral.

It is almost needless to observe, after the character already given of this primitive bishop, that his death was universally lamented; much less can we attempt any addition to it, we shall therefore only mention, that he was remarkable for an uncommon memory, which he improved by art. It is asserted, by the first writer of his life, Dr. Lawrence Humfrey, that he taught this art to Dr. Parkhurst his old tutor, while they were in exile at Zurich, and enabled him in the space of twenty-eight days, with only one hour's application each day, to repeat the whole Gospel of St. Matthew, and upon naming any separate verse, to recite the preceding and subsequent verses. As to his own sermons they were chiefly extempore, from heads put down in writing, on which he used to meditate while the bell was ringing to summon him to church. Several experiments were likewise made of the strength of his memory, which are related at large by the same writer, but it is of much more consequence for us to know, that his theological and polemical works, rendered his name celebrated all over Europe; and that all

his

his Englifh works, ftill held in efteem by divines, were publifhed together in Folio, at London in 1609.

⁎ *Authorities.* Wood's Athen. and hift. and antiq. of Oxford. Humfrey, and Featly's life of Jewel. Britifh biography.

The LIFE of

JOHN KNOX.

[A. D. 1505, to 1572.]

OUR chronological plan now conducts us to a review of the progrefs of the reformation in the church of Scotland, where it was manfully propagated by one of the moft eminent men of the age in which he lived, the celebrated John Knox, defcended from an ancient and honorable family. He was born at Giffard, near Haddington in Scotland in 1505, from whence he was removed at a proper age to the univerfity of St. Andrews, and placed under the tuition of the learned Mr. John Mair; and he applied with fuch uncommon diligence to the academical learning then in vogue, that, in a fhort time, and while yet very young, he obtained the degree of mafter of arts.

As the bent of his inclination led him ftrongly to the church, he turned the courfe of his ftudies very early to divinity, and, by the advantage of

his

his tutor's inſtructions, ſoon became remarkable for his knowledge in ſcholaſtic theology ; ſo that he took prieſt's orders before the period uſually allowed by the canons : and, from being a learner, began himſelf to teach with great applauſe, his beloved ſcience. But, after ſome time, upon a careful peruſal of the fathers of the church, and particularly the writings of St. Jerom and St. Auſtin, his ſentiments were entirely altered. He quitted the cobweb ſubtilty of the ſchools, and took to the ſtudy of plain, ſolid, rational divinity.

Having once embraced the ſcriptural doctrines of chriſtianity, he attended none but ſuch preachers, whom he knew to be of the ſame way of thinking, the moſt eminent of whom was Guilliam, a black-friar, whoſe ſermons were of extraordinary ſervice to him. This friar was provincial of his order in 1543, when the earl of Arran, then regent of Scotland, favoured the reformation ; and Mr. George Wiſhart, another celebrated reformer, coming from England in the ſucceeding year, with the commiſſioners ſent from king Henry VIII. Knox being of an inquiſitive nature, learned from him the principles of the Proteſtants ; with which he was ſo pleaſed, that he renounced the Romiſh religion, and became a zealous reformer, having left St. Andrews a little before, to be tutor to the ſons of the lairds of Ormiſtoun and Languidry, who were both favourers of the reformation.

Mr. Knox's ordinary reſidence was at Languidry, where he not only inſtructed his pupils in the different branches of academical learning, but was particularly careful to inſtil into their minds the principles of piety and of the proteſtant religion : this coming to the ears of David Beaton, the cardinal and archbiſhop of St. Andrews, that prelate prosecuted him with such severity, that he was frequently obliged to abscond, and fly from place to place. Whereupon, being wearied with such continual dangers, he resolved to retire to Germany, where the new opinions were spreading very fast; knowing that in England, though the pope's authority was suppressed, yet the greater part of the Romish tenets still prevailed, and had the sanction of the king's authority. But he was dissuaded from this step, by both the fathers of his pupils, and cardinal Beaton being assassinated by Norman and John Leslie, in the castle of St. Andrews, in 1546, in consequence of his having condemned and burnt their relation the venerable George Wishart for heresy; Knox was advised to take shelter with his pupils in the castle, now in possession of the Leslies, the determined friends of the reformed religion.

Here he began to teach his pupils in his usual manner. Besides the grammar, and the classical authors, he read a catechism to them, which he obliged them to give an account of publicly, in the parish-church of St. Andrews. He likewise continued to read to them the gospel of St. John, proceeding where he left off, at his departure from Languidry. This lecture he read at a certain hour, in the chapel within the castle, and was attended by several gentlemen of the place. Among these Mr. Henry Bolnaveis, and John Rough, a preacher there, being pleased with the manner of his doctrine, began earnestly to entreat him to take upon him the office of a preacher, but he absolutely refused; alledging, in a strain of humour, for which he was remarkable, " that he would not run where God had not called him." Hereupon, these gentlemen deliberating the matter in a consultation with Sir David Lindsay, of the Mount, lyon king at arms, a person of great probity and learning, it was concluded to give

Mr.

Mr. Knox a charge publicly by the mouth of Mr. Rough from the pulpit, to preach the gospel of Christ to the deluded multitude, at a time when they stood most in need of such able teachers; and this was accordingly done in a sermon composed for the occasion, the congregation at the same time joining with their minister, in declaring their belief that this was a holy vocation which he could not refuse.

Mr. Knox, with some reluctance consented, and after retiring for a few days from all society, he ascended the pulpit, and at once discovered that the protestant cause had now acquired a most intrepid leader, whose fortitude, eloquence and learning, would both astonish and confound his adversaries. Instead of trifling with the subject, he boldly laid the axe to the root of popery in his first sermon, proving to the satisfaction of his auditors, that the doctrine of the Romish church was contrary to the doctrine of Christ and his apostles.

This sermon made a great noise; and the popish clergy being much incensed at it, the abbot of Paisley, lately nominated to the see of St. Andrew's, and not yet consecrated, wrote a letter to the sub-prior, who, *sede vacante*, was vicar-general, expressing great surprize, that such heretical and schismatical doctrines were suffered to be taught without opposition.

Upon this rebuke, every official measure was taken to oppose Mr. Knox, but he carefully avoided incurring ecclesiastical censures, by a peculiar and happy address; in particular, the sub-prior having ordered all the learned divines in St. Andrew's to preach by rotation in the parish churches on Sundays; to avoid all controversial points, his discourses were properly guarded on the Sabbaths; but as the injunction did not extend

extend to other days, he made amends to his protestant auditors, by preaching frequently on weekdays, and with unbounded latitude against the errors of popery; and his public ministry at St. Andrew's was attended with that success, which always accompanies the doctrines of truth, delivered with manly eloquence and pious intrepidity: Popery sensibly lost ground, while converts to the reformed religion increased daily; and he was the first minister who ventured to administer the sacrament in Scotland, according to the rites of the reformed church, but such was the zeal he had inspired, that all the people in the castle and many of the inhabitants of the town joined in communion with him. But this rapid success only lasted from Easter to July 1547, when the castle was surrendered to the French, who were at war with Scotland.

Mr. Knox continued thus in the diligent discharge of his ministerial work, till July in that year, when the castle was surrendered to the French.

Mr. Knox was carried with the garrison to France, and remained a prisoner on board the gallies till the latter end of the year 1549; when, being set at liberty, he passed to England; and going to London, was there licensed, and appointed preacher, first at Berwick and next at Newcastle.

While he was thus employed, he received a summons in 1551, to appear before Cuthbert Tonstal, bishop of Durham, for preaching against the mass; but what was the event we are not informed; however in 1552, he was appointed one of the six chaplains, whom the council thought proper to retain in the service of Edward VI. not only to attend the court, but to be itinerary preachers

of

of the new religion all over the kingdom, and, the enfuing year, he had the grant of forty pounds per annum, till fome benefice in the church fhould be conferred on him. The fame year he came into fome trouble on account of a bold fermon preached at Newcaftle, upon Chriftmas-day, againft the obftinacy of the Papifts; after which he returned to London; and, being well efteemed by his majefty and fome of the court, for his zealous preaching againft the errors of the Romifh church, he was appointed to preach before the king and council at Weftminfter, and in his fermon he levelled fome fevere ftrokes with honeft freedom againft fome great men of the court, who were fecret abbettors of popery.

Yet it is evident, the council were not difpleafed, for about this time, the living of Allhallows, in London, was offered to him; but he refufed it, not caring to conform to the Englifh Liturgy as it then ftood.

He was called before the council on this refufal, and was told, that they were forry to find him of a contrary mind, to the common order. Knox replied, " he was forry the common order " was contrary to Chrift's inftitution," alluding to fome ceremonies ftill retained in the church of England, to which he objected, and on the fame ground, it is faid, he refufed a bifhopric, vehemently condemning all ecclefiaftical dignities. However, he ftill held his place of itinerary preacher; and, in the difcharge of that office, going to Buckinghamfhire, was greatly pleafed with his reception at fome towns, particularly at Amerfham, in that county; and he continued to preach there, and at other places, fome time after queen Mary's acceffion to the throne.

But, in the year 1554, he left England, and, croffing the fea to Dieppe, in France, went from thence

thence to Geneva; where he had not long resided, when he was called by the congregation of English refugees, then established at Frankfort, to be preacher to them. This vocation he obeyed, though unwillingly, at the command of John Calvin: and he continued at Frankfort till some of the principal persons of his congregation, finding it impossible to persuade him to use the English Liturgy, resolved to effect his removal from the place.

With that view, Dr. Cox, an English protestant exile (bishop of Ely, in the reign of Elizabeth) and his party, being determined to establish the church of England service at Frankfort, in opposition to that of Geneva, espoused by Knox; took the most ungenerous measures to oblige him to quit the city. Knox had published a treatise some time before in England, intitled, "An Admonition to Christians;" in which, with his usual boldness, he had said, that the emperor of Germany was as great an enemy to Christ as Nero; and his adversaries taking advantage of this and some other unguarded expressions in the treatise, accused him to the magistrates, of treason, committed both against their sovereign, the emperor of Germany, and also against their own sovereign in England, queen Mary; and the magistrates, not having it in their power to save him, if he should be demanded, either by the emperor, or, in his name, by queen Mary, gave him private notice thereof; which he no sooner received, than he set out for Geneva; where he arrived on the 26th of March, 1555, but staid there only till August following; when, resolving, after so long an absence, to make a visit to his native country, he went to Scotland.

Upon his arrival there, finding the professors of the reformed religion much increased in number, and

and formed into a society under the inspection of some teachers, he associated himself with them, and preached to them. Presently after this, he accompanied one of them, the laird of Dun, to his seat in the north; where he resided a month, teaching and preaching daily to considerable numbers who resorted thither; among whom were the chief gentlemen in that country.

From thence returning to Lothian, he lived, for the most part, in the house of Calder, with Sir James Sandilands, where he met with many persons of the first rank; with whom he conversed familiarly, and confirmed them in the truth of the protestant doctrine.

He afterwards preached for a considerable time at Edinburgh, and in 1556, he went to the west of Scotland, at the desire of some protestant gentlemen, and preached in many places in Kyle; in some, he also celebrated the Eucharist after the manner of the reformed churches. He likewise visited the earl of Glencairn, at his house of Fynlaiston in the county of Renfrew, and administered the sacrament to his lordship's family.

From these western parts he returned to the east, and resided some time at Calder, where many resorted to him both for doctrine and the benefit of the sacraments. From thence, he went a second time to the laird of Dun's house, in the county of Mearns, where he preached more publicly than before, and administered the sacraments to many persons of note at their desire.

The popish clergy being greatly alarmed at this success of Mr. Knox, in protecting the protestant cause, summoned him to appear before them in the church of the Black-Friars in Edinburgh, on the 15th of May, 1556; and several gentlemen of distinction, among whom was the laird of Dun, resolving to stand by him, he determined to obey the summons. But the prosecution was dropped when the bishops perceived such a considerable party in his favour. However, he went to Edinburgh on the day on which he was cited; where he preached to a greater audience than ever he had done before; and in the bishop of Dunkeld's house he instructed great numbers of people, who were desirous of embracing the protestant religion, twice a day, for ten days successively.

At this time, the earl of Glencairn prevailed with the earl mareshal, and his trustee, Henry Drummond, to hear one of Mr. Knox's sermons. They were extremely well satisfied with his discourse, and proposed to him to write to the queen-regent an earnest letter, to persuade her, if possible, to hear the protestant doctrine. He complied with their desire, and wrote to her the latter end of May, 1556. The letter was delivered by the earl of Glencairn. The queen read it and gave it to James Beauton, archbishop of Glasgow (nephew of the cardinal who was assassinated) with this sarcastic expression, "Please you, my lord, to read a pasquil?"

This gave occasion to Mr. Knox to make some additions to his letter, which he printed at Geneva in 1558.

While our reformer was thus occupied in Scotland, he received letters from the English congregation at Geneva, earnestly entreating him to come thither; and, having seriously considered this invitation, he determined to comply with it. Accordingly, in July, 1556, he left Scotland, went first to Dieppe, in France, and from thence to Geneva.

He had no sooner turned his back, than the bishops summoned him before them; and, upon his non-appearance, they passed sentence against him for heresy, and burned him in effigy at the cross

cross of Edinburgh. Against this process he afterwards printed, at Geneva, in 1558, his " famous appellation from the cruel and most unjust sentence pronounced against him by the false bishops and clergy of Scotland, with his supplication to the nobility, estates, and commonality of the said realm;" a master-piece of its kind, not only for the noble defence of religious independency contained in it, but for the elegance and purity of the style.

In March, 1557, several noblemen, the chief promoters of the reformation at that time in Scotland, judging their affairs to be in a pretty good posture, and being sensible of the usefulness of Mr. Knox for this purpose, sent him an express, earnestly desiring him to return home. This letter coming to his hands in May, 1557, he immediately communicated it to his congregation, who were very unwilling to part with him; but, having consulted with Calvin, and other ministers, they gave it, as their opinion, that he could not refuse such a plain call, unless he would declare himself rebellious to God, and unmerciful to his country. The congregation, upon this, yielded to his departure; and he wrote back by the messengers who brought the letter, that he would return to Scotland with all reasonable expedition.

Accordingly, having provided for his flock at Geneva, he left them about the end of September, and came to Dieppe, in his way to Scotland, in October. But there he unexpectedly met with letters from thence, contrary to the former, informing him, that new consultations were entered into, and advising him to stay at Dieppe till the conclusion of them. This was also farther explained in another letter, directed to a friend of Mr. Knox, wherein he was told, that many of those

those who had before joined in the invitation, were becoming inconstant, and began to draw back.

Upon the receipt of these advices, Mr. Knox wrote an expostulatory letter to the lords who had invited him, concerning their rashness; wherein he denounced judgments against such as should be inconstant in the religion they now professed. Besides which, he wrote several other letters from Dieppe, both to the nobility and to the professors of the reformed religion of an inferior degree; exhorting them to constancy in that doctrine, and giving some useful cautions against the errors of sectaries, which grew up about this time, both in Germany and in England.

In these letters he also enjoined them to give due obedience to authority in all lawful things: and they had such an effect on those who received them, that they, one and all, entered into an agreement to commit themselves, and whatsoever God had given them, into his hands, rather than suffer idolatry to reign; or the subjects to be defrauded of their religious liberties: and to secure each others fidelity to the protestant cause, a common bond, or covenant, was made and entered into by them, dated at Edinburgh, on the third of December, 1557; and from this period, they were known by the title of the CONGREGATION.

Mr. Knox returned to Geneva in the beginning of 1558, and the same year he printed there, his treatise, intitled, " The First Blast of the trum-
" pet against the monstrous regimen of women."
He designed to have written a subsequent piece, which was to have been called, " The Second
" Blast:" But queen Mary dying soon after the First was published; and having a great esteem for queen Elizabeth, whom he looked upon as an instrument

strument raised up, by the providence of God, for the good of the Protestants, he went no farther.

In 1559, he determined to return to his native country; and, having a strong desire, in his way thither, to visit those in England, to whom he had formerly preached the Gospel, he applied to Sir William Cecil, his old acquaintance, now secretary of state, to procure leave for that purpose. But this petition was so far from being granted, that the messenger, whom he sent to solicit that favour, very narrowly escaped imprisonment. For it appears, that Knox's doctrine, contained in his " First Blast," needed no sequel, and could not fail of giving great disgust to Elizabeth; for he asserts in it, " that it is unnatural, absurd, " and impious, for women in any country, to be " intrusted with the government of states and " kingdoms."

Hereupon, he made the best of his way to Scotland, where he arrived in May, and was very active in promoting the reformation there, as appears from the second book of his history, which contains a full account of his conduct till the Protestants were obliged to apply to England. For carrying on which transaction, in July of the same year, he was pitched upon to meet Sir William Cecil, incognito, at Stamford; but his journey being retarded by the danger of passing near the French, who lay at Dunbar, he was afterwards sent, in company with Mr. Robert Hamilton, another protestant minister, to negotiate these affairs between the Protestants in Scotland, and queen Elizabeth.

When they came to Berwick, they remained some days with Sir James Crofts, the governor, who undertook to manage their business for them, and advised them to return home, which they did. Secretary Cecil sent also an answer to the protestant nobility and gentry, concerning their proposals to queen Elizabeth; which was so cool that they were very near resolving to break off the negotiation, had not Mr. Knox interposed with so much earnestness, that they allowed him to write once more to the secretary. To this letter an answer was returned without loss of time, desiring that some persons of credit might be sent to confer with the English at Berwick; and the same dispatch informed them, that a sum of money was ready to be delivered for carrying on the common cause; assuring them, that, if the lords of the congregation were willing to enter into a league with queen Elizabeth, upon honourable terms, they neither should want men or money.

Upon this answer, Mr. Henry Balnavers, a man well respected in both kingdoms, was sent to Berwick, who soon returned with a sum of money, which defrayed the public expence till November; when John Cockburne, of Ormistoun, being sent for the second support, received it, but fell into the hands of earl Bothwell, who took the money from him.

The effect of these negotiations was, the sending of an English army under the command of the duke of Norfolk, to assist the Scotch protestants, and protect them against the persecutions of the queen-regent, dowager of James V. who was supported by the arms of France; but the duke of Norfolk's army being joined by almost all the great men in Scotland, a peace was procured and concluded between the three kingdoms, on the eighth of July, 1560.

The congregationers being freed by this peace from any disturbance, made several regulations towards propagating and establishing the new religion; and, in order to have the reformed doctrine preached

preached throughout the kingdom, a division was made thereof into twelve districts, (for the whole number of the reformed ministers at this time was only twelve); whereby the district of Edinburgh was assigned to Mr. Knox. These twelve ministers composed a confession of faith, which was afterwards ratified by parliament. They also compiled the first books of discipline for their new church, and thus the papal authority, and the Romish worship was abolished in the kingdom of Scotland.

In the following year, however, the celebrated Mary, queen of Scots, arrived in her native country, from which she had been absent thirteen years, though she was now but nineteen, and the widow of Francis II. king of France, who had been dead about a year. On the Sunday after her arrival, she commanded mass to be celebrated in the chapel of her palace, which step occasioned great murmurs among the protestants who attended the court, and Knox with his accustomed freedom and boldness, declared from the pulpit, that, "One mass was more frightful to "him, than ten thousand armed enemies landed "in the kingdom." And the animosity of the people against popery, being increased by the apprehension of seeing it restored again by royal authority was so great, that the queen's servants belonging to the chapel, were greatly insulted and abused; further violence in all probability would likewise have ensued; if the prior of St. Andrew's who was one of the heads of the protestant party, had not seasonably interposed. And by the persuasions of this gentleman, who brought over some of the most moderate of the protestant leaders to his opinion, the queen and her domestics were permitted to enjoy the free exercise of their religion unmolested. But Knox's freedom of speech was not so readily forgiven; it had given great offence to the queen, who sent for him, and they held a long conference together on different subjects, which only served to increase Mary's aversion to him: for, in answer to the queen's accusation, that he had written a book which tended to subvert her authority, he told her, in an uncourtly style: " That if the realm found no " inconvenience in being governed by a wo- " man, that which the people approved, he should " not disallow farther than within his own breast; " but should be as well content to live under her " Grace, as Paul was under Nero." " And my " hope is," continued he, " that so long as you " defile not your hands with the blood of the " saints of God, that neither I, nor my book " shall either hurt you, or your authority; for in " very deed, madam, the book was written a- " gainst that wicked Jezebel (Mary) of Eng- " land."

In 1562, we find him employed in reconciling the earls of Bothwell and Arran; which is an evidence how much he was regarded by the most eminent persons in the kingdom, and how much interest he had with them. The same year, the queen, being informed that her uncles were likely to recover their former interest at the court of France, received the news with great joy. Mr. Knox hearing of her behaviour, and apprehending that the power of her relations would produce dismal effects, in prejudice of the reformed interest in these parts, thought fit to preach a sermon, wherein he taxed the ignorance, vanity, and despite of princes against all virtue, and against all those in whom hatred of vice and love of virtue appeared. This, and other expressions, in reproof of dancing for joy, at the displeasure taken against God's people, coming to the ears of the queen, her majesty

jesty sent for him, and had a second conference with him.

This year also, he was appointed by the general assembly, commissioner to the counties of Kyle and Galloway; and, by his influence, several of the most eminent gentlemen entered into a covenant, which was subscribed on the fourth of September, 1562.

From the shire of Air he went to Nithsdale and Galloway, and had several conferences about matters of great importance with the master of Moxwell; and from this county he wrote to the duke of Chaterault, giving him cautions both against the bishop of St. Andrew's and the earl of Huntley, whose councils he judged might prove obnoxious to the Protestants. About this time he accepted a challenge, made by an eminent person among the Papists, to a public disputation upon the mass, which continued the space of three days, and was afterwards printed.

In the beginning of the queen's first parliament, held in 1563, Mr. Knox endeavoured to excite the earl of Murray to appear with zeal and courage to get the protestant religion firmly established by law; but finding him cooler than he expected, a breach ensued between them, which continued for a year and a half: and, after the bill was rejected, the parliament not being dissolved, he preached a sermon before a great many of the members, wherein he expressed his sense of that matter with vehemency: and, at the close, declared his abhorrence of the queen's design of marrying a papist. This gave great offence to the court; and her majesty, sending for him a third time, expressed much passion, and thought to have punished him, but was prevailed upon to desist at that time.

In 1565, lord Darnley being married to the queen

queen, was advised by the Protestants about court to hear Mr. Knox preach, as thinking it would contribute much to procure him the good will of the people. Darnley accordingly complied, but was so much offended at the sermon, that he complained to the council, who immediately ordered Mr. Knox before them, and silenced him for several days.

His text indeed was very remarkable, and his application of it still more striking. The words were, "*O Lord our God, other lords, besides thee, have had dominion over us;*" from which he took occasion to speak of the government of wicked princes, who for the sins of the people are sent as tyrants and scourges to plague them, and sometimes, said he, God sets over them, for their offences and ingratitude, BOYS and WOMEN.

The general assembly, which met in December this year, in their fourth session, appointed Mr. Knox to draw up a consolatory letter in their name, to encourage the ministers to continue in their vocations, which many were under temptation to leave for want of subsistence; and to exhort the professors of the realm to supply their necessities. He was also appointed by this assembly, to visit, preach, and plant the kirks of the south. But he requested the next general assembly, which met at Edinburgh in December, 1566, that he might have leave to go to England to visit two of his sons in that kingdom, and also to transact some other business there. The assembly granted his request, but limited his stay in England, to their next annual meeting: they then furnished him with ample testimonials of his life, doctrines, and public usefulness in the ministry, and a strong recommendation to all protestants. He also carried with him a letter from the assembly to the bishops of England,

England, drawn up by himself; complaining of their severe treatment of the English Puritans (Calvinists) and soliciting indulgence for them.

In 1567, Mr. Knox preached a sermon at the coronation of king James VI. of Scotland, afterwards James I. of England. This year was very remarkable in Scotland, on account of the great turn of affairs there, queen Mary being obliged to resign the government, on the appointment of the earl of Murray to be regent. The first parliament which was called by the earl met upon the 15th of December. It was a very numerous convention of all the estates, and Mr. Knox preached a very zealous sermon at the opening of it; he was also extremely afflicted at the regent's death in 1569.

In 1571, the Hamiltons and others, who had entered into a combination against the earl of Lenox, then regent, began to fortify the town of Edinburgh. While they were thus employed, a council was held by them in the castle on the fourth of May; where the laird of Grange, captain of the castle, proposed that they might give security for the person of Mr. Knox, which was also much desired by the town's people. The Hamiltons answered, That they could not promise him security upon their honour, because there were many in the town who loved him not, besides other disorderly people that might do him harm without their knowledge.

Upon this answer, which plainly shewed no good intention to Mr. Knox, his friends in the town, with Mr. Craig, his collegue, at their head, entreated him to leave the place; in compliance with their requests, he left Edinburgh on the fifth of May; he went first to Abbotshall in Fife, and thence to St. Andrew's, where he remained till the twenty-third of August 1572.

This year there was a convention of the ministers at Leith, where it was agreed, that a certain kind of episcopacy should be introduced into the church, which was zealously opposed by our reformer. The troubles of the country being much abated, and the people of Edinburgh, who had been obliged to leave it, being returned, they sent two of their number to St. Andrew's, to invite Mr. Knox to return to them, and to ask his advice about the choice of another minister to assist him during the time of the troubles. The superintendant of Lothian was with them, when they presented the letter; which, when Mr. Knox had perused, he consented to return, upon this condition, that he should not be desired in any sort to cease speaking against the treasonable dealings of those who held out the castle of Edinburgh; and this he desired them to signify to the whole brethren, lest they should afterwards repent; and, after his return, he repeated these words more than once, to his friends there, before he entered the pulpit: they answered, that they never meant to put a bridle on his tongue, but desired him to speak according to his conscience, as in former times. They also requested his advice upon the choice of a minister; and, after some debates, they agreed upon Mr. James Lawson, sub-principal of the king's college at Aberdeen.

Mr. Knox left St. Andrew's on the seventeenth of August, and came to Leith on the twenty-third. Upon the last day of that month, he preached in the great kirk; but his voice was become very weak, and therefore he desired another place to teach in; where his voice might be heard, if it were but by an hundred persons; which was granted: after which Mr. Knox continued to preach in the Tolbooth as long as he had strength; but his health received a great shock

shock from the news of the massacre of the protestants at Paris, about this time. However, he introduced it into his next sermon, with his usual denunciation of God's vengeance thereon, which he desired the French ambassador, monsieur La Crocque, might be acquainted with. On Sunday, November the ninth, 1572, he admitted Mr. Lawson to be minister of Edinburgh. But his voice was so weak, that very few could hear him; he declared the mutual duty between a minister and his flock; he praised God, that had given them one in his room, he being now unable to teach, and desired that God might augment his graces to him a thousand-fold above what he had possessed, if it were his pleasure, and ended with pronouncing the blessing.

From this time his approaching dissolution was observed with concern by all his friends; an unwearied application to study, continual agitation in business, during troublesome times, joined to the frequency and fervour of his public preaching, had worn out a constitution naturally strong, and had brought on a lingering decay; during the course of which, he discovered the greatest fortitude and resignation, constantly employing himself in acts of devotion, and comforting himself with the prospect of immortality, which not only preserves good men from despondency, but fills them with exultation in their last moments; thus in his death, which happened on the 24th of November, 1572, did he set a glorious example, as he had done in his life, to those whose principal director he had been in the laudable but arduous task of reforming them from the errors of superstition, ignorance and priestcraft.

A summary of the character of this extraordinary man is so admirably drawn up by the masterly pen of Dr. Robertson, that we cannot finish this article

ticle with greater propriety, than by borrowing it upon so justifiable an occasion as the embellishment of a work, which in its very nature disclaims originality, and can only stand indebted for its merit, to the judicious introduction of established authorities, and of the refined sentiments of celebrated writers.

"Knox was the prime instrument of spreading and establishing the reformed religion in Scotland. Zeal, intrepidity, disinterestedness, were virtues which he possessed in an eminent degree. He was acquainted too with the learning cultivated in that age; and excelled in that species of eloquence, which is calculated to rouse and to inflame. His maxims however, were often too severe, and the impetuosity of his temper excessive. Rigid and uncomplying himself, he shewed no indulgence to the infirmities of others. And regardless of the distinctions of rank and character, he uttered his admonitions with an acrimony and vehemence, more apt to irritate than to reclaim.

Those very qualities, however, which now render his character less amiable, fitted him to be the instrument of providence for advancing the reformation among a fierce people, and enabled him to face dangers, and to surmount opposition, from which a person of a more gentle spirit would have been apt to shrink back."

He was interred with with great solemnity in the kirk-yard of St. Giles's, the corpse being attended by several of the nobility then in Edinburgh, particularly by the earl of Morton, that day chosen regent, who, as soon as he was laid in his grave, said, "There lies a man who never in his life feared the face of a man, who hath been often threatened with dug and dagger, but yet hath ended his days in peace and honour. For he had God's providence watching over him in a special manner, when his very life was sought."

Dr.

Dr. Robertson justly observes, that this eulogium is the more honourable, as it came from one whom he had often censured with peculiar severity.

Mr. Knox was an author of considerable repute, for the time in which he lived, but the improvements since made in the systems of divinity render his works less valuable in the present age. They are theological, controversial and historical, comprised in one volume folio, printed at Edinburgh, the fourth edition, 1732. It is intitled, "The History of the Reformation of Religion, in the Realm of Scotland, &c."

*** *Authorities.* Biog. Britan. Mackenzie's lives of the Scotch writers; Dr. Robertson's History of Scotland.

The LIFE of

MATTHEW PARKER,

ARCHBISHOP of CANTERBURY.

[A. D. 1504, to 1575.]

Including Memoirs of George Browne, and of Hugh Corwin, Archbishops of Dublin.

THE æra of the complete and permanent establishment of the protestant religion in England, Scotland, and Ireland, comprizing the most interesting part of the ecclesiastical history of these kingdoms; it is hoped, the reader's patience will not be put to too severe a trial, by attending to the measures which were taken by queen Elizabeth and the eminent divine she placed at the head of the church of England, to

make

make that church, a distinct and permanent part of the constitution of the realm, a privilege it possesses at this time, under the denomination of "Our happy constitution in church and state."

The principal instrument for accomplishing this political union was, Matthew Parker, the son of a reputable citizen of Norwich, born there, in the year 1504. His father died when he was very young, but having ordered by his will, that he should be devoted to the church, his mother sent him at a proper age to Bennet, now Corpus Christi college, Cambridge; where his lively genius improved by assiduous application to those studies which are peculiarly adapted to the sacred function, established his reputation in early life, as a man of uncommon learning for his age; in 1527, he entered into priest's orders, took the degree of master of arts, and was chosen fellow of his college. At this time, a flattering testimony of his conspicuous abilities was given by cardinal Wolsey, who offered him one of the first fellowships in his new college, at Oxford, but for reasons best known to his friends, they advised him to reject this advantageous opportunity of throwing himself under the patronage of that great man; in compliance therefore, with their solicitations, he remained at Cambridge.

In the year 1533, he commenced preacher, and became so popular that his fame reached the ear of Cranmer, who, on enquiry, finding likewise, that his opinions favoured the reformation, sent him a special licence to preach in his diocese, and recommended him to the notice of Henry VIII. The king sent for him to court the same year, and his queen, Ann Boleyn, being highly pleased with a sermon preached before her, in which Parker avowed the principles of the reformed churches abroad, she
appointed

appointed him one of her chaplains, placed the greatest confidence in him ever after, and upon her fatal reverse of fortune, gave him several private injunctions respecting her daughter the princess Elizabeth, the care of whose education she particularly directed should be entrusted to him; and thus the basis was laid of the strong attachment of that princess to her learned and pious, spiritual guardian.

Mr. Parker's first benefice in the church, was the deanry of Stoke in Suffolk, which the king gave him on the queen's solicitation in 1534, and from this time, to the death of his royal patroness, we meet with nothing remarkable concerning him, except an accusation brought against him by the popish party, for exposing the errors of the Romish church with great freedom, in his sermons at St. Paul's Cross, but he defended himself in a most satisfactory manner, and was ordered by the lord chancellor Audley, who tried the charge, to persevere in so good a cause, regardless of the menaces or accusations of his adversaries.

King Henry made Mr. Parker one of his chaplains after the fall of Ann Boleyn, and during the remainder of this reign, he continued rising in the church, and in the university of Cambridge; the degree of doctor in divinity was conferred on him in 1538. In 1544, he was elected master of his college, and the following year, vice-chancellor.

Dr. Parker had indulged a sincere affection for a young lady, of the family of Harslestone in Norfolk, and a tender intercourse had been carried on for some years, but the bloody articles, one of which, forbad the marriages of the clergy, being put in force with uncommon rigour, about the time that this connection was formed, the happy union of
the

the parties was delayed till the statute was repealed on the accession of Edward VI. when they were married; and it should seem by the sequel, that the papists, his avowed enemies, always had their eye upon this expected event. Our divine, during the short reign of Edward, chiefly distinguished himself as a frequent and zealous preacher in support of the reformation, and consequently could not escape the notice of the opposite party, to whom he rendered himself extremely obnoxious, by the share he had in the suppression of the rebellion under Kett, the tanner of Norwich; for Dr. Parker being one of their countrymen, with great intrepidity went to their camp, and preached to the rebels from the oak of reformation, persuading them to submit to the king, and to return to their families and occupations, which had such an effect that many dispersed, and their army being considerably diminished, became an easier conquest to the king's forces, commanded by the earl of Warwick, who totally defeated them: this eminent service, however, was performed at the peril of his life, for some of the leaders, aware of the consequences of his sermon, which cooled the ardour of their men, were for sacrificing him on the spot, but a large party, better pleased with his friendly admonitions, conducted him safely out of the camp.

It is rather extraordinary, that Parker was not promoted in this reign, in which we do not find that he received any addition to the ecclesiastical preferments he enjoyed at the demise of Henry: we are told indeed, by Strype, that, " he was nominated to a bishopric, which he either refused, or others stepped in before him," but from the reluctance he afterwards shewed to accept the highest station in the church, it is most probable,

he

he declined the offer and preferred a private life, especially, as he was perfectly at ease in his circumstances at this period: but queen Mary no sooner ascended the throne, than his inveterate enemies availing themselves of his marriage, made him experience a total reverse of fortune; for he was deprived of all his preferments, and reduced with his wife and two sons, to the necessity of living with the utmost parsimony, and in the greatest privacy and obscurity, often changing their place of abode, to prevent his falling into the hands of the bloody persecutors of the reformed clergy; whose fury, however, he most fortunately escaped by his own vigilance, and the unwearied assiduity of his friends.

At length, he had the happiness to be called forth from his retreat, to new accessions of honour and fortune. Queen Elizabeth embracing the earliest opportunity to reward him for his services and his sufferings in the protestant cause, nominated him soon after she was proclaimed, to fill the archiepiscopal see of Canterbury, vacant by the death of Cardinal Pole. Dr. Parker, however, was so far from being elated at this most distinguishing mark of the approbation of his sovereign, that he requested the lord keeper Bacon to use his interest with the queen, to permit him to decline the acceptance of this great honour, alledging amongst other excuses, his bodily infirmities, particularly, a hurt which he had received by a fall from his horse, in flying by night, from some persons who were sent to apprehend him in the late reign; the injury he complained of was the consequence of a contusion on his breast, which made preaching very painful to him, and therefore, in his opinion, disqualified him for the most essential duties of his high station: but the queen persisting in her choice, he was

consecrated

consecrated at Lambeth in 1559; and it was soon perceived, that this appointment was one of the many which manifested the great penetration and political genius of the sovereign: for the archbishop being invested with full powers to establish the protestant religion, took a special care to recommend to the queen, such divines who had distinguished themselves for their piety, their learning, and their zeal, in promoting the reformation, to fill the vacant sees; and the other ecclesiastical benefices, of which the popish priests were soon after deprived, for not conforming to the new statutes and injunctions concerning religion.

Archbishop Parker likewise extended his influence and his concern, for the protestant interest, to the kingdom of Ireland, where religion had suffered the same revolutions as in England; the reformation having been set on foot during the administration of Cromwell, earl of Essex, in the reign of Henry VIII by George Browne, archbishop of Dublin, an Englishman, and an Augustine Friar of London, who was promoted to that see by Cromwell's recommendation; this prelate, was the first clergyman in Ireland who embraced the reformation; he proceeded in it with such zeal, that he carried the bill for establishing Henry's supremacy through the parliament of Ireland, at a time, when even the attempt was reckoned dangerous. He also removed all images and superstitious relics from the churches, and was the first who ordered the Lord's prayer, the creed, and the ten commandments, to be placed in their stead, at the altars; after which, he detected some conspirators who were sent from Rome, to raise a rebellion in Ireland, and to root out heresy. He continued to exert the same active zeal in the reign of Edward, but in the first year of Mary, being a married man, he was deprived, and died soon after. Popery

pery was then restored again in Ireland, but when archbishop Parker had settled the affairs of the church of England, he sent over proper instructions to Hugh Corwin, archbishop of Dublin, for completing the reformation of the church of Ireland, and he was to be supported by the earl of Sussex, newly appointed the queen's lieutenant of that kingdom. Accordingly, the litany was sung in English at the cathedral in Dublin, the earl and his court being present, which so exasperated the popish party, that they had recourse to the old sacriligious fraud of inventing a miracle. The particulars of this last effort to impose on the credulous, are very curious, and therefore, we shall give them in the words of Strype, who relates the story, as communicated in a letter from archbishop Corwin to archbishop Parker.

" There was in the cathedral, an image of Christ in marble, standing with a reed in his hand and a crown of thorns on his head; and while service was saying before the lord-lieutenant, the archbishop, the rest of the privy council, and the corporation of Dublin, (on the second Sunday of singing the English litany) blood was seen to run through the crevices of the crown of thorns, trickling down the face of the image. The people did not perceive it at first; therefore, some who were in the fraud, cried out to one another, and bad them see, how our Saviour's image sweat blood. Whereat several of the common people fell down with their beads in their hands, and prayed to the image. Vast numbers flocked to the sight, and one present, who indeed was the contriver, and formerly belonged to the priory of the cathedral, told the people the cause, *viz.* that he could not chuse but sweat blood, whilst heresy was then come into the church. The confusion hereupon was so great, that the assembly broke up.
But

But the people still fell upon their knees, thumping their breasts; and particularly one of the aldermen, the mayor of the city, whose name was Sedgrave, and who had been at the English service, drew forth his beads and prayed with the rest before the image. The earl of Sussex, and those of the privy council, hasted out of the choir, fearing some harm. But the archbishop being displeased, caused a form to be brought out of the choir, and bad the sexton to stand thereon, and to search and wash the image, and see if it would bleed afresh. The man soon perceived the cheat, observing a sponge within the hollow of the image's head. This sponge, one Leigh, the person above mentioned, had soaked in a bowl of blood, and, early on Sunday morning, watching his opportunity, placed the said sponge so swoln and heavy with blood, over the head of the image within the crown; and so, by little and little, the blood soaked through upon the face. The sponge was presently brought down and shewn to these worshippers; who began to be ashamed, and some of them cursed father Leigh, who was soon discovered, and three or four others, who had been the contrivers of it." These were exposed and punished, and the archbishop ordered the image to be removed.

Ridiculous as this story must appear, it had a very happy effect at the time, in England, for archbishop Parker caused it to be universally circulated, to cool the ardour of those who still retained a veneration for images, a folly which seems to have adhered to queen Elizabeth for some time after her accession, though many writers impute it to policy. However this be, the sight of this letter, backed by several passages produced from scripture by our protestant divines,

overcame

overcame her scruples, and she consented to have them taken down throughout the kingdom, and demolished.

But still the great work of fixing the religion of the state on a permanent footing, and as consonant to the civil polity of the kingdom as possible, suffered many impediments and obstructions: not indeed from the Romish persuasion, who had now lost all hopes, but the desperate one of cutting off the secular power, that presumed to countenance and established heresy: the opposition arose from the disciples of Calvin, and other sectaries, who though they were protestants, objected as much as the papists to some of the doctrines, and more generally to the worship of the church of England, as it was then just established by the act of uniformity. Some of these rejected infant baptism, and were styled *Anabaptists*, others denied the unity of the Godhead in the Trinity, and were called *Arians:* some again affirmed, while others denied, the doctrines of *free-will* and *predestination*, and administered the sacraments in their own manner; these likewise branched out into many other distinctions, and Calvin supported their pretensions to a share in the ecclesiastical part of our constitution, by writing a polite, but artful letter to archbishop Parker, requesting him to prevail with the queen to call a general assembly of all the protestant clergy wheresoever dispersed, that they might agree upon one common form of worship and of church government, to be established not only within her dominions, but also among all the reformed and evangelical churches abroad: but the English exiles who lived abroad, during the reign of Mary, some of whom were men of great piety and learning, as well ecclesiastics as laics, having already

already shewn great diversity of opinions on this delicate subject; some having contended (as we have noticed in the life of Knox) for the service of the church of England, and others for that of Geneva, the privy-council wisely considering, that the church of England in this its infant state, required some support from spiritual authority, resolved to maintain episcopacy, and this resolution Parker was ordered to transmit to Calvin, thanking him at the same time for his candid offers.

A more effectual method could not be taken to silence Calvin, who was a bitter enemy to any episcopal government of Christ's church; accordingly, he made no farther application to the British court, but he secretly encouraged all the English dissenters from the worship of the church of England; who, upon their separation from that church upon the publication of the act of uniformity, were called *Puritans*, from their laying claim to a purer form of worship and church discipline, in their idea, than that which was now established in England.

Another prejudice still retained by queen Elizabeth, was a strong aversion to the marriages of priests, upon which subject she would certainly have come to a rupture with the archbishop, if Cecil had not compromised matters between them, by getting Parker, who was as tenacious of his opinions as her Majesty, to agree to a royal injunction, that no head or member of any college or cathedral should bring a wife, or any other woman, into the precincts of it, to abide in the same, on pain of forfeiture of all ecclesiastical preferments. It should seem as if the queen and our archbishop had determined to plague each other on the subject of matrimony, for Parker had written a letter to her majesty, exhorting

horting her to enter into that holy state, to which he had procured the signature of some other prelates, and now upon his application to her, to revoke this injunction, she treated the institution with severe satire and marked contempt, telling the archbishop she repented having made any married men bishops; which mortified him not a little, and occasioned his writing a sharp letter to the secretary of state, in which he informed him, that the bishops were all dissatisfied with the queen, and that for his part he repented his having accepted the station he now held.

This misunderstanding, however, was no sooner adjusted, than a religious quarrel of another nature broke out among the clergy of the established church, which threatened an alarming and dangerous schism, and could not fail of giving cause of scandal to all well disposed christians: since even the bishops were divided in opinion, and formed themselves into distinct parties.

The queen, in consequence of a clause in the act of uniformity, which impowered her to add any rites and ceremonies she thought proper to the established church, had enjoined particular ecclesiastical habits to be worn by the different orders of the clergy; to these regulations some implicitly conformed, others rejected part of their dress, and not a few the whole, as the relics of popish superstition. Surplices and copes in particular, were strongly objected to; and this difference in opinion had such an effect upon the congregations, that divine service was almost deserted by those who had a prepossession in favour of these habits, if the priest of the parish was of a contrary opinion; and the same happened in parishes where the people abhorred these garments, and their pastors persisted in wearing them. In short, as it happens

happens in all public disputes, which give rise to parties; the infection spread to private families, and caused domestic altercations. And, as the majority of the laity were against these habits, the clergy who wore them were subjected to the insults of the vulgar, who considered them as hypocrites, believing them to be papists at heart, and conformists to the new religion only from worldly motives. This spirit in the people, increased with their aversion to popery, and our archbishop whose advice the queen chiefly followed, was severely censured as the principal author of these disturbances, but neither Parker nor the rest of the prelates in his party made any concession to quiet the minds of the dissatisfied, on the contrary, when the two archbishops were sent for to court, and commanded to restore the peace of the church, they immediately pursued such measures as were calculated to inforce obedience from the clergy, and the laity were totally left out of the question, unless they thought proper to conform to the ordinances now drawn up by Parker and his associates, for due order in preaching and administering the sacraments, and for the apparel of persons ecclesiastical.

In consequence of these regulations, the breach was widened, and has not been closed to this hour: for all the licences for preaching were directly cancelled, and no new ones granted but to such of the clergy as would subscribe to the queen's original injunctions concerning the ecclesiastical habits, and to the ordinances set forth by Parker, containing some articles to which many of the clergy, and a considerable body of the laity could by no means be brought to conform. Among other things, the principal minister was to wear a cope when he administered the sacrament: at prayers they were all to wear
surplices,

surplices, in the parish churches, and in cathedrals, hoods, in which they were to preach: the communion table was to be placed in the east, and no person permitted to receive the sacrament in any other posture but kneeling. And finally, no person was to be ordained, who had not taken degrees at Oxford or Cambridge.

A violent schism ensued, and such numbers of the clergy resigned their benefices and cures, that the two universities could not supply men of tolerable abilities to fill up the vacancies; the bishops were therefore obliged to procure degrees for, and to ordain many illiterate persons who had barely the qualifications of common clerks, but whom they found ready to comply with any forms or ceremonies by which they might be inducted to valuable livings.

But among the clergy who refused to conform were many persons of the first reputation, for piety, learning, and moral character, for whom the candid and disinterested in general, conceived the highest veneration, these had considerable interest at court; and they were countenanced by a few of the moderate bishops, particularly by Jewel, bishop of Salisbury, and Pilkington, bishop of Durham, who, as they had been exiles for their profession of the protestant faith in the worst of times, could not be suspected of want of zeal, and therefore they wrote with great freedom and intrepidity to the earl of Leicester, the reigning court favourite, representing that the reformed countries abroad had cast off popish apparel with the pope, that in things indifferent in themselves, compulsion should not be used, by any means, and that so many ministers were resolved to leave their livings, rather than comply, that it would be impossible to find proper teachers, the realm being

being scarce of them, and many places entirely destitute of any. Leicester, already inclined to favour the cause of the non-conformists, gained over several other courtiers, and their representations had such an effect on the queen, that she resolved to withdraw the royal sanction, and leave the ordinances to the ecclesiastical court, which had sufficient authority over the inferior clergy by the canon law, to inforce obedience if it was judged necessary to exert it, and thus the odium of a spiritual persecution against the puritans was taken off from the crown, and thrown upon the archbishops and their party.

Parker, exasperated at this measure, openly declared, that the queen had ordered him to draw up the injunctions and the ordinances, and resolved to abide by them; he now published them under the title of advertisements, and soon gave the clergy to understand that he would inforce them with rigour, in the spiritual court; for he cited Sampson dean of Christ's church Oxford, and Humphreys president of Magdalen college, to appear before him, and other ecclesiastical commissioners, and after trying every persuasive argument to induce them to conform, they were menaced with deprivation in case of refusal, and a short time was allowed them to give in their answer; this however, they employed in writing an elaborate letter to the commissioners in defence of their conduct, and in support of religious liberty: with great coolness and judgement they expressed their concern, that such a dissention should arise for so trifling a subject, *propter lanam et linum*; meaning, the square cap, and the surplice, and only required the same indulgence for their opinions, which they were ready to grant to those, who differed from them. This law, concerning the restoring the ceremonies of the church of Rome, they said,

appeared

appeared to them, to be joined with the hazard of slavery, necessity and superstition; "But because this does not seem so to you, you are not to be condemned by us; because this does seem so to us, we are not to be vexed by you." These and other arguments, equally fraught with the spirit of primitive christianity, charity and affection, had no weight with the commissioners, who acted under the influence of the archbishop, and he was determined to make an example of these two divines, who were universally esteemed for their great learning; their zeal in the protestant cause, and their sufferings on that account in the reign of queen Mary, being of the number of the unfortunate exiles, who were reduced to great extremities abroad, subsisting solely on the charity of the foreign protestants. Accordingly, on their second appearance, they were ordered to comply in a peremptory manner by the archbishop, and on their refusal, they were taken into custody, and confined in the archbishop's palace at Lambeth, with a view of terrifying the inferior clergy; but this proceeding not having the desired effect, they were deprived, and then released.

Soon after, the archbishop ordered the whole body of the London clergy to appear before him, and some of the ecclesiastical commissioners at Lambeth, on a certain day, to subscribe their conformity to the injunctions and ordinances, and having given proper notice of his intention to the court, he requested secretary Cecil, and some of the privy council to be present, but he could not obtain their consent; however, he found means to procure a royal proclamation, requiring uniformity in the habits of the clergy, under pain, upon refusal, of being silenced and deprived.

When the London clergy appeared in court, they were admonished to follow the pious example of one Thomas Cole; who overcoming his scruples, by the force of persuasions, had conformed, and being dressed in the habits required by the injunctions, was placed in a conspicuous manner near the commissioners. The archbishop's chancellor, then addressed them in these words, as related by Strype, in his life of Grindal, bishop of London.

"My masters, and ye ministers of London! the council's pleasure is, that strictly ye keep the unity of apparel, like to this man (pointing to Mr. Cole) that is, wear a square cap, and a scholar's gown, priest like, a tippet, and in the church, a linnen surplice, and inviolably observe, the rubric of the book of common prayer, and the queen's majesty's injunctions, and the book of convocation (the thirty-nine articles) ye, that will subscribe, write *Volo*. Those that will not subscribe, write *Nolo*. Be brief, make no words." And when some of the clergy offered to speak, he interrupted them, crying, "Peace, peace,—apparitor call over the churches, and ye masters answer presently *sub pœna contemptus*, and set your names." Of ninety-eight present, sixty-one subscribed, and when the rest presented a paper to the archbishop, assigning their reasons for refusing, his grace told them, that it was no part of the duty of the commissioners to debate; adding, "he did not doubt, but when they had felt the smart of want and poverty, they would comply; for the wood as yet was but green."

It would be a tedious and unsatisfactory task to follow the archbishop through all his inquisitorial proceedings against the non-conforming clergy, in which he persisted to the last; nor should we have dwelt so long upon this article, if it had not enabled us to trace the origin of the subscriptions required from the clergy to the thirty-nine articles;
and

and other canonical ordinances, a subject which is become interesting in our day, by the vigorous but ineffectual applications lately made to parliament for relief, from this act of religious thraldom.

We are likewise indebted to this part of our history, for the rise of that respectable body of dissenters from the church of England, who have ever since approved themselves the zealous and steady friends of the religious and civil liberties of their country.

For, the archbishop did not stop here; but finding that the books and pamphlets published by the deprived clergy, who with the dissenting laity were now styled *Puritans*, were written with manly freedom, and contained unanswerable arguments in favour of their refusal to comply with ceremonies retained from the Romish church; he complained to the privy council, that the queen's injunctions were disobeyed, and the schism in the church increased by the publication of heterodox libels. This application to the government produced an order from that arbitrary tribunal the star chamber, prohibiting all books and pamphlets in which any thing was advanced against the injunctions, the ordinances, or the established mode of worship of the church of England; the wardens of the stationers company were likewise empowered to search the booksellers shops and the printing-houses for such works, and to bring the offenders before the ecclesiastical commissioners. Thus was the finishing hand put, to a total separation of the conscientious Puritans, from the new church of England. On the merits of the controversy no impartial decision can be made at this distance of time, though some hundreds of volumes have been published on both sides: But we may venture one remark; that, as the difference arose only from external ceremonies, both parties agreeing in the fundamental doctrines and mysteries of christianity, the extremes to which it was carried, could only be the effect of passion, prejudice, and selfishness, which prevails to this hour, and prevents that desirable union in religion which ought to be the result of the extension of human knowledge, and of the liberal, refined sentiments, that prevail all over Europe, with respect to all other sciences but that of divinity.

The archbishop's zeal at length carried him beyond the limits of his duty, for he wanted to influence the house of commons to submit all matters concerning religion to the bishops, but two renowned patriots of those days, Mr. Strickland and Mr. Wentworth, strenuously opposed this arbitrary proceeding, in which the queen was impoliticly concerned; and, after very warm debates, the commons were obliged to agree to her majesty's pretensions, though by no means well founded, that as supreme head of the church, the ordering of all things thereunto belonging, was a branch of her royal prerogative; and Mr. Wentworth, for his freedom of speech in this debate, was sent to the Tower. The queen then committed this prerogative into the hands of Parker, and the prelates of his party, who not content with requiring subscription to the thirty-nine articles, exceeded the penalties prescribed by law for refusal. And to crown the whole, the archbishop made a personal visitation in the Isle of Wight, at that time chiefly inhabited by foreign protestants of different persuasions, who had fled from Romish persecution: it had been the policy of government hitherto to let these strangers enjoy religious toleration, especially as there were amongst them many Calvinists; but Parker having information, that not a few of the non-conforming clergy had found an asylum, and an hospitable reception in this island, he resolved

ARCHBISHOP of CANTERBURY.

solved to enforce the act of uniformity there, never thought of before, and upon meeting with almost a general refusal, he deprived the clergy, and ordered the churches to be shut up. This intemperate zeal, when it came to be known at court, highly displeased the queen, who justly considered, that as this place was resorted to by mariners of different nations, her reputation would soon suffer in foreign countries; where these proceedings would astonish the protestants, and give the Roman catholics an opportunity of retorting the charge of persecution upon the church of England. About the same time the bishop of Winchester remonstrated, that the archbishop in a visitation of his diocese, had infringed on his privileges, and established an inquisitorial power over his clergy. The council upon these complaints, declared their disapprobation of the archbishop's conduct, and advised her majesty to order the churches to be opened in the Isle of Wight, and the ministers to be restored, without subscribing, unless they did it voluntarily, which was accordingly done, and when Parker came to court, the queen publicly reprimanded him. But the mischief was done, the spirit of superiority, of ecclesiastical pride, and of disdain for their protestant brethren of different persuasions, which remains to this hour a reproach to the dignified clergy of the church of England as a body, had disseminated itself in all parts of the kingdom, never to be eradicated.

Parker could but ill brook any coolness from the queen, or her ministry, as he always pretended that the warmth of his zeal, was for the advancement of her majesty's honour, and the support of her royal prerogative, and therefore he retired from court, and wrote a very sharp letter to Cecil lord Burleigh,

Burleigh, now high treasurer, and first minister of state, expressing his discontent at the opposition formed against his measures, and declaring both the church and the state to be in danger of dissolution from the countenance given to the Puritans; but he did not long survive this letter, for being severely afflicted with the stone, and its common attendant the stranguary, he was taken off by a violent fit of the last in May 1575.

This prelate however, with all his faults, must be considered as a principal agent in adding to the lustre of the reign of Elizabeth, by fixing the protestant religion, on such a permanent footing, as left not the least probability of the restoration of popery, to which the people, from the natural inconstancy of their dispositions, so readily returned after the death of Edward VI. A circumstance which will be hereafter enumerated with the rest of the signal advantages obtained for this kingdom, by her prudent and successful administration.

His reputation, as an author, and a useful antiquarian, still preserves his name with veneration in the learned world. He was a diligent researcher after Saxon and British antiquities, he spared neither labour nor expence to collect and preserve the writings of the most ancient authors of our own country, and according to Strype, one of his agents only procured for him no less than 6700 volumes, in four years. His controversial works are but few and of small estimation, but his folio edition of the Bible in English, published by him in 1568, is in high estimation: it is called the Bishop's Bible, because he was assisted in the translation by some of the bishops: it is now very scarce, but there is a copy in excellent preservation at the British Museum, and, by the best critics
this

this tranflation is preferred to that which is in common ufe, being the laft tranflation made in the reign of James I. and by that Prince ordered to be ufed in all churches inftead of Parker's, or the bifhop's bible. The archbifhop likewife publifhed editions of four of our ancient Englifh hiftorians; Matthew of Weftminfter, Matthew Paris, Afler's Life of Alfred, and Thomas Walfingham's hiftory from Edward I. to Henry V. with his account of Normandy. To thefe we may add the lives of his predeceffors the archbifhops of Canterbury, the joint labour of Parker and Joceline one of his chaplains. The beft edition of this work is that by Dr. Samuel Drake, London, 1729.

*** *Authorities.* Life of Matthew Parker by Strype, M. A. Neale's Hiftory of the Puritans. Warner's Ecclefiaftical Hiftory of England. Sir James Ware's Hiftory of the Bifhops of Ireland. Stow's Chronicle.

The LIFE of

Sir THOMAS GRESHAM,

Merchant and Citizen of LONDON.

[A. D. 1519, to 1579.]

THE Revolutions in the commercial affairs of Europe, form as ftriking a picture of the glorious age of Elizabeth as thofe of religion, with which they were at this period intimately connected, ed, and perhaps, there is not to be found in the history of any nation such a concurrence of happy events as those, which at almost one and the same instant, contributed to insure the prosperity of England, and to fix the renown of its sovereign during this glorious æra.

It is impossible to illustrate the truth of these historical remarks, in more precise terms than those of the celebrated Voltaire, in his universal history; and as he makes honourable mention of the eminent citizen and patriot, to whose life they are applied, the reader cannot be presented with a more beautiful and apt introduction.

"From the first beginning of Elizabeth's reign, the English applied themselves to manufactures: the Flemings being persecuted by Philip II. king of Spain, (who permitted his governor of the low countries, now the Austrian Netherlands, to exercise every act of cruelty for the extirpation of heresy) removed to London, bringing with them an increase of inhabitants, industry and riches. This capital, which enjoyed the blessings of peace under Elizabeth, cultivated likewise the liberal arts, which are the badges and consequences of plenty. London was enlarged, civilized, and embellished; and, in a short time, one half of the little island of Great Britain, was able to counterbalance the whole power of Spain. The English now figured as the second nation in the world in industry, as in liberty they were the first; and a private merchant in London, was rich enough to build the Royal Exchange, and to found and endow a college for the education of the children of his fellow citizens."

By what means England attained this accession of national power, splendor, and riches, will be developed in the life of this illustrious citizen,

Sir THOMAS GRESHAM.

tizen, and of those great statesmen, warriors and navigators, who by their signal services in their different stations of life, at once immortalized their own reputations, and aggrandised their native country.

Mr. Thomas Gresham was the descendant of an ancient family, who, according to Camden, took their name from a town so called in Norfolk, and this family had produced several eminent men in the earlier periods of the British history, nor was the father of this gentleman, Sir Richard Gresham, of less note than his ancestors: for being fortunate in the business of a mercer, and enabled to purchase considerable estates, he became sheriff of London in 1531, and recommended himself to Henry VIII. who conferred upon him the honour of knighthood, and made him his principal agent for the negociation of his mercantile concerns and loans at Antwerp, during his wars with France, and he was afterwards mayor; but Sir Richard is still more memorable as a citizen, for obtaining the privilege for private merchants to be bankers, and to negociate bills of exchange without applying for a special licence, which was before required; and as this privilege was first exercised by merchants residing in Lombard-street, this made that situation so well known afterwards for this business, and here it was that Sir Richard proposed to build a bourse or exchange, but this honour however, was reserved for his son Thomas; but he purchased the chapel of St. Thomas of Acres now Mercer's chapel for that company. It is observable, that at this period and long after, no person could belong to any other company but that of the trade he followed, which bred an attachment, friendship and society among citizens of the same trade, and occasioned valuable gifts

gifts and legacies to the several companies from their respective members; whereas at present, one of the principal uses of such companies is destroyed, for a fishmonger by trade, may be a clothworker in his corporate capacity; a lawyer a goldsmith, and a peer a sadler, to the destruction of all order, and of the original design of instituting such fraternities.

Sir Richard Gresham had two sons, the eldest, John Gresham, was an eminent citizen in the reign of Edward VI. and though bred to his father's business, accompanied the protector Somerset, in his expedition to Scotland, and was knighted by the duke on the spot, after the victory he obtained over the Scots in Mussleborough field in 1547; he died in the reign of queen Mary in 1560. The youngest son, our famous merchant, was born at London in 1519, and for some particular view as we imagine, was bound apprentice to a mercer when he was very young, but he certainly did not follow the business as an apprentice, for we find him passing some years in his studies at Caius college, under the celebrated founder Dr. Caius, who in commendation of his application and proficiency, styled him *Doctissimus Mercator*, the very learned merchant. However, the profits of trade were then so great and such large estates had been raised by it in his own family, that he also engaged in it, and was made free of the mercers company in 1543. It is supposed, that Mr. Gresham married about this time, the daughter of William Fernley of Suffolk, relict of William Reade, Esq; of Middlesex, for he had a son named Richard, in honour of his grandfather, born some time before the death of Sir Richard, which happened in 1548.

Sir William Dansell succeeded Mr. Gresham's father as the king's agent at Antwerp, but by his bad manage-

management, instead of supplying the king with money, he brought him so considerably in debt, that the merchants at Antwerp would not make any further advances, which greatly embarrassed the king's affairs at home, and occasioned a letter of recall, which Dansell refused to obey; hereupon our merchant was sent for by the council, and his opinion required by what means his majesty might best be enabled to discharge the debt, amounting to 260,000 *l.* or put it in such a state of liquidation and security, that his loans might go on in the usual channel at Antwerp. His sentiments upon this point, must have been very satisfactory, for without any request on his part, he was appointed agent, and removed with his family to Antwerp in 1551, where he soon found himself involved in very troublesome and uneasy circumstances; but his fertile genius enabled him to extricate himself with great honour. The money that had been borrowed by the late agent for the king's use, not being repaid at the stipulated times, he found himself under a necessity to procure an additional term of prolongation, but this the avaritious Flemings would by no means agree to, unless his majesty would purchase jewels, or some other rich commodities, to a considerable amount, on which they might gain immense profits, besides the interest, at that time rated at 16 *per cent.* on the value, till paid for.

And it deserves the reader's notice, that the principal commerce of Antwerp at this early period, consisted in the importation of diamonds, pearls and other precious stones, and of wool; together with the negociation of loans of money and exchanges. The persecution of the duke of Alva, drove the manufacturers, and the merchants trafficking in bulky commodities, most liable to seizure and confiscation, from this ancient mart of com-

commerce, but many of the diamond merchants, and money agents remained, whose descendants have preserved this city from a total decline, by keeping alive the two branches of the diamond trade, and negociating bills of exchange, for both of which, Antwerp is at this day famous, being the cheapest European market for jewels, and so remarkable, with respect to exchanges, that a well known merchant, or gentleman, either native or foreigner, may get a bill discounted, drawn on the remotest part of the habitable globe.

Mr. Gresham did not judge it compatible, either with the king's honour, or his own credit as his agent, to comply with the venal proposals of the Flemings, he therefore peremptorily rejected them, and transmitted a plan to England for discharging the king's debts at Antwerp in two years. He proposed that the council should immediately remit about 1300 *l*. to a friend in their interest with the utmost privacy, and he would make such a discretional use of this sum thus thrown into the market as to prevent the artful fall of the exchange with England. The council approved his design and remitted the money, with which small sum he contrived to take up 200 *l*. every week upon his own credit, on bills of exchange drawn at double usance on England, and thus he gained time, and negociated 72,000 *l*. in one year. In addition to this scheme, he proposed, that the king should take the commerce of the lead mines with Antwerp, into his own hands, and issue a proclamation, forbidding the exportation of this article, except on the king's account for five years. This measure being taken had the desired effect, the king's agents engrossed the lead, which caused the price to rise considerably at the Flemish markets, and at the enhanced value, they supplied Antwerp discretionally; so that by these two mercantile stratagems.

gems the balance was turned in favour of England, and the king's debts honourably discharged within the term proposed by Mr. Gresham. And the credit of the crown of England, which before his time, was considered by the Flemish merchants as very slender, rose to such a height of reputation, that Mr. Gresham could borrow what sums he thought proper, on equitable terms, either on his master's, or his own private credit.

The demise of king Edward, retarded for a time, the honours due to this great man for his eminent services, for upon the accession of queen Mary, he was recalled, but he had been enabled to live very comfortably as a private gentleman by the munificence of his royal master, who, besides lands, to the yearly value of 300 *l.* settled a pension of 100 *l.* on him and his heirs for ever, about three weeks before he died, making use of these words, among other honourable expressions in the patent, " You shall know that you have served a king."

However, his friends importuned him, to present a memorial to the queen, stating the signal services performed by his father and himself to the crown in their public characters, often at the risk of their lives and fortunes, and making particular mention of a heavy loss sustained by our merchant on his return to England, the vessel in which his houshold furniture, plate, and the wearing apparel of himself and his lady was embarked being shipwrecked, and not one article saved, yet no indemnification had been given him for a misfortune incurred, while he was employed in the public service. It appears, that this memorial procured him the restoration of his former employ, and other commissions from the queen, for the management of her affairs in the Low-countries, which are inserted in the 15th volume of *Rymer's Fœdera.* When queen Elizabeth succeeded to the crown,

crown, he was one of the first of her loyal citizens taken into favour; she employed him soon after her accession to buy up, and furnish the royal arsenals with arms; and the year following, her majesty conferred on him the honour of knighthood, and appointed him her agent in foreign parts. Being now in the highest esteem with his fellow citizens and in great credit at court, he thought proper to fix his residence in the city, and to live there in a manner suitable to his rank and fortune: for this purpose, says *Stow*, " he built " that large and sumptuous house for his own " dwelling on the west side of Bishopsgate-street, which, after the demise of his lady, was converted into a college, pursuant to his will, called Gresham college, and has since been pulled down, being in a ruinous condition, to build the New Excise Office. Here he maintained a post becoming his character and station."

But the joy which prosperity naturally inspires, was checked by a family misfortune about this time, by the sickness and death of Richard Gresham his only son, who died in 1564.

The merchants of London still continuing to meet in Lombard-street in the open air, exposed to the inclemencies of the weather, Sir Thomas resolved to revive his father's plan of building for them a commodious bourse, on the plan of the bourse at Antwerp. With this view he generously proposed to his fellow citizens, to erect this public edifice at his own expence, if the corporation would assign over to him a proper spot of ground, sufficiently spacious, to render it both useful and convenient. Such an instance of urbanity is but rarely to be met with, and therefore the city most readily and gratefully accepted this offer, in consequence of which they purchased eighty houses in Cornhill, situated in the three allies, then called, Swan's,

Swan's, New, and St. Chriſtopher's allies, for which the corporation paid to the ſeveral owners, in the year 1566, the ſum of 3532 *l*. and immediately ſold the houſes under contract, to pull them down and remove the materials in three months, for the trifling ſum of 478 *l*. This done, the ground plot was laid out at the expence of the city, and poſſeſſion given to Sir Thomas, who in the deed of aſſignment, is ſtyled " Agent to the " queen's highneſs;" and on the 7th of June, 1567, the founder laid the firſt ſtone of the edifice, accompanied by ſome of the aldermen, who laid eight pieces of gold upon the bricks for the workmen, and after this ceremony was over, they ſeemed to vie with each other in expreſſing their gratitude, for they proceeded on the building with ſuch amazing diligence and diſpatch, that in November the roof was covered in, and the timber work, which had been framed and fitted for putting up at Batisford near Ipſwich, was completed ſoon after.

The plan of this bourſe, or exchange, was an oblong ſquare, with piazzas on the north and ſouth ſides, ſupported by ten pillars of marble on each ſide; and thoſe on the eaſt and weſt ends were ſupported by ſeven pillars on each ſide: under theſe piazzas, ſhops, to the number of 120, were neatly fitted up, which were lett by Sir Thomas, upon an average at 4 *l*. 10 *s*. *per annum*. Other ſhops were fitted up at firſt in the vaults under ground, but the darkneſs and damp rendered them ſo unwholeſome and inconvenient, that they were very ſoon removed, and the vaults lett for ſuitable uſes. Upon four pinnacles at each corner of the roof was placed a graſhopper, the creſt of the arms of the Greſham family; and in honour of Sir Thomas, a very large graſhopper was placed on the turret of the new Royal Exchange, which

ſerves

serves likewise as a vane. The old building was burnt in the great fire of 1666, and the present noble structure was erected at the joint expence of the city and of the mercers company. It cost 80,000 *l.* and was finished in the year 1670.

Sir Thomas Gresham's exchange was entirely completed, and the shops opened in 1569, and in January, 1570, queen Elizabeth, attended by her nobility, came from Somerset-house, and passing by Temple Bar, through Fleet-street, Cheap, and the north side of the new bourse, to Sir Thomas's house in Bishopsgate-street, dined there, and after dinner, returning through Cornhill, entered the bourse on the south side, and having viewed every part thereof above ground, especially the Pawn, (the ranges of shops) which was richly furnished with all sorts of the finest wares in the city, she caused the bourse, by a trumpet and a herald, to be proclaimed the ROYAL EXCHANGE, and so to be called from thence forth, and not otherwise. A ridiculous tradition is handed down to this time, founded on no historical evidence whatever, that in honour of his royal visitor, and in proof of his great wealth, Sir Thomas Gresham, ordered a pearl of immense value to be reduced to powder, and thrown into a glass of wine, which he drank to the queen's health. It seems to have been only a poetical licence, taken from an historical play, in two acts, composed to compliment the queen upon two great events in her reign; the building of the Royal Exchange, and the destruction of the Spanish Armada. The lines in the drama are—

> Here fifteen hundred pound at one clap goes.
> Instead of sugar, Gresham drinks this pearl,
> Unto his queen and mistress: pledge it lords.

The judicious critic will likewise reflect, that Gresham's fortune had suffered in the reign of queen Mary, it is therefore highly improbable, that in the course of twelve years, in the infancy of the British commerce, he should have gained such immense wealth, as to enable him to commit such an act of idle extravagance.

But the situation of public affairs, from the time of his forming a design of building an exchange, to the date of its completion, totally discredits this fable; for in this interval Sir Thomas Gresham had been sent to Antwerp to borrow about 8000 *l.* sterling, and to procure further time for the payment of two old debts of the crown, amounting together to about 22,000 *l.* sterling: this business he successfully negotiated in 1566; and by this time fully convinced that her Majesty might borrow money of her own subjects, on more advantageous terms, than those required by the Flemings, he presented a memorial to the ministry upon this subject, on his return from Flanders; but this salutary advice was not followed till the year 1569, when the rupture between England and Spain absolutely forced administration into a measure, which sound policy and domestic œconomy should have induced them to have adopted much eariler.

The duke of Alva, by order of Philip II. king of Spain, prohibited all commerce in Flanders with the English; upon which, our merchants and factors left Antwep, and retired to Hamburgh; and Cecil, the secretary of state, and lord treasurer, apprehensive that the merchants would not have money sufficient to carry on their trade at their new settlement, where their credit was not yet established, and consequently that the import duties at home, especially on woollen cloths, would fall short, the
queen's

queen's only resource for discharging her foreign debts, communicated his sentiments, in this embarrassed situation, to Sir Thomas Gresham; who, being well acquainted with the circumstances of the English merchants at Hamburgh, and the state of their commercial transactions, dispelled the minister's fears, by assuring him, that if the queen could contrive to pay the London merchants the first payment, being one half of her debt to them, they would thereby be enabled to make such remittances to Hamburgh, as would firmly establish the credit of the English merchants settled there; and before the second payment, enable them to ship from thence for England, commodities to the amount of 100,000 *l*. which, with the exports for Hamburgh then ready to be shipped and estimated at 200,000 *l*. would produce duties to the amount of 10,000 *l*. and remove every doubt of the queen's ability to pay her creditors.

Sir Thomas further added, that the demand for English commodities was so great, that the merchants at Hamburgh would have plenty of money, as well as full credit to obtain any quantity of foreign commodities for England, after they had received the merchandize now shipping from London; but in the mean time, lest these should be retarded by any unforeseen accident, he advised Cecil to remit money to Hamburgh, to enable them to fulfill the contracts they had made for goods sent to England on their first settlement, before they could receive any returns: this being done, the credit of the queen and the English merchants was in such high repute, that the duke of Alva, who foresaw his own ruin, in that of the Flemish commerce, " quaked for fear." The persecution set on foot by the duke of Alva has been already noticed; but besides this scourge, he laid a heavy imposition on commerce,

commerce, demanding the tenth penny upon the value of all goods brought into the Low-countries for sale, which completed the ruin of the commerce of those countries, and removed it to Amsterdam, Hamburgh, and London. The prudent measure of procuring loans from her own subjects for the public service, was next carried into execution; but the laudable project received a considerable check at first from the corporation of Merchants Adventurers, who, at a general court rejected the queen's demand of a loan, which the queen highly resented, in a letter written by Cecil to the company at her express command; however, the sum being only 16,000 *l.* was obtained through Gresham's interest in the city from some of the aldermen, and other merchants, at *six per cent.* for six months; and at the expiration of that term, a prolongation was readily agreed to. This happened in the year 1572, and is a revolution in the finance operations of government, which adds another wreath of fame to the annals of this reign.

To remedy the scarcity of silver coin, which obstructed inland trade, our patriotic merchant, ever zealous in the service of his country, knowing that one Reggio, an Italian merchant, had lodged thirty thousand Flemish ducatoons in the Tower for security, and that he had likewise a considerable quantity of the same pieces in the hands of private friends in London, advised the queen to purchase them of Reggio, and to coin them into English shillings and sixpences, by which she would gain three or four thousand pounds, and keep all this fine silver in her realm: (many of these shillings and sixpences are still to be met with in the cabinets of the curious in high preservation) the ducatoons were accordingly purchased of the Italian, and the queen borrowed the amount of the London merchants for

two

two years, at moderate interest. At the same time Sir Thomas sent five sacks of new Spanish ryals, his own property, to the Mint; and this example encouraged others, so that when the new coinage was issued, silver currency became very plentiful at home, and the greatest part of the queen's debts in Flanders were paid with it; the residue being soon after remitted in bills of exchange on Hamburgh, to the great honour of the queen, and the further advancement of the commercial credit of the kingdom in foreign countries.

These wise regulations of course, abolished the office of queen's agent for money matters in foreign parts; but the queen, to shew her high regard for Sir Thomas Gresham, and that he might not lose the dignity of a public character in the city, put him into the commission with the archbishop of Canterbury, the bishop of London, and some lords of the council, who, in this reign, were usually appointed assistants to the Lord Mayor in the government of the city, during the queen's summer progresses through the kingdom. This honour he held as occasion required, from 1572 to 1578.

Sir Thomas Gresham's active life would not permit him to be long absent from the bustle of the mercantile world; he loved to visit his favourite exchange, and to associate with merchants: upon which account, he would not retire to any of the considerable estates he had purchased in the remoter counties, but built a magnificent seat at Osterley Park, near Brentford in Middlesex.

Here he indulged himself with short intervals of relaxation, but his mind was always so full of plans for the public good, and the promotion of useful industry, that even here he mixed utility with recreation, and made business part of his amusement:

for

for within his park, he erected paper, oil, and corn mills, thus finding constant employment of various sorts of workmen, who were constantly devoted to his service, he being likewise a liberal master, the wonderful part of the following anecdote falls to the ground; and it appears highly probable, though we have but slender authority to support the fact as it is related by Fuller in his Worthies of Middlesex. According to him, "Queen Elizabeth, having been once very magnificently entertained and lodged at Osterley Park, she found fault with the court before it, as being too large, and said it would appear better, if divided by a wall in the middle: he took the hint, and sent for workmen from London," (rather from Brentford) "who in the night built up the wall with such privacy and expedition, that the next morning the queen, to her great surprise, found the court divided, in the manner she had proposed the day before."

The greatest part of the very ample fortune which Sir Thomas Gresham had acquired by his close application to, and consummate skill in mercantile transactions, he now resolved to devote to the benefit of his fellow-citizens, and their children's children, having no legitimate heir to inherit it after his decease. He had indeed a natural daughter, by a Flemish woman, while he resided at Bruges in Flanders; but having given her in marriage to Nathaniel Bacon, the second son of the lord keeper of the great seal, with a portion suitable to his own circumstances, and the rank of the gentleman who had married her, he thought himself free from all family claims, after he had made a comfortable provision for his lady, in case she survived him. Accordingly, he made no secret of his laudable design, to have his mansion-house (as it was then called) converted into a college, for the profession of the seven liberal sciences, and to endow it with the revenues of the Royal Exchange, after his own and his lady's decease. As soon as this was known, the university of Cambridge, at which place he had been educated, ordered their public orator, Mr. Richard Bridgewater, to write him an elegant Latin letter, reminding him of a promise he had formerly made (as the university were informed) to give them 500*l*. either towards building a new college, or repairing an old one at Cambridge, for the same purposes. This letter was expedited the beginning of March, 1575; and before the end of the month they wrote him another, acquainting him, that they had heard, he had positively declared his intention of founding a college to Lady Burleigh; and as there were but three convenient situations, in their opinion, for such a foundation, London, Oxford, and Cambridge, they hoped a superior regard for Cambridge would determine him to give that university the preference. At the same time, they wrote to Lady Burleigh, requesting her interest with him upon this occasion. But these letters failed of the desired effect, owing to very just and prudent causes. London, at this time, had no similar institution, and the want of liberal education made the principal merchants, obstinate and tenacious of every idle prejudice adopted from custom. This Sir Thomas had experienced, in the trouble they had given him, by opposing his very rational plan of establishing a reciprocal union of interests and attachment between them and the government, by supplying the public loans instead of foreigners. Another motive, undoubtedly, was that immortal fame, which every public spirited, every good citizen should have in view, whereby, as he was venerated while living, so, in after ages, his memory might be gratefully preserved, in that community of which he was a respectable member.

Persisting therefore, in the resolution of fixing the college in his dwelling-house, he executed a deed of settlement, dated May 20, 1575, disposing of his several manors, lands, tenements, and hereditaments, with such limitations and restrictions, particularly as to the Royal Exchange, and his house in Bishopsgate-street, as might best secure his views with respect to the purposes for which they were intended. This deed, which was an indenture quadripartite, was succeeded by two wills, the one bearing date July 4, and the other the following day, of the same year: by the first, he bequeaths to his wife, whom he appoints his sole executrix, all his personal estate, consisting of cash, plate, jewels, chains of gold, and flocks of sheep, with other cattle; except several legacies to his relations, friends, and servants, amounting to upwards of 2000*l.* and a few small annuities. By the second, he gives one moiety of the Royal Exchange to the mayor and commonalty of the city of London, and the other to the Mercer's company, for the salaries of seven professors, one for each of the liberal sciences, to be chosen by them, " being meet and sufficiently learned," to read public lectures in divinity, law, physic, astronomy, geometry, music, and rhetoric, for which they are to receive a salary of 50*l. per annum*, and to be provided with apartments for their residence, in his said mansion-house. He likewise bequeaths 53*l.* 6*s.* 8*d.* yearly, to be divided equally between eight poor persons, inhabiting the like number of alms-houses built by him, behind his house. Also 10*l. per annum* to the prisons of Newgate, Ludgate, the King's-bench, the Marshalsea, and the two Compters; with the like annuity to the hospitals of Christ, St. Bartholomew, Bedlam, and St. Thomas. Also 100*l.* annually, to provide a dinner for the whole company of Mercers in their hall, on every quarter-day, at 25*l.* for each dinner.

These dispositions were made conformable to the produce of the rents of the Royal Exchange, and the fines for alienations which exceeded at the time, the annual payments appointed by the will, so that the two corporations had more than sufficient investments for the trusts they were to execute. But as the lady Anne, his wife, was to enjoy the mansion, and the rents of the Royal Exchange for her life, in case she survived him, they were both vested (after her decease) in the two corporations for the term of fifty years; which limitation was made on account of the statutes of *Mortmain*, prohibiting the alienation of lands or tenements to any corporation, without licence first obtained from the crown; the procuring of which, the testator not only recommended in the strongest terms, but by a prudential clause, in some measure secured; for the estates were to revert to his heirs at law, if no licence was obtained within the time limited. The two corporations however, in conformity to the conditions of their trust, applied for a patent, which was granted to them by James I. in the year 1614, to hold the bequeathed estates for ever, for the uses declared in the will.

His worldly concerns being thus adjusted in a manner that could not but afford him much secret satisfaction, and the most pleasing reflections, it is most probable that he lived a retired life, enjoying the happy tranquillity, which affluence acquired by honest industry, and peace of mind, the result of pious and benevolent actions always afford, for no particular memoirs of the four last years of his life are handed down to us; all the account we have of him, after the year 1575, is, that on the 29th of November, 1579, this great and good man was taken off in an apoplectic fit: Hollingshed says, " that coming," (or, more properly, being come) " from the Royal Exchange to his house in Bishopsgategate-street, he suddenly fell down in the kitchen, and being taken up was found speechless, and presently died."

By his death, many large estates in several counties of England, amounting to the yearly value of 2388*l.* an amazing income, in those days, devolved to his lady for her life; and as she survived him many years, this accounts for the late date of the patent to the corporations, Lady Gresham residing in winter at the mansion-house in Bishopsgate-street, and in summer at Osterley Park.

His obsequies were performed in a public and solemn manner, and his charitable works followed him to his very grave; for he had ordered by his will, that his corpse should be attended by one hundred poor men, and the same number of poor women cloathed in black cloth gowns, at his expence. His remains were deposited at the north-east corner of St. Helens, his parish church, in a vault which he had long since provided for himself and family. The funeral charges amounted to 800*l.* Over the vault is a large, curious marble tomb, on the south and west sides of which are his own arms, and on the north and east, the same empaled with those of his lady; the arms of Sir Thomas, with those of the city of London, and of the Mercer's company, are likewise painted on glass, in the east-window of the church, above the tomb, which remained without any inscription upon it till the year 1736, when for the information of the curious, the following words, taken from the parish register, were cut on the stone that covers it. *Sir Thomas Gresham, Knight, was buried* December 15, 1579.

To the copious account already given of the principal events in the life of this generous citizen, we have only to add, from Ward's summary of his character, the following particulars. He was well acquainted with the ancient and several modern languages, and he was a liberal patron to learned men, both natives and foreigners, which is acknowledged in the dedications of their works to him, by different authors, particularly by John Fox, the celebrated martyrologist; Hugh Goughe, writer of the history of the Ottoman Turks, &c. He transacted queen Elizabeth's affairs so constantly, that he was commonly called, "The Royal Merchant." And he had the very signal honour, upon many occasions, to be appointed to receive foreign princes on their first arrival in England, and to entertain them at his house, till they were presented at court. In fine, having no son to keep up his name, he took the most effectual method to perpetuate it, in the highest degree of grateful veneration, as long as the city of London exists as a corporation.

*** *Authorities.* Camden's Britan. edit. 1720. Journal of Edw. VI. of his own writing in the Coton. library at the Museum. Rymer's Fœdera, vol. 15. Ward's life of Gresham.

The LIFE of
ROBERT DUDLEY,
EARL of LEICESTER.

[A. D. 1532, to 1588.]

Including Memoirs of Sir Philip Sydney, and Sir Robert Dudley.

SOME mention has already been made of this gentleman, in the life of the duke of Northumberland, Vol. I. p. 170. It is therefore only necessary to add, as to the juvenile part of his life, that he was the duke's fifth son, by Jane, the daughter and heiress of Sir Edward Guilford. The exact time of his birth is not recorded, but it is supposed to have been in the year 1532; and in the year 1550, he was married to Amy, the daughter of Sir John Robart, when, as a compliment to his father, the king was present at the nuptials; and it is remarkable, that from early youth to the last hour of his life, he was a successful courtier. Upon the king's death, he engaged with his father, in support of lady Jane Grey's title to the crown, and attended upon him in his expedition into Norfolk; but upon the duke's being arrested at Cambridge, he he fled to queen Mary's camp, and furrendered; from whence he was brought up prifoner to London, and confined in the Tower, on the twenty-fixth of July 1553, and on the fifteenth of January following, was arraigned of high treafon at the Guild-hall of London, confeffed the indictment, and was adjudged by the earl of Suffex to be hanged, drawn, and quartered. But the lords interceding for him with the queen, fhe reftored him and his bretern, (except the lord Guilford) in blood, received him into favour, and made him mafter of the Englifh ordnance at the fiege of St. Quintin, in 1557.

As foon as queen Elizabeth afcended the throne, fhe advanced him to one of the higheft pofts of honour near her perfon, making him her mafter of the horfe, and in the fecond year of her reign, to the great furprize of his rival courtiers, her Majefty advanced him to the dignity of privy counfellor, and honoured him with the noble order of the garter.

Encouraged by thefe favours, he gave into the opinion, that, if he could get rid of his wife, he need not defpair of foon rendering himfelf perfonally agreeable to her Majefty. The lady was difpatched into the country, to the houfe of one of his dependants, where, it is faid, he firft attempted to have taken her off by poifon; but, failing in this defign, he caufed her to be thrown down from the top of a ftair-cafe, and murdered by the fall. She was at firft obfcurely buried, but that having given occafion to cenfure, he ordered her body to be taken up, and fhe was interred again in St. Mary's church at Oxford, with all imaginable pomp and folemnity.

Ambition and luft were the ruling paffions of Dudley; and his perfonal accomplifhments, derived both from nature and polite education, infpired him with confummate vanity: nor muft Elizabeth pafs
uncen-

uncensured, for it appears, that even before the death of his wife, she exceeded the bounds of female decorum in her conduct towards him, insomuch, that at foreign courts her reputation was but slightly treated, and her ambassadors complained of it, in their dispatches to the ministry at home. But after this tragical event, it was observed that he met with a more favourable reception than ever from the queen; and though she did not openly countenance his pretensions of marriage, yet she seemed not at all displeased with the overture; and when her marriage with him was moved by the French ambassador, she only objected that he was not of the royal blood, nor could she think of raising a dependant to the rank of a companion. But envy and hatred are the sure attendants upon greatness, and Dudley, by being thus distinguished above the rest in her Majesty's favour, drew upon himself the odium of the courtiers: and, it is possible, that about this time, the history of Reynard the Fox, now in the hands of every child, was written, as a satire against his lordship.

Yet it must be noticed, in justice to the queen's political character, that notwithstanding her blameable partiality to him as a favourite, which sometimes gave him a prevailing interest at the councilboard, she never confided to him the general administration of affairs; and this may be accounted for, by admitting that Cecil's great abilities as a statesman, enabled him to undermine the voluptuous Dudley, whose sensuality checked the progress of his ambition. Yet his skilful antagonist, that he might seem to gratify him even in this passion, while he was attempting either his removal from court, or a diminution of his influence, suggested to her Majesty the propriety of a match between Dudley and Mary queen of Scots, then about to form a foreign alliance, which must be prejudicial to England. The crown of Scotland in poffeffion, and the right of inheritance to the crown of England, were moft alluring baits; and Cecil knew, that fhould he be over-earneft in the purfuit of the match propofed, he would be infallibly loft in the good graces of the queen; at the fame time, he was under no apprehenfion, from the known temper of the queen of Scots, that a perfon of his lordfhip's extraction could ever render himfelf acceptable to her. Elizabeth, whatever was her motive, gave ear to this propofal, and fent immediate inftructions to Randolph, her ambaffador in Scotland, to open the matter to Mary; but that queen refolved to reject the offer, though fhe feared to come to an open rupture with Elizabeth. She difpatched Sir James Melvil to London, with inftructions full of friendlinefs and regard. But when Elizabeth enquired if the queen of Scots had fent any anfwer to the propofition of marriage fhe had made her, the ambaffador gave an evafive anfwer. Her Majefty then entered upon the commendation of lord Robert Dudley, declared fhe would marry him herfelf, if fhe had not been determined to end her days in virginity: and fhe further told Sir James Melvil, "fhe wifhed that the queen her fifter might marry him, as meet ft of all other with whom fhe could find in her heart to declare her fecond perfon. For being matched with him, it would beft remove out of her mind all fears and fufpicions to be offended by any ufurpation before her death. Being affured, that he was fo loving and trufty, that he would never permit any fuch thing to be attempted during her time." In the courfe of this curious converfation, given at large by Sir James Melvil, in his memoirs, Sir James had named the earl of Bedford as firft commiffioner to be fent to Scotland, to fettle all differences between the two crowns; and lord Robert Dudley only as his fecond. The queen

queen took fire at this, vowed she would make him a far greater earl than Bedford, and desired the ambassador to stay till he should see him made earl of Leicester, and baron Denbigh, which was accordingly done at Westminster on the 29th of September 1564, with great solemnity, the queen herself assisting at the ceremony. And not long after, upon the resignation of Sir J. Mason, he was made chancellor of the university of Oxford.

The earl, however, seemed now rather to decline the match, than desire it; he excused himself to the Scottish ambassador, from having ever entertained so proud a pretence, declared his sense of his own unworthiness, and begged her Majesty would not be offended, nor impute a matter to him, which the malice of his enemies had devised for his destruction: within a few days after, Sir James Melvil obtained his dispatch, with a more ample declaration of the queen's mind, upon the subject of his embassy.

In the mean time, the earl of Leicester wrote letters to the earl of Murray, to excuse him to the queen of Scots. And that he might the better recommend himself at court, by shewing his zeal in the service of his royal mistress, he accused Sir Nicholas Bacon to Elizabeth, that he had intermeddled in the affair of the succession, and assisted in the publication of a book against the queen of Scot's title. The queen was highly offended, the author, Hales, was taken up and imprisoned, and Sir Nicholas Bacon would have infallibly lost his office, if Leicester could have persuaded Sir Anthony Brown to have accepted it.

In November following, the earl of Bedford and Mr. Randolph, the earl of Murray and secretary Lidington, commissioners on both sides, met near Berwick, to treat of the marriage, but with slenderer offers, and less effectual dealing, than was expected.

The

The earl of Leicester's behaviour, and the prudence and discretion, which appeared in the letters he had written to the earl of Murray, had made an impression upon the queen of Scots, and she seemed so far to approve of the match, that queen Elizabeth began to be afraid it might take effect. Under these apprehensions, and at the solicitation of secretary Cecil, she permitted lord Darnley to take a journey into Scotland, in hope, that his presence might be more prevalent than Leicester's absence. And the earl of Leicester, perceiving the queen's inclination, wrote private letters to the earl of Bedford, to desist from prosecuting his proposed match any farther. The queen of Scots was soon after solemnly married to lord Darnley, in the royal chapel of Holyrood-house, and the next day he was publicly proclaimed king, and associated with her Majesty in the government.

In 1565, application was again made to queen Elizabeth to think seriously of marriage, by this means to weaken the party of the queen of Scots in England, and to strengthen the interest of the protestant religion. The emperor Maximilian proposed his brother, the arch-duke Charles, with very honourable conditions. The earl of Sussex favoured the match; but Leicester, presuming upon his power with the queen, took pains to prevent it. This opposition was ill digested by the earl of Sussex, who was of an high spirit, and nobly descended. The honesty of his nature led him to a professed enmity, which divided the whole court; and whenever the two earls went abroad, they were attended with a retinue of armed followers; insomuch, that the queen was obliged to interpose her authority to make up the breach: but Sussex continued his aversion till his death; and, in his last sickness, is said to have addressed his friends to this purpose: " I am now passing into another world, and

and muft leave you to your fortunes, and to the queen's grace and goodnefs; but beware of the gypfie (meaning Leicefter) for he will be too hard for you all; you know not the beaft fo well as I do."

The ground of this quarrel, however, is more fully explained in Cecil lord Burleigh's papers, wherein it appears, that the queen permitted it to be debated in council, whether fhe fhould marry the arch-duke or Leicefter? Suffex and his friends drew up the reafons why fhe fhould not marry Leicefter. And from this very meafure we may judge of the real intentions of Elizabeth, which were to gain the confent of Mary and her minifters to the propofed match between the queen of Scots and Leicefter, that it might not appear derogatory to her honour to marry him after another queen had agreed to accept his hand; but the Englifh council prudently over-ruled her fecret inclinations.

We have already obferved, that the earl of Leicefter was made chancellor of the univerfity of Oxford, towards the end of the preceding year. At this æra, the univerfity was in a moft deplorable condition: their difcipline had long been neglected, and their learning moft miferably impoverifhed. The whole univerfity could furnifh only three preachers; and in the abfence of two of them, the audience was frequently put off with very lame performances. To give the reader an inftance: The congregation being one Sunday deftitute of a preacher, Taverner of Woodeaton, the fheriff of the county, enters St. Mary's, with his fword by his fide, and his gold chain about his neck, mounts the pulpit, and harangues the fcholars in the following ftrain: "Arriving at the mount of St. Mary's in the ftony ftage, where I now ftand, I have brought you fome fine bifcuits, baked in the oven of charity, carefully conferved for the chickens
of

of the church, the sparrows of the spirit, and the sweet swallows of salvation." This Taverner, it seems, had been brought up in the cardinal's college, was an inceptor in arts, and in deacon's orders, and a person at that time in esteem for his learning in the university; so that from this specimen it appears to how low a character their studies were reduced.

The earl of Leicester laboured by all possible means to introduce an improvement in literature, and give a new turn to the face of affairs in the university. By his letters he recommended to them the practice of religion and learning, and pressed them to a more close observance of their duty. This application was not without its effect; provision was immediately made for reforming abuses in graces and dispensations, lectures and public exercises were enforced by statute, and the habits brought under regulation; the earl continuing to patronize and regulate the university upon every occasion.

In the beginning of the year 1566, monsieur Ramboullet was dispatched into England to queen Elizabeth, by Charles IX. king of France, with the order of St. Michael, to be conferred on two English noblemen, such as should be most agreeable to her Majesty. The queen made choice of the duke of Norfolk and the earl of Leicester, the one distinguished by his high birth, and the other by her Majesty's favour. And on the twenty-fourth of January, they were invested in the royal chapel at Whitehall, with very great solemnity; no Englishman having ever been admitted before into this order, except king Henry VIII. king Edward VI. and Charles Brandon duke of Suffolk.

This summer the queen made her first progress into the country, a laudable custom which she afterwards kept up, the greatest part of her reign; and upon her return she visited Oxford. She was
attended

attended by the earl of Leicester, who previously informing the university of her design, desired they would consult their own credit upon this occasion, and make an honourable provision for her Majesty's reception. On the twenty-ninth of August his lordship, with some others of the nobility, were dispatched before by her Majesty, to give notice, that she would be there within two days. The vice-chancellor and the heads of houses came out to meet them on horseback, and entertained them with Latin orations addressed to their chancellor and secretary Cecil. And in the afternoon the lords returned to Woodstock, where the court lay, and expressed their satisfaction at their honourable reception.

On the thirty-first of August in the forenoon, the earls of Leicester and Huntingdon were present at Dr. Humphrey's lectures in the schools, who read as queen's professor in divinity, and then they attended at the public disputations. Towards evening, as her Majesty approached, she was met at Wolvercote, where the jurisdiction of the university ends, by the chancellor the earl of Leicester, by four doctors, and the vice-chancellor, in their scarlet robes and hoods; and by eight masters of arts, who were heads of colleges or halls. The chancellor then delivered the staffs of the three superior beadles into her Majesty's hands, and having received them again from her, and likewise restored them to their respective officers, the canon of Christ-church made an elegant speech to her Majesty upon the occasion. She then held out her hand to the orator and the doctors, and as Dr. Humphreys drew near to kiss it, "Mr. doctor," says the queen, smiling, "that loose gown becomes you mighty well, I wonder your notions should be so narrow." This Humphreys, it seems, was at the head of the puritan party, and had opposed the ecclesiastical habits with violent zeal.

As she entered the town, the streets were lined with scholars from Bocardo to Quatervois, who, as her Majesty passed along, fell down upon their knees, and with one voice cried out, "Long live the queen!" At Quatervois the Greek professor addressed her Majesty in a Greek oration, and the queen answered him in the same language, and commended his performance. From hence she was conveyed with the like pomp to Christ-church, where she was received by Mr. Kinsmill, the public orator; who, in the name of the university, congratulated her Majesty on her arrival among them.

For seven days together the queen was magnificently entertained by the university, and expressed an extreme delight in the lectures, disputations; public exercises, and shews; which she constantly heard and saw. On the sixth day she declared her satisfaction in a Latin speech, and assured them of her favour and protection. The day after she took her leave, and was conducted by the heads as far as Shotover-hill, when the earl of Leicester gave her notice, that they had accompanied her to the limits of their jurisdiction. Mr. Roger Marbeck then made an oration to her Majesty, and having laid open the difficulties under which learning had formerly laboured, he gratefully acknowledged the encouragements it had lately received, and the prospect of its arising to a superior degree of splendor under her Majesty's most gracious administration. The queen heard him with pleasure, returned a very favourable answer; and casting her eyes back upon Oxford, with all possible marks of tenderness and affection, she bade him farewell. Here it may not be amiss to observe, that the queen's countenance, and the earl of Leicester's care,

care, had such an effect upon the diligence of this learned body, that, within a few years after, it produced more eminent men in every branch of science, than in any preceding age.

Upon the queen's return to London, the parliament met on the first of November, fell into warm debates, and seemed resolved to insist upon her Majesty's immediate marriage, or the declaration of a successor. The earl of Leicester had earnestly supported the title of the queen of Scots; but, not meeting with the success he desired, he said that an husband ought to be imposed on the queen, or a successor appointed by parliament against her inclination. Wherein he was openly joined by the earl of Pembroke, and privately by the duke of Norfolk. But the queen was highly incensed at this behaviour, and, for some time, they were all excluded the presence-chamber, and prohibited access to her person: however, it was not long before they submitted, and obtained her Majesty's pardon.

During this disgrace, Leicester is charged with having entered into a traiterous correspondence with the Irish, who had just before broken out into an open rebellion. His letters are said to have been found upon a person of distinction, who was killed in battle; but, before the discovery could be made, he was reconciled to the queen, and placed above the reach of any private accusation.

The next year, count Stolberg was dispatched into England, by the emperor, to renew the treaty of marriage between his brother, the archduke Charles, and the queen. The earl of Sussex had not long before been sent to his imperial Majesty upon this subject, and had used his utmost efforts that her Majesty might be married to a foreign prince: but Leicester took care to supplant him in his designs, and privately engaged the lord North, who

who attended him in his journey, to be a spy upon his actions, and to break the measures he should enter into, by adverse insinuations. In the mean time, he discouraged her Majesty from the attempt, by laying before her the inconveniences that would necessarily arise from a foreign match: and the archduke, not long after, married the daughter of the duke of Bavaria; and Leicester was now no longer under any apprehension that the queen would marry a foreigner; indeed, the difficulties with respect to religion were a sufficient bar, if no other impediment had stood in the way, to the success of future negociations, as it had been in the case of the archduke.

In 1568, the queen of Scots fled into England; and Leicester appears to have continued strongly attached to her interest. He even stands charged with having entered into a conspiracy against secretary Cecil, because he suspected him to favour the succession of the house of Suffolk.

Mary at this period was a widow for the third time, her second husband, lord Darnley, having been first murdered, as it is conjectured, and then blown up by gun-powder, with all his attendants, at his hunting-seat, in 1566: Bothwell, the supposed chief conspirator, and the queen's favourite, was tried for the murder, but by her influence acquitted; and that no room might be left to doubt who was the real contriver of this foul treason, Mary married Bothwell soon after; upon which the earl of Murray, and other lords, raised an army against her, took her prisoner, and obliged her to resign her crown to her son, by lord Darnley, an infant of thirteen months old, who was thereupon crowned by the title of James VI. and Murray was appointed regent: as to Bothwell, he fled to Denmark, where he died obscurely, and Mary escaping, took refuge in England.

Here

Here Leicester contrived a new plan to restore the unfortunate, guilty queen, by proposing a marriage between her and the duke of Norfolk. He took upon him to propound the matter to the duke; extenuated the crimes she was accused of; and wrote letters to Mary in commendation of Norfolk; in which he earnestly persuaded her to approve of the marriage: and, farther, he drew up certain articles, which he sent to her by the bishop of Rosse, promising, upon her acceptance of the proposed conditions, to procure for her the crown of Scotland in present possession, and the crown of England in reversion.

Whilst affairs were in this situation, and the earl of Leicester was waiting for a convenient opportunity of opening the design to his mistress, the earl of Murray sent secret advice to her Majesty of the whole transaction, and charged the duke of Norfolk with having engaged in private practices to get the present possession of the two crowns by means of this marriage. This report, though very foreign to the duke's inclinations, was supported by circumstantial evidence, and raised the queen's jealousy, to a high degree, against the duke and the lords that were concerned with him: which, when Norfolk understood, he would have persuaded the earl to impart the scheme to her Majesty without delay; but Leicester put it off from time to time, till, at length falling sick at Titchfield, or, at least, pretending sickness; for he was a complete master of the courtly art of dissimulation; and being there visited by Elizabeth, he declared the whole matter to her, begging forgiveness with sighs and tears: and, not long after, the duke and the lords being taken into custody, the earl of Leicester was examined before the queen and council; where he gave such an account of his proceedings, and behaved in such a manner, that he easily obtained her Majesty's pardon.

In 1571, died, in a strange manner, Sir Nicholas Throgmorton, who had been at the head of Leicester's party, against Cecil secretary of state, but had lately gone over to him. Being at Leicester's house, as he was at supper, he was seized, in a most violent manner, with an imposthumation in his lungs, and died in a few days, but not without suspicion of poison. It is said, that, on his changing sides, the earl was apprehensive he might make a discovery of his secret practices, and for this reason took care to dispatch him. And, he likewise bore him a secret grudge for a former message sent over to queen Elizabeth, whilst her ambassador in France, that he had heard it reported at the duke of Montmorency's table, that her Majesty was about to marry her horse-keeper, meaning Leicester her master of the horse.

The day before his death, Throgmorton is said to have declared the cause of his distemper to be a poisoned sallad he eat at the earl's; and he broke out into bitter invectives against his cruelty. The earl, however, made a mighty shew of lamentation over him; and, in a letter to Sir Francis Walsingham, then ambassador in France, he thus expresses himself upon the occasion. " We have lost, on Monday, our good friend Sir Nicholas Throgmorton, who died in my house, being there taken suddenly in great extremity on Tuesday before. His lungs were perished, but a sudden cold he had taken was the cause of his speedy death. God hath his soul, and we, his friends, great loss of his body."

About this time, a marriage was proposed between queen Elizabeth and the duke of Anjou; and the earl of Leicester appears to have laid aside his pretensions to the queen upon this occasion, and to have solicited the marriage with zeal. But the

the duke infisting upon a toleration in the exercise of his own religion, the queen absolutely refused to comply.

With a view to prevent any farther attempts in favour of the queen of Scots, a law was now made, prohibiting, under a severe penalty, the declaring any person whatsoever to be heir or successor of the queen, except it were the natural issue of her body. This expression, as it was uncustomary in statutes of this nature, and the term Natural was usually applied by the lawyers to such children as were born out of wedlock, gave great occasion to censure; and loud clamours were raised against Leicester, as if, by inserting this clause in the statute, he had designed to involve the realm in new disputes about the succession: for it was urged, that no possible reason could be imagined, why the usual form of Lawful Issue should be changed into Natural Issue, unless with a view to reflect upon the honour of her Majesty, and to obtrude hereafter upon the English some bastard son of his own, as the Natural Issue of the queen.

From this time, it appears, that Leicester was universally detested, and very justly, for his pride and venality offended all the great officers of state, and his other crimes drew upon him the odium of the people. He had quarrelled openly with archbishop Parker and the bishop of London, for refusing to grant a dispensation for a child to hold a valuable benefice, whose father had bribed Leicester to obtain this favour. He had likewise private gifts on the disposal of bishoprics, besides lucrative grants from the crown; and to preserve his extensive influence at court, he was assiduous in his attendance on the queen, with whom he once sat up the whole night, when she was ill. Thus highly favoured, he carried his insolence to such a pitch to other courtiers, that even in the queen's presence,

presence, he treated them with great indignity: a privy-counsellor, we are told, unable to contain his resentment at such usage, struck him; upon which the queen told him, "he had forfeited his hand;" but the gentleman, with great presence of mind, and noble intrepidity, falling on his knees, "intreated her Majesty to suspend this judgment, till the traitor, who better deserved it, had lost his head."

The year 1572, is but too fatally memorable, for the barbarous massacre of Paris, called the massacre of St. Bartholomew, because the bloody business commenced on the eve of St. Bartholomew. This plot was laid with as deep dissimulation, as the action itself was horrid; and whether we consider the high dignity of the persons who projected it, the high rank of the victims sacrificed to bigotry, or the innocence of the slaughtered multitude, we shall find no traces in modern history of such examples of perfidy and cruelty as Charles IX. Catharine of Medicis his mother, and Pope Gregory XIII. the perpetrators of this inhuman butchery.

The particulars in brief ought to find a place, in all memoirs of these times, written by protestants, at the remotest ages, from the melancholy event; that they may never lose sight of the invariable maxims of dissimulation, constantly practised by the church of Rome, to conceal her hatred of, and cruelty to the professors of the reformed religion of every denomination, whom her rulers are interested to undermine and extirpate. The queen-dowager of Navarre was decoyed to Paris, by a proposal of marriage between her son, afterwards Henry IV. of France, and the princess Margaret, sister to Charles IX. The same pretext drew thither Henry prince of Bearn, and his uncle the prince of Condé. The famous admiral of France, Coligni, was invited by by the king, with a promise to declare him his general in a war against Spain, and the other chiefs of the Huguenots (French Protestants) depending upon the peace that had been lately granted them, accompanied him. The queen of Navarre was taken off by poison. Coligni was shot at, as he was going home at noon, by a villain hired for the purpose, but he was only wounded. And in the evening, the duke of Guise communicated the king's secret intentions to Charron, intendant of Paris, who ordered the captains of the different wards to arm the burghers privately; giving orders, that the Roman Catholic citizens, as soon as they heard an alarm struck on the bell of the palace clock, should place lights in their windows by way of distinction, and then breaking into the houses of all the Huguenots, put them to the sword, without regard to sex or age.

At midnight, Guise, accompanied by the duke D'Amaule, grand prior of France, a number of officers, and three hundred chosen soldiers, marched to the admiral's hotel, broke open the gates, and entered the house; a colonel and two subaltern officers dispatched the wounded Coligni, and threw his body from his chamber-window into the street. All his domestics were assassinated, without mercy; and while this was transacting, the alarm was struck on the bell, and the militia joining with the soldiers, a general massacre ensued; two thousand persons were put to the sword before morning, and a great number in the course of the ensuing day; at the same time, by orders from the court, the Huguenots, in all the capital cities of the kingdom of France, shared the same fate: but in two or three garrison-towns they were spared, the governors refusing to execute the bloody mandates, excusing themselves, by saying, the king must be out of his senses when he gave them. The mangled body

body of the admiral was infulted by the bigotted populace, and hung upon the gibbet of Montfaucon; and the young king of Navarre, the prince of Bearn, and the prince of Condé, were clofetted by Charles and his favage mother, who told them, that if they did not embrace the Roman Catholic religion, they fhould not live three days; by fair promifes they gained time, and made their efcape.

But according to Camden, it was intended to have involved England in the fate of this evil day; for he fays, that the earl of Leicefter, and Cecil, then lord Burleigh, were invited to the nuptials, and were to have been cut off, being the fupporters of the Proteftant intereft both in England and in France, by their councils and affiftance: and the truth of this is juftified by the conduct of the French ambaffador foon after, who haughtily demanded, that all the French Proteftants, who had fled to England, on hearing of the maffacre of Paris, fhould be delivered up as rebellious fubjects, which the queen, with equal humanity and refolution, abfolutely refufed.

To return to Leicefter, moft hiftorians agree, that it was in the courfe of this year he privately married lady Douglas, dowager-baronefs of Sheffield; and though fome fecret memoirs of the adventures of this unfortunate lady, whom he would never own as his wife, were handed about, yet the affair did not reach the queen's ear. But the wits of the court, after his marriage with the countefs dowager of Effex was known, ftyled thefe two ladies, Leicefter's two teftaments, calling lady Douglas the old, and lady Effex the new teftament. Unable, however, to make lady Douglas defift from her pretenfions, he endeavoured, fays Dugdale, to take her off by poifon, and fhe narrowly efcaped death, with the lofs of her hair and her nails.

Yet

Yet all the reports and representations made to the queen of the earl's reprehensible conduct and bad character, had so little effect upon the queen, that in 1575, her Majesty made him a visit at his castle of Kenelworth, which had been granted to his lordship and his heirs, by the queen's letters patents, ever since the fifth year of her reign; and his expence in enlarging and adorning it, amounted to no less than 60,000*l*. Here he entertained the queen and her court with all imaginable magnificence, for seventeen days.

"At her first entrance, a floating island was discerned upon a large pool, glittering with torches; on which sat the lady of the lake, attended by two nymphs, who addressed her Majesty in verse with an historical account of the antiquity and owners of the castle; and the speech was closed with the sound of cornets, and other instruments of loud music. Within the lower court was erected a stately bridge, twenty feet wide, and seventy feet long, over which the queen was to pass; and on each side stood columns, with presents upon them to her Majesty from the gods. Silvanus offered a cage of wild-fowl, and Pomona divers sorts of fruits; Ceres gave corn, and Bacchus wine; Neptune presented sea-fish, Mars the habiliments of war, and Phœbus all kinds of musical instruments.

"During her stay, variety of sports and shews were daily exhibited. In the chase was a savage man with satyrs; there were bear-baitings, fireworks, Italian tumblers, and a country wake, running at the quintain, and morrice-dancing. And, that no sort of diversion might be omitted, the Coventry men came, and acted the ancient play, so long since used in their city, called Hocks-Tuesday, representing the destruction of the Danes in the reign of king Ethelred; which proved so agreeable to her Majesty, that she ordered them a brace of bucks, and five marks in money, to defray the charges of the feast. There were, besides, on the pool, a triton riding on a mermaid eighteen feet long, and Arion upon a dolphin."

An estimate may be formed of the expence from the quantity of beer that was drank upon this occasion, which amounted to 320 hogsheads.

Towards the close of this year, Walter D'Evereux, earl of Essex, was, by lord Leicester's management, commanded to resign his authority in Ireland; and returned into England, after having sustained a considerable loss in his private fortunes. But expressing his resentment with too much eagerness against Leicester, to whose under-hand dealings he imputed the whole cause of his misfortunes, he was again sent back into Ireland by his procurement, with the unprofitable title of earl-marshal of the country. And here he continued not long before he died of a bloody-flux in the midst of incredible torments.

The death of this nobleman carried with it a suspicion of poison, and was charged upon the earl of Leicester. Two of Essex's own servants, are reported to have been confederates in the murder: and it is said, that a pious lady, whom the earl much valued, was accidentally poisoned at the same time. It is farther alledged, that his lordship's page, who was accustomed to taste of his drink before he gave it him, very hardly escaped with life, and not without the loss of his hair, though he drank but a small quantity; and that the earl, in compassion to the boy, called for a cup of drink a little before his death, and drank to him in a friendly manner, saying, " I drink to " thee, my Robin; but ben't afraid, 'tis a better " cup of drink than that thou tookest to 'taste " when we both were poisoned."

This

This report however, was contradicted by Sir Henry Sidney, the lord-deputy of Ireland; yet the suspicion was increased soon after, when Leicester married the countess dowager of Essex, an event which he wished to conceal, but the French ambassador Simier, pressing the queen's marriage with the duke of Anjou, and imagining her private attachment to Leicester was the only obstacle to it, revealed the earl's marriage to her, and she was so intemperate in her rage upon this occasion, that she forbad him the court, and would have committed him to the Tower, if the earl of Sussex had not prevented it, on prudential reasons.

It is suggested, but with no shadow of reason, that Leicester plotted against the life of Simier in resentment of this discovery; for the suspicion was founded on two circumstances; the one was a proclamation issued by the queen, that no person should presume to offer any affront to the French ambassador or his servants, but this is accounted for from the extreme aversion of the people to the proposed marriage. The other was that, as Simier was attending the queen in a barge upon the river, a gun was fired, the shot from which passing the ambassador's barge shot one of the queen's watermen through both arms, but upon the clearest evidence it appeared, the gun was fired by accident.

In 1579, the duke of Anjou came over to England, thinking thereby the better to forward his suit; but for a long time he met with no better success than his ambassador, at length, however, as he was one day entertaining her majesty with amorous discourse, she drew a ring from off her finger, and placed it upon his, on certain private conditions, which had been agreed between them. The company present mistook it for a contract of marriage; and the earl of Leicester, and the rest of his faction, who had spared no pains to render the design abortive, cried, The queen, the realm, and religion, were undone. The ladies of honour, who were all in his interest, broke out into bitter lamentations, and so terrified the queen, that, early the next morning, she sent for the duke of Anjou, and, after some private conversation with him, dismissed him her court, after he had staid in England three years. To do him honour, the queen attended him as far as Canterbury, and ordered the earl of Leicester, and some others of her nobility, to wait upon him to Antwerp, to which place he retired in 1582.

From this time, to 1585, we meet with nothing material in Leicester's transactions, except his subscribing an association with the rest of the nobility to defend queen Elizabeth at the hazard of their lives and fortunes, against the open, violence, and secret machinations of her enemies.

In 1585, the estates in the Netherlands, who had lately thrown off the Spanish yoke, being greatly distressed, made application to queen Elizabeth, and desired her majesty to accept of the government of the United provinces, and to take them into her protection. The queen heard their deputies favourably; however, she refused the sovereignty, and only entered into a treaty, by which she engaged to furnish them with a large supply of men and money, which she sent to them, soon after, under the conduct of her general, the earl of Leicester.

On the eighth of December he embarked, attended by several persons of distinction. His fleet consisted of fifty sail of ships and transports; and, on the tenth, he arrived at Flushing, where, with his whole train, his person being guarded by fifty archers, fifty halberdiers, and fifty musqueteers, he was magnificently entertained by Sir Philip Sidney,

his

his nephew, governor of the town for her majesty; by Grave Maurice, second son to William of Nassau, prince of Orange, then lately deceased; by the magistracy of the city; and by the queen's ambassador. This town, with the castle of *Ramilies*, and the town of *Tervere* in Zealand, and the *Brille* in the province of Holland, had been delivered to Elizabeth, as a security for the repayment of the expences she had been at, to enable the united provinces to maintain their new republic, independent of Spain, and they are thence styled in history, *The Cautionary Towns*.

The same splendid and honourable reception was given to the earl throughout his progress to the Hague; every town endeavouring to outvie the other in demonstrations of respect; all manner of shews and entertainments by land and on their canals were exhibited; the detail of which is very prolix, and of little use in these days of refinement in every species of amusement; and the reader will be pleased to observe, that to indemnify him for the omission of the account of all this idle pomp and parade, (which he will find at large in *Aitzema*'s History of Holland) the more material historical events of Elizabeth's reign, connected with the life of Leicester, are introduced by the present editor.

At the Hague, the States desirous of engaging queen Elizabeth still further in their defence, as a compliment to her majesty, conferred on her favourite, the highest honour that republic can bestow: they made him governor and captain general of the United Provinces, gave him a guard, in the same manner as had been the custom for the prince of Orange, and permitted him to keep a court, to which the states, and the magistracy repaired to pay their compliments, and in most respects he was treated as their sovereign.

But

But this step had a contrary effect to what the states expected, for the queen had given a strict charge to Leicester before his departure, not to exceed his commission, which was so limited, that his acceptance of these honours highly militated against his secret instructions, as well as his commission; her majesty therefore considered her personal honour as injured, rather than complimented by the extravagant reception her lieutenant had met with, and thought the states, who were considerably indebted to her, might have found a better use for their money, than to expend it on pageants, triumphal arches, and feasts; she therefore severely reprimanded them in a letter written with her own hand, and to Leicester she sent her vice-chamberlain to check his ambition, by personal reproof.

The states returned a submissive answer, excused what they had done by the necessity they lay under, to shew her representative all possible tokens of respect. The earl of Leicester, too, lamenting his hard fate in having disobliged her, so wrought upon her easy disposition by his feigned sorrow, that she overlooked the offence, and even acquiesced in the title given him by the states.

The earl then proceeded to the exercise of his high authority, and having appointed natives of Holland to be his deputies in every province, he put the whole army, both Dutch and English, under such excellent regulations, that the prince of Parma, general of the Spanish forces, began to consider him as a formidable enemy, and to despair of recovering these provinces for the crown of Spain, though not long before he had boasted, that he should make them an easy conquest. Several skirmishes now happened, in which the English forces gained the advantage; and the prince of Parma having laid siege to Grave, Norris, who
was

was Leicester's lieutenant general, and count Hollack, repulsed him with considerable loss, but Van Hemart, a young Dutch nobleman, the governor, basely surrendered it, for which he lost his head. However, upon the whole, the English were so successful, that in honour of their victories, Leicester determined to celebrate the festival of St. George at Utrecht, where he had his head quarters, with the same ridiculous ostentation, a fondness for which was one of his great foibles. And this fresh proof of his vanity, embroiled him again with his royal mistress, whose frequent remission of his offences, has been always urged as the strongest proof, by foreign historians, of a criminal attachment to him.

But the future success of the campaign not answering to the high expectations formed by the Dutch, on the first enterprises of the English, the miscarriages were imputed to Leicester's want of military courage and conduct, especially after the failure of the siege of *Zutphen*, a town in possession of the Spaniards, and of the most importance of any they held in the Netherlands.

The strength of this place consisted in a fort built upon the river Yssel. This Leicester endeavoured to block up by batteries erected against it, and he reduced the governor to such extremities, that he was obliged to send to the prince of Parma, then besieging Rhinberg for succours. The prince at the head of a strong detachment, flew to his assistance, and at this critical juncture, by some unaccountable misconduct, Leicester neglected to send money to the Count de Meurs, to pay two thousand German mercenaries whom the count had hastily levied and brought into Holland for the service of the states, and the prince of Parma being informed that the men were on the point to mutiny, shewed his generalship, by surrounding

rounding them in this temper, whereupon some threw down their arms, and the rest entered into the Spanish service. After which he contrived to throw succours into the fort at Zutphen.

But the flower of the English volunteers being in the field, and among them many persons of high rank, particularly the gallant Sir Philip Sidney, Sir William Stanley, Sir William Russel, and Sir John Norris, they resolved to pursue the enterprize, notwithstanding this discouragement; and rather to die for the honour of their country, than raise the siege. With such sentiments, it is not surprising that they performed prodigies of valour, but all their efforts proved ineffectual, for Leicester again sacrificed to his idol vanity in this famous battle; having taken a chapel which stood in the field of battle, he employed too much time and attention, in securing this post which he had taken in erson, by a trench, instead of inspecting the motions of the enemy, who had broke through the line of the English foot, and supported by a strong fire from their cavalry, had made dreadful havock; but seeing Leicester chiefly intent on his trifling acquisition, the enemy directed their attack with three thousand men against the general's favourite chapel, which occasioned a bloody contest, the Spaniards gaining possession of it; but at length, they were driven with considerable slaughter to their intrenchments; however, the advantages which had been gained by the English in other quarters were lost by this manoeuvre, and time was given to the prince of Parma, who had hitherto left the fate of the day to the marquis of Vasto, to advance with his main force against the English, just as they were preparing to force the intrenchments. Then it was that the lieutenant-general Norris, observing the design of the prince of Parma, which was to flank the English, advised Leicester either to call off the

troops

troops under Sir William Pelham, from their attack on the intrenchments, to support the body of the English against the prince, or to order a retreat. Leicester unfortunately chose the latter; and Zutphen remained in the hands of the Spaniards.

In the battle, the English in general, gave signal proofs of their military skill and personal valour; but Sir Philip Sidney surpassed all others. This gallant officer, who was the son of Sir Henry Sidney, by Mary, the eldest daughter of John Dudley duke of Northumberland, distinguished himself very early at the court of Elizabeth; for after having made the tour of Europe, he was esteemed such an accomplished young gentleman, that in the year 1576, when he was but in the twenty-second year of his age, he was sent by the queen to congratulate Rodolphus II. emperor of Germany, on his accession to the imperial throne. And in his way home, he visited Don John of Austria, governor of the Low-countries, a most haughty prince, accustomed to treat all foreigners with insolent contempt; Sir Philip Sidney therefore met with a very cool reception, but afterwards, upon the report of his courtiers, that he was a gentleman of great learning and knowledge of the world, though so young, he condescended to converse with him, and from that time he shewed him every possible mark of respect and esteem.

He possessed the ancient spirit of British freedom, which he exerted manfully upon all occasions, particularly when a quarrel happened between him and the earl of Oxford at the royal tennis-court, which was carried to such lengths that the queen interposed, and told Sidney " to consider the difference in degree between earls and gentlemen, adding, that princes were under a necessity to support the privileges of those on whom they conferred titles and dignities; and that, if gentlemen contemned the

the nobility, it would teach peasants to insult both." To which he made the following reply, with due reverence: " That rank was never intended for privilege to wrong; witness her Majesty herself, who, how sovereign soever she were by throne, birth, education, and nature, yet was she content to cast her own affections into the same moulds with her subjects, and govern all her prerogatives by their laws. And he besought her Majesty to consider, that although the earl of Oxford were a great lord by birth, alliance, and favour, yet he was no lord over him; and therefore the difference in degrees between freemen, could challenge no other homage but precedency."

With the same independent spirit he wrote an elegant Latin letter to the queen, containing the soundest arguments, founded on the principles of general policy, and the constitution of the kingdom, dissuading her from the marriage then nearly concluded between her Majesty and the duke of Anjou; which letter was well received, and is preserved in the queen's library at the Museum.

But his natural fire and vivacity made him scorn the idle life of a courtier, and led him on to the field of military glory; the queen therefore, by the recommendation of Walsingham, whose daughter he had married, and of his uncle the earl of Leicester, appointed him governor of Flushing, and lieutenant-general of the horse. Arrived in Zealand, he formed a close friendship and intimacy with Maurice, son of the prince of Orange; and in conjunction with him, entered Flanders, and took Axel by surprise. Though the prince is named in this enterprize, yet the honour of the contrivance, and the execution of it, is generally ascribed to Sidney, who revived the ancient discipline of silent order on the march; and by this conduct, his soldiers were enabled to scale the

walls

walls in the dead of night, when no enemy was expected. Having succeeded so far, a chosen band made directly to the guard-chamber on the market-place, took the officers prisoners, and thus became masters of the place before the commandant, who had the keys of the town in his bed-chamber, had the least notice of the surprize.

Encouraged by this success, he made an attempt upon Graveline; but the design proved abortive, through the treachery of La Motte, the commanding officer. His next and last service was at the siege of Zutphen; here he was constantly engaged in the heat of the action, and signalized himself by prodigies of valour. He had two horses killed under him, and was mounting a third, when he was wounded by a musket shot from the trenches, which broke the bone of one of his thighs; and being then unable to manage his horse, he bore him from the field; "the noblest bier to carry a martial commander to his grave." In this agonizing situation, he rode to the camp, near a mile and half distant, and passing by the rest of the army, faint with the loss of blood, he called for drink; but when it was brought to him, as he was putting the bottle to his mouth, he saw a poor soldier carried along more dangerously wounded, who cast a longing eye towards the bottle, which the generous, heroic Sidney observing, he gave it to the soldier, before he had tasted a drop himself, saying, "thy necessity is yet greater than mine." He drank however after the soldier, and was then carried to *Arnheim*, where the principal surgeons were: during sixteen days they entertained hopes of his recovery, but at last finding they were not able to extract the ball, this brave man prepared to meet death with a pious fortitude and resignation, correspondent to the great actions of his life. He expired in the arms of his brother, Sir Robert Sidney,

Sidney, on the 17th of October, 1586, in the thirty-second year of his age; to whose memory we cannot pay a greater tribute of honour, than by styling him the Wolfe of those times.

The States of Zeeland requested of the queen that they might have the honour of burying him, but this was refused; and her Majesty, in consideration of his uncommon merit, ordered the body to be embarked for England, which was accordingly done, with the usual military honours; it was received with the same at the Tower, and after lying in state several days, was interred with great pomp in St. Paul's cathedral. But besides his military fame, he left an unfading memorial of his fine genius, in his celebrated romance, entitled, Arcadia.

The loss of this promising hero, in the bloom of youth, combined with the ill fortune of the day, occasioned loud murmurs in the army, and alienated the esteem of the Dutch, who now openly arraigned Leicester, and did not scruple to charge him with want of military skill, if not of personal valour.

When therefore he arrived at the Hague, after this campaign, the states being then assembled, they received him with coldness, and soon broke out in expostulation and complaint; in a moderate way desiring redress. But Leicester, in return, entered upon a justification of his proceedings, strove to remove their supposed misconstructions and mistakes, and at last endeavoured to dissolve the assembly; but not being able to effect it, he declared his resolution of returning to England, and left them in an angry manner. However, he seems afterwards to have been brought to temper, and to have told the states, that by his journey into England, he should be the better enabled to assist them in their affairs, and provide a remedy for all grievances.

When

When the day came for his departure, by a public act, he gave up the care of the provinces into the hands of the council of state; but privately, the same day, by an act of restriction, he reserved an authority to himself over all governors of provinces, forts and cities; and farther took away from the council and the presidents of provinces, their accustomed jurisdiction. And then he set sail for England.

But whatever might be the pretence for Leicester's leaving the Low-countries at this conjuncture, his presence in England seems now to have been desired secretly by Elizabeth, who wanted him near her person at this juncture: for the late conspiracies, which had been formed in favour of the queen of Scots, had made a deep impression upon her Majesty, and she now resolved to sacrifice her to her own safety; but the difficulty lay in what manner it should be done; and she knew she could securely rely upon Leicester's fidelity. When the matter was brought before the council, his lordship is said to have advised to take her off by poison; but this base design being openly opposed by secretary Walsingham, it was determined to proceed against her by public trial, the proceedings and issue whereof, the reader will find in the life of Cecil lord Burleigh.

In the mean time, the affairs of the Low-countries were in a very unprosperous condition. And the governors of the provinces gave in loud complaints against the earl of Leicester's administration. During his stay in England, they called together the states general, and to preserve their country, they agreed to invest prince Maurice with the full power and authority of Stadtholder. Pursuant to this determination, they obliged all the officers to receive a new commission from him, and to take a new oath to the states, and discharged all recusants whatsoever from the service.

Queen

Queen Elizabeth was highly displeased with these alterations in the government. She immediately sent over lord Buckhurst to enquire into the matter, to complain of the innovations they had introduced in the earl of Leicester's absence, and to settle all differences between them. The states in return, assured her Majesty, that their proceedings were but provisional, and enforced through fear of a general revolt in consequence of their losses; and that at his lordship's return they would readily acknowledge both him and his authority; for the states were too well acquainted with the share Leicester bore in her Majesty's affection, to abide by any accusation against him. But notwithstanding many outward professions of regard, they inwardly hated him, and privately proceeded in the execution of their projects, to limit his power.

The queen however, openly espousing the cause of her favourite, Leicester went over to Holland again, where by his professions of zeal for the protestant religion, he formed a strong party among the divines and devotees, and thus raised two factions in the country, by which the states were greatly distressed, the magistrates and persons of rank only being of their party, while the mass of the people, with the clergy, were devoted to Leicester: from this embarrassing situation, they were fortunately relieved by Leicester's recall in 1588, when England was in a general consternation on account of the intended invasion, by the Spanish Armada. And to the astonishment of the Dutch minister in England, as well as of the whole English nation, though lord Buckhurst now delivered in accusations against him at the council-board, for mal-administration in the Low-countries, supported by the states, who were exasperated at the loss of Sluys, and the general bad success of the campaign in 1587, the queen interposed; and as a token of her great esteem for, and

and confidence in the earl, she made him lieutenant-general of the army, which had marched to Tilbury to prevent the landing of the Spaniards. As her Majesty intended to put herself at the head of this army, if the Spaniards had made a descent on the coast, no greater honour could be conferred on a subject, nor could a greater proof be given of blind favouritism; for Leicester certainly wanted many of the talents requisite to form a great general, and it is not without reason that he is supposed to have been deficient in personal bravery. Indeed it can hardly be imagined, that cool reflection, temper and courage, could subsist in a mind over-charged with the remembrance of crimes of the deepest dye.

Yet Elizabeth, when she reviewed this army, bestowed the highest encomiums on him, in her memorable speech, which, considering the great occasion, and the dignity of the speaker, claims a place in this work, without abridgment, or alteration.

In imitation of the celebrated generals of ancient Greece and Rome, the illustrious English heroine thus harangued her troops:

" MY LOVING PEOPLE,

" We have been persuaded by some, that are careful of our safety, to take heed how we commit ourselves to armed multitudes, for fear of treachery; but I assure you, I do not desire to live to distrust my faithful and loving people. Let tyrants fear, I have always so behaved myself, that, under God, I have placed my chiefest strength and safeguard in the loyal hearts and good-will of my subjects. And therefore I am come amongst you, as you see, at this time, not for my recreation and disport, but being resolved, in the midst and heat of the battle, to live and die amongst you all; to lay down

down for my God, and for my kingdom, and for my people, my honour and my blood, even in the dust. I know I have the body but of a weak and feeble woman, but I have the heart and stomach of a king, and of a king of England too; and think it foul scorn that Parma, or Spain, or any prince of Europe, should dare to invade the borders of my realm; to which, rather than any dishonour shall grow by me, I myself will take up arms, I myself will be your general, judge, and rewarder of every one of your virtues in the field. I know already, for your forwardness, you have deserved rewards and crowns; and we do assure you, on the word of a prince, they shall be duly paid you.

In the mean time, my lieutenant-general shall be in my stead, than whom never prince commanded a more noble or worthy subject, not doubting but by your obedience to my general, by your concord in the camp, and your valour in the field, we shall shortly have a famous victory over those enemies of my God, of my kingdom, and of my people."

The Spanish invasion was providentially prevented by a violent storm which dispersed their fleet, and it was afterwards defeated; but for the account of this engagement, we refer to the lives of the lord high admiral, Charles Howard earl of Nottingham, and of Sir Francis Drake.

This was the last expedition in which the earl of Leicester was engaged; for retiring soon after to his castle at Kenelworth, as he was upon his journey, he was taken ill of a fever at Cornbury Park, in Oxfordshire; of which he died on the 4th of September 1588.

His death, according to some authors, was hastened by poison, and the crime is imputed to Sir James Crofts, in revenge for some injury done by
the

the earl to his father. His corpse was removed to Warwick, and magnificently interred in a chapel, adjoining to the choir of the collegiate church, and over it an handsome monument was erected to his memory.

His character is given in few words, by Camden; " he was a most accomplished courtier, free and bountiful to soldiers and students; a cunning time-server, and respecter of his own advantages; of a disposition ready and apt to please; crafty and subtle towards his adversaries; much given formerly to women, and in his latter days doating extremely upon marriage. But, whilst he preferred power and greatness, which is subject to be envied, before solid virtue, his detracting emulators found large matter to speak reproachfully of him; and, even when he was in his most flourishing condition, spared not disgracefully to defame him by libels, not without a mixture of some untruths."

But certain it is, that he was well skilled in and a frequent practiser of the diabolical art of poisoning; which formed part of the Machiavelian accomplishments of a courtier in most courts of Europe at this æra.

The earl of Leicester left only one son, to whom he bequeathed the greatest part of his real estate, by the title of *his base son Robert*, on account of his having always denied his marriage with the lady Douglas, his mother; but the young gentleman, with great reason, laid claim to legitimacy, and to the hereditary honours of his family, in the beginning of the reign of James I. and commenced a suit for that purpose in the ecclesiastical court; and when he had proceeded so far as to prove the marriage of his mother, by indubitable evidence, the cause, through the influence of the dowager countess of Leicester, (formerly countess of Essex) now married to a third husband, Sir Christopher Blunt,

Blunt, was amoved into the ſtar-chamber, where the king in an arbitrary manner put an end to the ſuit, by ordering the examinations of the witneſſes to be locked up, and no copies to be taken without the royal licence.

This act of injuſtice determined Sir Robert Dudley to leave his native country, and at this time he was eſteemed one of the moſt accompliſhed gentlemen of his age. The Dudley family, for three deſcents, had furniſhed men of very great abilities; but this reputed *baſe* ſon, in learning, ſurpaſſed them all, eſpecially in the uſeful part of mathematics. And in the laſt years of Elizabeth, he had fitted out ſome ſhips, and made ſome valuable diſcoveries in navigation: he alſo took and deſtroyed nine ſail of Spaniſh ſhips; and he behaved ſo gallantly at the ſiege of Calais, that the queen conferred on him the honour of knighthood; but he certainly did not receive the encouragement he appears to have merited, either in her reign, or that of her ſucceſſor.

Diſguſted at the Engliſh court, he obtained a licence to travel for three years; but upon the death of his uncle the earl of Warwick, he aſſumed his title abroad, which giving offence to king James, he was ordered home, and not thinking it prudent to comply, his eſtate was confiſcated, for his life, to the crown.

Upon this reverſe of fortune he retired to Florence, where he was kindly received by Coſmo II. great duke of Tuſcany; and for his eminent ſervices to the manufactures and commerce of that country, the emperor, on the recommendation of the archducheſs, to whom he had been appointed chamberlain, created him a duke of the Holy Roman Empire in 1620; and he then aſſumed his grandfather's title, duke of Northumberland.

He

He died at his country-feat near Florence in 1639, leaving a great character in the learned world for his skill in philosophy, chemistry, and medicine; and in the means of applying them for the benefit of mankind.

He was an author of some repute; and his principal work, entitled, *Del Arcano del mare*, &c. printed at Florence in 1630, and again in 1646, is highly valuable and very scarce. He was also the inventor of a sudorific powder, for a long time known, under the name of the earl of Warwick's powder.

⁂ Authorities. Camden's Annals and Birch's Life of Queen Elizabeth. Dugdale's Antiquities of Warwickshire. Fuller's Worthies of Surry. Melvil's Memoirs, edit. 1752. Hakluyt's Collection of Voyages, Travels, and Discoveries of the English Nation, fol. edit. 1580.

THE LIFE OF SIR FRANCIS WALSINGHAM,

Secretary of State to Queen ELIZABETH.

[A. D. 1536, to 1590.]

FRANCIS WALSINGHAM was descended of an ancient and good family, born about the year 1536; he was educated at King's-college in the university of Cambridge: his friends sent him to travel in foreign countries while he was very

very young; and it was owing to this happy circumstance, that he remained abroad during the persecuting administration of queen Mary, to whose sanguinary zeal he might otherwise have fallen a victim for his declared attachment, while he was at the university, to the reformed religion.

A genius for political knowledge, directed his attention in early life, to the study of the forms of government, legislations, manners and customs of the different nations of Europe; and of these he acquired such a competent knowledge, that on his return to England in the beginning of the reign of Elizabeth, her Majesty soon discovered his talents for public business, and desired Sir William Cecil, then secretary of state, to employ him, in some honourable station under him. Cecil accordingly received him at first into his office, as his under-secretary; and afterwards, as he became better acquainted with his profound skill in politics, he confided to him the most interesting negociations of state, and advised with him on the propriety of the measures he had taken in his concerns with foreign powers. Walsingham, by these advances, led the way to the high honour which was conferred on him in the year 1570, when he was sent ambassador to France, where he served queen Elizabeth with great fidelity and address; but, by his vast expences in procuring intelligence at that critical period, he involved himself so deeply in debt, that he was obliged to solicit his recall; which he obtained in 1573.

The hardships he had undergone, during his late embassy, a scarcity of provisions, amounting nearly to a famine, having happened while he resided at Paris, joined to a consciousness of having failed in her promises of remittances, which had exposed him to great difficulties, obliged the queen in honour, to make him some recompence on his return,

she

she took the most prudent method to cancel the obligation, and to serve herself at the same time, by appointing him to be one of her principal secretaries of state; the same year, he was also sworn of the privy-council, and soon after he received the honour of knighthood.

It was on the promotion of his constant friend and patron Sir William Cecil, now created a peer, and made lord-treasurer, that Walsingham was raised to his new dignity; but still he was the junior secretary, till the death of Sir Thomas Smith, which happened in 1577; from which time Sir Francis Walsingham may be considered as second in the administration of public affairs, and the firm, grateful supporter of Cecil lord Burleigh's power and influence, against Leicester and his party. And though it will appear, in the life of Cecil, that he was the principal in all the great transactions of Elizabeth's reign till the year 1598, yet in justice to Walsingham, it must be observed, that without the assistance of the particular cast of political abilities possessed by him, Cecil in all probability must have fallen a victim to the sinister designs of his numerous enemies.

Sir Francis was peculiarly happy, in the discovery of court intrigues and treasonable conspiracies at home; and he was no less successful in procuring the earliest and most authentic intelligence of the secret designs of the principal powers of Europe.

Dr. Lloyd mentions the means he made use of to secure private advices from abroad; "he maintained fifty-three agents and eighteen spies in foreign courts," and this at a trifling expence; whereas, in the present times of political error, we have only one lordly minister at every court, with the extravagant yearly salary of 3000 *l*. whose chief employment is to dress, to give sumptuous entertainments, and to introduce British travellers of rank and fortune

tune at the court where he resides; thus passing an agreeable life of dissipation, they know nothing of the state affairs of the country, but what they pick up at card-tables, or from opera girls; and the best political intelligence is transmitted home from private persons, unpensioned, unemployed, and we are sorry to add, often unthanked.

This experienced statesman was sent over to Holland in 1578, to assist at the congress held by the Protestant states of the provinces of *Holland, Zealand, Friezland,* and *Utrecht*; he acted as the representative of queen Elizabeth at their meetings, but those writers who style this private agency an embassy, forgot that the republic was not yet established, or in a capacity to receive ambassadors; Walsingham however contributed by his political talents and influence to the formation of the alliance entered into by these provinces, the beginning of the following year, styled, *The union of* UTRECHT, which was the object of his commission.

On his return home, he was consulted by the queen and Cecil on the conditions of the proposed marriage between her Majesty and the duke of Anjou; and these being adjusted, he was appointed ambassador to the court of France, for the third time, and he repaired thither in 1581; but Henry III. of France, rejecting the proposals, the embassy proved unsuccessful; Walsingham was recalled towards the close of the year; and the duke of Anjou finally quitted England, as we have related more amply, in the life of Leicester.

Upon every occasion, when skilful address and political intrigue were essentially requisite, Walsingham was sure to be employed; as soon therefore as the queen received intelligence that the young king of Scotland, afterwards James I. of England, had shewn a strong attachment to the earl of Arran, and had made him his chief confident, Walsingham was

Sir FRANCIS WALSINGHAM.

was difpatched to Scotland, to endeavour to remove the earl; or if that could not be effected, to form a party at court and in the kingdom againft him. The latter he accomplifhed, and at the fame time, he purfued another fecret defign of Elizabeth, "which was to obtain from a man of Walfingham's penetration and difcernment, the real character of James:" this we give on the authority of Hume, who further adds, "that Walfingham was greatly deceived upon this occafion, entertaining higher ideas of his talents for public bufinefs than they merited." But this does not impeach the judgment of our ftatefman, who at the time of his arrival in Scotland, and during his refidence there, was in a very bad and declining ftate of health: and in this fituation, James, who knew his fame as a man of letters, engaged him chiefly in converfations which tended to fhew his own fcholaftic learning; and Walfingham, fays Lloyd, "fitted the humour of the king by paffages out of Xenophon, Thucydides, Plutarch, or Tacitus," in fuch literary conferences, the young monarch took great delight, and he generally exerted himfelf upon fuch occafions; fo that from his critical knowledge of ancient hiftory and other branches of fcience, Walfingham was warranted to draw a conclufion, that he would not prove fo miferably deficient, as we fhall find he was, in the application of his knowledge to practice.

In 1586, by his peculiar fagacity and management, he unravelled the whole plot of Babington, and others, againft the life of the queen.

Soon after this, he was appointed one of the commiffioners for the trial of the queen of Scots, having before oppofed the advice of the earl of Leicefter, who was inclined to difpatch her by poifon, and had privately fent a court-divine to fecretary Walfingham, to perfuade him to confent; but the latter perfifted in his opinion, that fuch a method of proceeding was not only unjust, but likewise dangerous and dishonourable to their royal mistress.

In the course of the trial, queen Mary charged him with counterfeiting her cyphers, and with practising against her's and her son's life. Whereupon Walsingham, rising from his seat with great earnestness, protested that his heart was free from all malice against the queen—he called God to witness that, in his private character, he had done nothing unbecoming an honest man, nor in his public capacity any thing unworthy of his station. He owned indeed, that out of his great care for the personal safety of his royal mistress, and the security of her realm, he had curiously endeavoured to search and sift out all plots and designs against both. And he added, that in this view, if Ballard, though an accomplice with Babington, had offered him his service in the discovery of the plot, he would not only have accepted it, but have rewarded him for it. Mary seemed to be satisfied with this vindication of himself, and expressed her concern that she should have credited every idle report to his disadvantage.

In 1587, the king of Spain having made vast preparations, which surprised and kept all Europe in suspense, not knowing on what nation the storm would break, Walsingham employed his utmost endeavours for the discovery of this important secret; and accordingly procured intelligence from Madrid, that the king had informed his council of his having sent an express to Rome, with a letter under his own hand to the pope, acquainting him with the true design of his preparations, and begging his blessing upon it; which, for some reasons, he could not disclose to the council till the return of the courier. The secret being thus lodged with the pope, Walsingham, by the means of a Venetian priest retained at Rome as his spy, got a copy of the original letter, which was stolen out of the pope's pope's cabinet by a gentleman of the bed-chamber, who took the key out of the pope's pocket while he slept.

After this, by his dextrous management, he caused the Spaniards bills to be protested at Genoa, which should have supplied them with money for their extraordinary preparations; and, by this means, he happily retarded this formidable invasion for a whole year.

This seems to have been the last public transaction in which he was concerned, and as to his private life we have no interesting anecdotes relative to it. We shall therefore only observe, before we drop the curtain on this true patriot, that every attempt to promote the trade and navigation of this country, met with his protection and encouragement. Hakluyt's voyages and discoveries in foreign parts, and Gilbert's settling of Newfoundland, were promoted by him; and he assisted these adventurers from his private purse, which accounts for his poverty. He likewise founded a divinity-lecture at Oxford, and a library at King's-college, Cambridge.

Yet after all his eminent services to his country, this great man gave a remarkable proof at his death (which happened on the sixth of April, 1590,) how far he preferred the public to his own interest; for, though, besides his post of secretary of state, he was chancellor to the dutchy of Lancaster, and to the order of the garter; he died so poor, that his friends were obliged to bury him by night in St. Paul's church, left his body should be arrested for debt: a circumstance, of which we have few or no examples; nor is it likely that any of our modern statesmen will make such sacrifices of their fortunes, acquired in the public service, to the public good.

In fine, let every generous British youth bear in grateful remembrance, that the head, the heart, and the purse of Walsingham, were devoted to his country—that he laid the foundation of the protestant religion as by law established—ruined the machinations of Rome to undermine it—and by his encouragement of navigation, arts, and manufactures, extended the commerce of England to various regions of the habitable globe, till his time unknown by our countrymen.

His negotiations, or state-papers, were collected by Sir Dudley Digges, master of the rolls, and published in 1655, folio. A work is likewise ascribed to him, intitled, *Arcana Aulica*, or Walsingham's manual of prudential maxims, which has been often printed; but we have no certain authority that he was the author.

A maxim however, which was undoubtedly his, being adapted to persons of all ranks, and of every age, may supply the place, with advantage, of the engraver's tail-piece:

KNOWLEDGE

IS

NEVER TOO DEAR.

*** *Authorities.* Camden's Annals. Lloyd's State Worthies. Melvil's Memoirs. Biog. Britan.

The

The LIFE of SIR JOHN PERROT.

[A. D. 1527, to 1592.]

WE are now to present to the reader one of those genuine English military characters with which our history abounds, whose rough, unconquerable valour, noble fierceness, and manly spirit, untempered by the softer passions, or the moral and social virtues, could only recommend them to future ages and enrol their names on the registers of fame, by heroic actions in the service of their country, performed at some particular crisis, when its welfare depended in a great measure on the existence of such eccentric beings.

The French style them savage, brutal and feroce, but Englishmen will know how to set a proper value on those uncivilized sons of Mars and Neptune, whose daring intrepidity has often been the salvation of their country; and they will cast a veil over the dissipation and libertinage of their domestic lives, in consideration of their glorious actions in the field.

Such indulgence must we claim, for sir John Perrot, the reputed son of Thomas Perrot, esq; of South Wales, by Mary the daughter and heiress of James Berkley, esq; second son to the lord Berkley; but it was generally believed, (according to Lloyd) and many circumstances in his life will confirm it, that he was the natural son of Henry VIII. whom he greatly resembled both in his person and his difposition. An intimacy of a fufpicious nature had fubfifted between the king and his mother, a fhort time before fhe was married to Mr. Perrot, and it is remarkable that we have no certain indication of the time of his birth, being obliged to compute it only from the æra of his being placed under the care of the marquis of Winchefter, lord high treafurer, about the year 1545, and it is generally allowed, he was then eighteen years of age, which calculation fixes his birth to the year we have affigned it.

The marquis following the example of Wolfey, and other ftatefmen of thofe times, received young gentlemen of rank and fortune into his houfe, to complete their education, efpecially fuch as were deftined for public life. Young Perrot's reputation for perfonal valour, ftrength, and dexterity in martial exercifes, which had been his chief rural fports, reached London before him, and it ferved to introduce an extraordinary fcene in lord Winchefter's houfe on his arrival, which at once difcovered the caft of his difpofition.

One of the young noblemen, the lord of Abergavenny, was fo fierce and hafty, that no fervant or gentleman in the family could continue quiet for him: but, when young Perrot came, his lordfhip was told, there was now a youth arrived, who would be more than a match for him. "Is there fuch a one?" faid he. "Let me fee him." Upon which, being brought where Perrot was, for the firft falutation, he afked him, "What, "Sir, are you the kill-cow that muft match "me?" "No," faid Mr. Perrot, "I am no "butcher; but, if you ufe me no better, you "fhall find I can give you a butcher's blow." "Can you fo?" faid he, "I will fee that." And fo being both angry, they fell to blows, till lord Abergavenny found himfelf overmatched, and
was

was willing to be parted from him; after which, the serving men, and others, when they found the young lord unruly, would threaten him with Mr. Perrot.

But this trial of their skill produced for a time, a respectful behaviour to each other, which ripened into a short lived friendship: being founded however, only on a forced restraint of their fiery tempers, it was not likely to be permanent. Accordingly, having agreed to make a joint entertainment for their common acquaintance; on the day appointed, they quarrelled, upon what subject is not known, and repairing to the buffet, wherein they had provided good store of glasses, before their guests came, they broke them all about each other's ears, so that when they arrived, instead of wine, they found blood spilled in the chamber, and the reproaches of their mutual friends only served to widen the breach between them.

Shortly after, it was Mr. Perrot's fortune to go into Southwark (as it was supposed to a house of pleasure) taking only a page with him, where he fell out with two of the king's yeomen. They both drew on him; but he defended himself so valiantly, that the king, being then at Winchester-house, near the place, was told how lustily a young gentleman had fought with two of his majesty's servants. Henry being desirous to see him, sent for him, demanded his name, country, and kindred. This being boldly by him related, it pleased the king very well to see so much valour and audacity in so young a man; and therefore he desired him to repair to the court, where he would bestow preferment on him.

It is highly probable, that Perrot took this opportunity of giving the king some intimation of his affinity to him; for it will appear by the sequel,

quel, that he all along knew it himself; and it is most likely his mother, in this view, had contrived to get him placed in the house of the marquis of Winchester, a step which a private gentleman of Wales would hardly have thought of, if he had not been influenced by his wife, whose secret motive he could not suspect.

Henry died soon after this interview, and it is beyond a doubt, by the early notice taken of him at the court of Edward VI. that he left some private instructions concerning this youth. For, at the coronation he was made a knight of the Bath; and soon after, when the marquis of Southampton went into France to treat of a marriage betwixt king Edward and the French king's daughter, Sir John Perrot accompanied him.

"The marquis being a nobleman who delighted much in all feats of activity, keeping the most excellent men that could be found for most kinds of sport, the king of France understanding it, engaged him to hunt the wild boar; and, in the chace, it fell out, that a gentleman, charging the boar, did not hit right, so that the beast was ready to run in upon him; upon which Sir John Perrot perceiving him to be in danger, came in to his rescue; and, with a broad sword, gave the boar such a blow as almost parted the head from the shoulders."

"The king of France, who saw this, came presently to him, took him about the middle, and, embracing him, called him *Beau-foile*. Our English knight thinking the king came to try his strength, took his majesty also about the middle, and lifted him up from the ground; with which the king was so far from being displeased, that he offered him a good pension to serve him. To this compliment Sir John Perrot nobly replied, That, he humbly thanked his majesty, but he was a gentleman

tleman that had means of his own; or, if not, he knew he served a gracious prince who would not see him want, and to whom he had vowed his service during life."

Shortly after, Sir John returned from France, and residing chiefly at court, he lived at so extravagant a rate, that he involved himself in debt, and could not extricate himself, though he mortgaged his estate.

Thus reduced, he fell upon a stratagem to attract the king's attention to his situation. He placed himself in a bye-part of the court, where he pretended to think himself out of hearing; and there, in a melancholy tone of voice, he began to reproach himself for his prodigality, and to argue the case with himself, whether he should continue at court, or seek his fortune in the army. The king, as he very well knew, overheard most of his soliloquy, having passed that way and stepped behind him. At length discovering himself, his majesty thus accosted him, " How now, Perrot, " what is the matter that you make this great " moan?" To whom Sir John replied with well affected surprise, " So please your majesty, I did " not think that your highness had been there." " Yes," said the king, " we heard you well " enough : and have you spent your living in our " service; and is the king so young, and under " government, that he cannot give you any thing " in recompence? Spy out somewhat, and you " shall see whether the king hath not power to " bestow it on you." Then he most humbly thanked his majesty, and shortly after found out a concealment of some lands or other effects that had been forfeited to the crown, and on his petition the king bestowed them on him; wherewith he paid the greatest part of his debts, and ever after became a more frugal manager.

Soon after the acceffion of queen Mary, Sir John Perrot was committed to the Fleet prifon, for harbouring heretics at his houfe in Wales, but through the intereft of his friends, and the queen's perfonal favour, he was releafed, to the great mortification of one Gaderne, his countryman, a bigotted papift, who had lodged the information againft him. Shortly after he went to St. Quintin, where he had a command under the earl of Pembroke; who at this time lived in the ftricteft friendfhip with him; but after their return to England, Sir John foon found, that no ties of friendfhip could reftrain his lordfhip's zeal for popery. The earl being prefident of Wales, received an order from the queen, not to fuffer any heretics to remain in Wales, and his friend, Sir John Perrot being with him at the time, he required his affiftance in carrying it into execution. Perrot refufing, on confcientious principles, a quarrel enfued, which came to blows, and they were never after reconciled.

Intelligence of this affair foon reached the court, and the bigotted queen was highly difpleafed; infomuch, that Sir John, having at that time a fuit for the caftle and lordfhip of Carew, and a promife of the grant being given him; when he came to court fhe would fcarce look on him, much lefs give him any good anfwer; which he perceiving, determined not to be baulked with auftere looks, but preffed fo near to the queen, that he fell upon her train, befeeching her majefty to remember her promife made to him for Carew; wherewith fhe feemed highly offended, and in angry fort afked, " What! Perrot, will you offer violence to our " perfon?" Then he befought of her pardon for his boldnefs; but fhe departed with much indignation. Yet foon after, Sir John Perrot found friends about the queen, who advifed her to remit what

was

was paſt, and to refer his ſuit to the lords of the privy-council.

When he came before the council to know their pleaſures, whether he ſhould have Carew, according to the queen's promiſe, Gardiner, biſhop of Wincheſter began very ſharply to cenſure him, ſaying, " Sir John Perrot, do you come to ſeek " ſuits of the queen? I tell you, except you alter " your heretical religion, it were more fit the " queen ſhould beſtow faggots than any living on " you?" But, when it came to the turn of the earl of Pembroke to deliver his opinion, he with a truly noble generoſity eſpouſed his cauſe, in the following terms, " My lords, I muſt tell you my " opinion of this man, and of the matter. For " the man, I think he would, at this time, if he " could, eat my heart with ſalt; but yet, not- " withſtanding his ſtomach towards me, I will " give him his due; I hold him to be a man of " good worth, and one who hath deſerved of her " majeſty in her ſervice, as good a matter as this " which he ſeeketh; and will, no doubt, deſerve " better if he reform his religion: therefore, ſince " the queen hath paſſed her gracious promiſe, I ſee " no reaſon but he ſhould have that which he " ſeeketh." When they heard the earl of Pembroke ſo favourable, who they thought would have been moſt vehement againſt him, all the reſt were content; and ſo her majeſty ſhortly after granted him his ſuit.

From this time, the better to avoid all future queſtion concerning his religion, which might put his life in jeopardy, he prudently retired into the country; but his ambition and his hopes revived on the acceſſion of queen Elizabeth, from whom he met with a moſt gracious reception, and he had the honour to aſſiſt at her coronation, being one of the knights who ſupported her canopy of ſtate in the procession. And in the first year of this reign, Sir John was the principal actor in a romantic, rural entertainment, given by the queen and her court, to the French ambassador in Greenwich-park. The particulars of which are thus recorded. " Tents being set up, and a banquet provided, her majesty accompanied by the ambassador, and the principal officers of her court entered the Park.

" As she passed through the gate, a page presented a speech to her, signifying, that there were certain knights come from a far country, who had dedicated their services to their several mistresses, being ladies for beauty, virtue, and other excellencies, incomparable; and, therefore, they had vowed to advance their fame through the world, and to adventure combat with such as should be so hardy as to affirm, that there were any ladies so excellent as the saints which they served. And, hearing great fame of a lady which kept her court thereabouts, both for her own excellency, and the worthiness of many renowned knights which she kept, they were come to try, whether any of her knights would encounter them for the defence of the honour of their mistresses.

When this speech was ended, the queen told the page, " Sir Dwarf, you give me very short " warning, but I hope your knights shall be " answered." And then looking about, she asked the lord-chamberlain, " Shall we be out-bragged " by a dwarf?" " No, may it please your majesty," answered he : " Let but a trumpet be sounded, and " it shall be seen, that you keep men at arms enough " to answer any proud challenge." Then was the trumpet sounded, and immediately there issued out of the east lane at Greenwich, several pensioners gallantly armed and mounted.

" The challengers were, the earl of Ormond, the lord North, and Sir John Perrot. Presently, upon

upon their coming forth, the challengers prepared themselves. Amongst the rest, there was one Mr. Cornwallis, to whose turn it fell, at length, to run against Sir John Perrot. As they both encountered, Sir John, through the unsteadiness of his horse, and uncertainty of the courses in the field, chanced to run Mr. Cornwallis, through the hose, razing his thigh, and somewhat hurting his horse; wherewith he being offended, and Sir John discontented, as they were both choleric, they fell into a challenge to run with sharp lances, without armour, in the presence of the queen; which her majesty hearing of, she would not suffer; so they were reconciled, and the combat ended after certain courses performed on both sides by the challengers and defendants.

"After finishing these exercises, her majesty invited the French ambassador to partake of the banquet, but a courier arriving, who brought his excellency an account of the tragical end of the king his master, Henry II. of France, he craved pardon of her majesty, and retired."

It is very remarkable, that the French monarch was accidentally killed at a tournament, given on account of the marriage of the Dauphin, afterwards Francis II. with Mary queen of Scots; and this melancholy event principally contributed to the suppression of these warlike entertainments; at one of which, a Turkish ambassador being present, he observed, "that if the combatants were "in earnest, it was not enough; if they were in jest, "it was too much." *Hainault's Hist. of France.*

From this time to the year 1572, nothing memorable is related concerning our hero, but in that year, his valour and activity were properly employed, not in idle feats of chivalry, but in the service of his country: he was appointed Lord President of the province of Munster in Ireland.

This

This province was in a desolate condition, having been laid waste by the earl of Desmond and his accomplices, who were in actual rebellion against the queen, as were many other provinces of that kingdom.

But the principal author of the cruel devastations in the province of Munster, was one Fitz-Morris, the earl of Desmond's lieutenant.

Sir John Perrot landed at Waterford the first of March 1572, and three days after, the rebel Fitz-Morris, by way of defiance, burned the town of Kyllmalog, hanged the chief magistrate, and others of the townsmen, at the high cross in the market-place, and carried all the plate and wealth of the town with him; with which entertainment our new president, was much discontented, and therefore he hastened to Dublin to take his oath before the lord deputy, Sir Henry Sidney, in order to qualify him to proceed with vigour, and without delay against this cruel, and arrogant rebel.

Upon his return to Corke, about the tenth of April following, he instantly marched with the forces under his command to Kyllmalog, where he took up his quarters in a house that had been partly burnt down, and then issued a proclamation, inviting all the inhabitants who had fled, to return home; which they did accordingly, and began to build their gates, to repair the town walls, and to rebuild their houses.

After he had properly fortified this place and restored good order and tranquillity, he pursued the rebels from place to place, with such intrepidity and diligence, and with such good fortune, that they never chose to come to a regular, decisive battle with him, only hazarding slight skirmishes, where they had the advantage of situation. " Which, Sir John Perrot observing, he pursued " them night and day without remission, even in
" the

"the midst of winter, and lay out many nights
"in the field both in frost and snow, enduring
"such hardships, as would harldly have been be-
"lieved, if two of his followers, men of great
"credit, had not related them."

The detail of his military exploits in a rude, uncultivated country, would be both tedious, as well as uninteresting at this distant period; we shall therefore only mention, that in less than the space of a year, by continual pursuits, by harrasing the rebel army, and by cutting off their communications, so that they could not procure supplies either of money, ammunition, or provisions, he entirely dispersed the power of Fitz-Morris, and made him glad to sue for pardon, offering to submit himself to the queen's mercy. Which at length Sir John Perrot consented to grant, but in the following humiliating manner, which indeed was a proper punishment for a poltroon, who after agreeing to accept a challenge from Sir John to decide the war by single combat, had refused to meet him.

Fitz-Morris came to Killmallock, where in the church, the lord-president caused him to lie prostrate, putting the point of his sword to his heart, in token that he had received his life at the queen's hands. Then he took a solemn oath to continue a true subject to the crown of England, whereby the province of Munster was restored to, and maintained in as good a state of peace and obedience, as any part of Ireland.

The severity he had been obliged to exercise in the course of his campaigns, in order to put an end to the rebellion, particularly his hanging up some merchants, who supplied the rebel forces with provisions and brandy, and his obliging the earl of Thomond, with other Irish noblemen, whom he suspected to be secret favourers of the rebellion, to follow his camp, occasioned some heavy complaints to be sent home against him, accusing him of abuse of authority and arbitrary proceedings. His temper took fire upon the first reproofs transmitted to him from the ministry of England, and following the natural bent of it, without waiting for leave of absence, he took such steps as he judged most prudent, for the preservation of the public peace in Munster, made up his accounts, and suddenly embarked for England in March 1573.

When Sir John Perrot came to court it was thought that the queen would have been highly offended at his coming over without licence. Yet as soon as he appeared before her, and had related the state of Ireland, the particulars of his services, and the cause of his coming over; her majesty commended his conduct, and desired him to return speedily to his charge, lest in his absence some disturbance might arise. To which Sir John answered, That for the general state of the province, it was so well settled, that no new commotion on a sudden need to be feared. Yet there were many particulars which might be amended without any great difficulty: which being allowed by her highness, he was ready to serve her there, whensoever it should please her to appoint him. And that the same might be the better understood, he presented a plan to the queen to be considered by her majesty, and her privy-council.

In general, it contained many excellent regulations, but the carrying some of them into execution, was likely to be attended with greater inconveniences than those he intended to remove, and he himself owned the difficulty of accomplishing some points; the fact is, he was a better soldier than a statesman; but being unable to brook opposition, on the council's rejecting his plan, he
desired

desired leave to retire for his health to his estate in Wales.

Sir John Perrot had enjoyed his retirement but a few years, when upon intelligence that Fitz-Morris, since his submission, had been in Spain, and procured the promise of ships and men to invade Ireland, especially the province of Munster, the queen and her privy-council sent for him to take the command of such ships and pinnaces as should be made ready to intercept, or interrupt the Spanish fleet and forces which were designed for Ireland. Sir John made such speed in his journey, that he came from Pembrokeshire to Greenwich in less than three days. The queen, when she saw him, told him, she thought he had not heard from her so soon: " Yes, madam, answered he, and have made as much haste as I might to come unto your majesty. Some thinks, said the queen, but how have you done to settle your affairs in the country? May it please your majesty, said Sir John, I have taken this care for all; that setting private business aside, in respect of your majesty's service, I have appointed the white sheep to keep the black: for I may well enough venture them, when I am willing to venture my life in your majesty's service." With which answer the queen was well pleased, and she conferred with him privately for some time; then dismissed him, and appointed him to receive farther directions for that service from the lords of her privy-council.

After this interview with the queen, he prepared for his expedition with all convenient speed, and the fleet being ready, Sir John left London about August, 1578, and went from thence in his barge, accompanied by several noblemen and gentlemen. As they lay against Greenwich, where the queen kept

kept her court, Sir John sent one of his gentlemen on shore, with a diamond, as a token to Mrs. Blanch Parry, willing him to tell her, that a diamond coming unlooked for, did always bring good luck with it: which the queen hearing, sent Sir John a fair jewel hung by a white cypress; signifying, that as long as he wore that for her sake, she believed, with God's help, he should have no harm. The message and jewel Sir John received joyfully, and he returned answer to the queen, "That he would wear that for his sovereign's sake, "and doubted not, with God's favour, to return "her ships in safety, and either to bring the Spa- "niards (if they came in his way) as prisoners, "or else to sink them in the seas." As Sir John passed by in his barge, the queen looking out at the window shook her fan, and put out her hand towards him, upon which he made a low obeysance, while he put the scarf and jewel about his neck; and then repaired to his squadron, which was riding at anchor off Gillingham, and consisted of three ships of the line and three pinnaces; he sailed from thence to the Downs, and passing by Falmouth and Plymouth put to sea for Ireland, where they arrived at Baltimore, a sea-port town in the province of Munster. The people in grateful remembrance of his former government of this country, appeared in great numbers upon the shore, upon his landing, some embracing his legs, and others pressing to touch any part of the body of their deliverer from the cruelties of Desmond and Fitz-Morris, but these marks of their affection had nearly produced fatal consequences, for the vice-admiral, mistaking them for some hostile intention, had pointed his guns to fire upon them, which Sir John perceiving, instantly sent off a boat with proper signals, to invite him on shore, where they were kindly entertained.

The

The squadron remained on the coast till the season was far advanced, and intelligence was received that the Spaniards had laid aside their design for that year, when it was ordered home. In the course of his voyage, Sir John met with one Derryfield, a noted pirate, whom he took, but in the chace he very narrowly escaped shipwreck: and a second accident happened to him on entering the Downs, when his ship struck on the Kentish-knocks, from which she was got off, with great difficulty.

Sir John Perrot was graciously received at court, and permitted to retire to his estate in Wales; but the affairs of Ireland still remained in a turbulent, unsettled state, except in the province of Munster; in other parts, rebellion and lawless licentiousness destroyed all order, and rendered private property, as well as the lives of the inhabitants, insecure: in this situation of things, Sir Henry Sidney, the lord deputy, who had found that post full of trouble and danger, without any proportion of reputation or profit, solicited leave to resign; and having obtained it, Sir William Drury was advanced to that dignity; and in 1579, the first year of his administration, the Spaniards, to the number of 1500, made a descent on the coast, and joined the rebels under the earl of Desmond; but they were all taken prisoners, and put to the sword the following year, and Desmond suffered death as a traitor; yet his party continued to carry on the rebellion in his name. In short, the troubles of the country increasing daily, and no commander being to be found of equal intrepidity and capacity for his service, Sir John Perrot, by the advice of Walsingham, who continually corresponded with him on Irish affairs, was appointed lord deputy of Ireland in 1583; and taking with him the earl of Ormond, a veteran in the Irish service, and who besides had

great

great interest there, he embarked at Milford-haven, and arrived at Dublin in the spring of the year.

Sir John Perrot, before his departure, had drawn up a plan for the government of Ireland, which had been approved by the queen and council; and as the kingdom was confessedly in a state of anarchy, which required severe measures to restore tranquillity, the approbation given at this time to his plan, is a justification of his character, in a great measure, from the imputations of arbitrary and cruel conduct, which we shall find hereafter laid to his charge.

As if there had been magic in his very name, his landing in Ireland struck the rebels of every faction with a panic; but when it was known that he proposed to make a progress through the country, many considerable parties came to Dublin, and made their submission, taking the oaths to the queen, and giving hostages for their future good behaviour.

But O'Neale, O'Donnel, Conaught, and several other considerable Irish chiefs, still remained in arms, and were supported from Rome by the pope with money, while the Spaniards occasionally landed small detachments of men, headed by veteran officers, to discipline the raw Irish rebels.

A resolution therefore, which had been taken in England to proceed in a summary way with the rebels, both with respect to their persons and their estates, was carried into execution with great rigour, and many innocent persons suffering with the guilty, this raised a great clamour against the lord deputy, who was charged with exceeding the bounds of his commission. His commission impowered him to execute the rebels as traitors by martial law, when found in arms, and to sell their estates on the spot to any adventurers, at easy rates, who would undertake to cultivate and improve the land:

land: this brought over many followers of fortune from England, men often of bad characters, but possessed of money to buy the forfeited estates; and the lord Deputy was accused of favouring the rapacity of these purchasers, and of hanging some considerable men, whose guilt was not very apparent, in his choler, that he might put an end to the rebellion on their extensive estates, by the sale of the lands to English purchasers. The charges however, though vague and ill-supported, were founded upon the abuses of the purchasers. Whole baronies were exposed to sale (into which the Irish counties are divided, as the English are into hundreds) and the new proprietors turned the innocent Irish as well as the guilty out of their possessions. Yet the measure was political, for the chiefs, seeing that they should not only ruin themselves, but all their posterity, by remaining in arms against the queen, came in bodies to the lord deputy on his progress, to surrender in time, particularly O'Neale and all his adherents, and the lords of Ulster, who upon their knees swore fidelity to the queen, and gave hostages, that they would raise troops for her service against the other rebels.

But Sir John Perrot's temper was suited only to the field; his haughtiness and impatience of controul in the council, made him unfit for the milder duties of civil government; and therefore every remonstrance from the queen and her ministry, founded on complaints sent home against him, exasperated him beyond measure; and upon these occasions, he would vent his wrath in the most disrespectful and indecent terms, forgetting not only his duty to her Majesty as his sovereign, but even the decorum due to her sex.

These unguarded expressions were taken down in writing by Williamson his secretary, who had been bought over by the lord chancellor of Ireland

and

and by the archbishop of Dublin, who sent over an impeachment against him, little regarded by him; for he relied so much on the merit of his military services, that he did not take any pains to secure any evidences in Ireland, to appear in his favour.

At length however, partly owing to the delicate situation of affairs, and partly to his own haughty disposition, he displeased the English as well as the Irish; for the queen having sent over a proclamation to repress the rapaciousness of the former, with respect to abuses in the purchases and possession of the forfeited estates, he executed it with such rigour, that the country reaped the benefit, many of the natives being re-instated; but it made the English outrageous against him: and as to the Irish nobility, their nearest relations having been either executed by him, or deprived of their estates, they secretly sought his ruin; in a word, he met with the fate of all conquerors, he was detested; but he had this consolation, that he did not conquer for himself, but for his sovereign, who certainly should have over looked his passionate temper, in consideration of his delivering her from very imminent danger, the rebels in Ireland being all along supported by her foreign and domestic enemies. At the same time, Sir John Perrot was highly culpable for slighting the rebukes he received from England upon some occasions, and for resenting them at others, instead of condescending to justify himself in his dispatches. At length, the discontent against him ran so high in Ireland, and the queen herself was so displeased with his ill-behaviour to her, that she recalled him in 1588. And this led him into another error, the consequence of his proud spirit; instead of embarking for London, and making use of his remaining interest at court, he set sail from Dublin for his castle

of

of Carew in Pembrokeshire, and arrived there with a numerous and splendid retinue.

Such a step could not fail of alarming the queen, especially as it was now reported, and afterwards made an article of his impeachment, that he held a secret correspondence with the duke of Parma and the queen's foreign enemies.

The articles sent over from Ireland, were therefore laid before the privy council, the attorney-general was ordered to prepare an indictment of high-treason upon them, and he was taken into custody: at first, he was brought to the lord treasurer's house, and confined there, but how long is uncertain; nor are we able to account for a space of near four years, between his arrival at the castle of Carew and his trial: all that we can find on record is, that he was committed to the Tower, and from thence brought to his trial, on the 27th of April, 1592, in Westminster-hall, a special commission being granted for that purpose to the lord chancellor, and the two chief justices.

The only charge proved against him was, his having treated the person and character of the queen contumeliously; but by the artful management of Popham the attorney-general, who admitted men of the most abandoned principles and characters to be evidences against him, he was convicted upon the other articles of the accusation, which were, that he had relieved popish priests—that he held a secret correspondence with the queen's foreign enemies—and that he had fostered the commotions in Ireland; nothing could be more absurd than the last article, since it was evident to the contrary, that Ireland had never been in such a state of tranquillity and of allegiance to the queen, as when he presided over it. But the true motive of his condemnation was, his own imprudent

imprudent boastings, that he was the queen's brother, that she knew his value in Ireland too well to let him fall a sacrifice to his frisking adversaries; and that whenever the Spaniards landed a force in Ireland to join the disaffected there, he should then be cherished again, and be once more, one of her white boys.

In a word, finding he had deceived himself by an ill-grounded confidence in the secret of his birth, and his great military services, his violent passions; after sentence of death was passed on him, which happened in June, preyed on his constitution, and in September following he died in the Tower, and left it doubtful whether Elizabeth intended to have pardoned him.

Thus fell Sir John Perrot, the introducer of military discipline amongst the natives of Ireland; and thus have we given a short sketch of the state of affairs in that kingdom, the better to complete our annals of the reign of Elizabeth.

⁂ *Authorities.* Cox's Hist. of Ireland. Life of Sir John Perrot, edit. 1728. Biog. Britan. Salmon's Chron. Hist.

The Life of

Sir FRANCIS DRAKE.

[A. D. 1545, to 1596.]

THIS celebrated English navigator, and brave naval officer, was the son of Edmund Drake, a mariner, and was born at a village near Tavistock in Devonshire, in the year 1545. He was the eldest of twelve brethren, and the father being distressed by so large a family, captain Hawkins, his mother's relation, (afterwards the famous admiral Sir John Hawkins) whose life immediately succeeds that of his ward, kindly took him under his patronage, and gave him an education suitable to the sea service. Through the interest of his patron, at the age of eighteen, he was made purser of a ship trading to the Bay of Biscay. At twenty, he made a voyage to Guinea; at the age of twenty-two, he was appointed captain of the Judith; and, in that capacity, he was in the harbour of St. John de Ulloa, in the gulph of Mexico; where he behaved very gallantly in the glorious action under Sir John Hawkins; and returned with him to England with a rising reputation, but totally destitute, having lost the little property he had acquired in his former station, by this unfortunate expedition.

Soon

Soon after this, he conceived a design of making reprisals on the king of Spain; which, according to some, was put into his head by the chaplain of the ship: and, indeed, the case was clear in sea-divinity, says Dr. Campbell, "that the subjects of the king of Spain had undone Mr. Drake, and therefore he was at liberty to take the best satisfaction he could on them in return.". This doctrine, however roughly preached, was very taking in England; and, therefore, no sooner did he publish his design, than he had numbers of volunteers ready to accompany him, though not actuated by the same motives, and without any such pretence to colour their proceedings as he had.

In 1570, he made his first voyage with two ships, the Dragon and the Swan; and the next year, in the Swan alone: from which last expedition he returned safe, if not rich. Though we have no particular account of these two voyages, or what Drake performed in them, yet nothing is clearer than that captain Drake had two great points in view: the one was, to inform himself perfectly of the situation and strength of certain places in the Spanish West-Indies; the other, to convince his countrymen, that, notwithstanding what had happened to captain Hawkins, in his last voyage, it was a thing very practicable to sail into these parts, and return in safety: for it is to be observed, that Hawkins and Drake separated in the West-Indies; and, that the former, finding it impossible to bring all his crew home to England, had set part of them, with their own consent, ashore in the bay of Mexico; and, indeed, few of these finding their way home, the terror of such a captivity as they were known to endure, had disheartened our seamen. But captain Drake, in these two voyages, having very wisely avoided coming to blows with the Spaniards, and bringing home sufficient returns to satisfy his owners,

owners, dissipated these apprehensions, and established his own character: so that, at his return from his second voyage, he found it no difficult matter to raise such a force as might enable him to perform what he had long meditated in his own mind, which otherwise he would never have been able to effect.

And, therefore, without loss of time, he laid the plan of a more important design; which he put in execution on the 25th of March, 1572: for, on that day, he sailed from Plymouth, in a ship called the Paseta, burden seventy tons; and his brother, John Drake, in the Swan, of twenty-five tons; their whole strength consisting of only seventy-three men and boys: but they were all provided with ammunition and provisions, and in case of an accident happening to either of the ships, or an occasion presenting of approaching nearer to any place, than the ships could lie, they had three pinnaces on board, framed and fitted in such a dextrous manner, that they could easily be put together, by the ship-carpenters, when wanted: and with this small armament, on the 22d of July, in the year following, they attacked the town of Nombre de Dios, which then served the Spaniards for the same purposes as Porto-Bello does now. He took it in a few hours by storm, but they made little or no advantage of this conquest, owing to the cowardice of part of his followers, who were ordered to guard the pinnaces, while the rest were taking possession of the immense wealth contained in the king's treasury; in one room they saw bars of silver piled up against the wall: as near as they could guess, each bar weighing about thirty or forty pounds, and the pile measuring 70 feet in length, 10 in breadth, and 12 in height: but the town being still full of people, the English sailors in the pinnaces mistook the flying parties, for large detachments,

tachments, who were coming to overpower them, and to cut off their communication with their ships.

Drake however, sent his brother to pacify them; but nearly at the same time, this gallant officer fainted with loss of blood from a dangerous wound he had received in his leg, during the assault, which he had till then carefully concealed, that he might not dishearten his people: upon his recovery, he insisted on completing their victory, by making themselves masters of the treasure; but the major part of his followers, apprehensive for their own safety, in case they should lose their commander, partly by intreaties and partly by force, carried him off to the pinnaces, and then set sail for the ships, content with the spoils they had taken, but abandoning the richest, says Lediard, that ever raised the expectations of such adventurers, amounting, as they were afterwards informed, to 360 tons of silver, besides several iron chests of gold, of far greater value.

His next attempt was to plunder the mules laden with silver, which passed from Vera Cruz to Nombre de Dios; but in this too he failed: however, attacking the former town, he carried it, and got some little plunder. In their return, they unexpectedly met with fifty mules laden with plate; of which they carried off as much as possible, and buried the rest. In these enterprises he was very greatly assisted by a nation of Indians, perpetually engaged in war with the Spaniards. The prince, or captain of this tribe, whose name was Pedro, captain Drake presented with a fine cutlass, which he saw the Indian admired. In return, Pedro gave him four large wedges of gold; which captain Drake threw into the common stock, saying, he thought it but just, that such as bore the charge of so uncertain a voyage, on his credit, should share all the advantages

tages that voyage produced. Then embarking his men, with a very confiderable booty, he bore away for England; and, in twenty-three days, failed from Cape Florida to the ifles of Scilly; and from thence arrived fafe at Plymouth in Auguft 1573.

His fuccefs in this expedition, joined to his generous behaviour to his owners, gained him great reputation; and, in 1575, fitting out three frigates at his own expence, he failed with them to Ireland; where, in the capacity of a volunteer, under Walter earl of Effex, the father of the unfortunate favourite, he performed many gallant exploits, and was fo highly in favour with the earl, that he recommended him to Sir Chriftopher Hatton, vice-chamberlain to the queen, in a letter written but a fhort time before his death, which ferved him as an introduction to her Majefty in 1576, who from this time took him under her own immediate protection. Thus countenanced at court, his fellow-citizens were ftill more animated to engage in any adventure he fhould project, and he was enabled to undertake that grand expedition which will immortalize his name. The firft thing he propofed was a voyage into the South-Seas, through the Straits of Magellan, hitherto unattempted by any Englifhman. This project was well received at court, and captain Drake foon faw himfelf at the height of his wifhes; for, in his former voyage, having had a diftant profpect of the South-Seas, he ardently prayed to God that he might fail an Englifh fhip in them; which now he found an opportunity of attempting.

The fmall fleet with which he failed on this extraordinary enterprize, confifted of the following fhips: viz. The Pelican, of 100 tons, commanded by himfelf; the Elizabeth, vice-admiral, of 80 tons, under the command of captain John Winter; the Marygold, a bark of 50 tons, under captain

John Thomas; the Swan, a fly-boat of 30 tons; and the Chriftopher, a pinnace of 15 tons, under captain Thomas Moon. In this fleet the whole number of hands embarked, amounted to no more than 164 able men, with all neceffary provifions for fo long and dangerous a voyage; the intent of which was, however, not publicly declared, but given out to be for Alexandria, though it was generally fufpected, and many knew, that it was defigned for America.

On the 15th of November 1577, captain Drake failed from Plymouth, but was forced, by a violent ftorm, into Falmouth, in a very bad condition; but fuch was his activity and diligence, that he put to fea again, on the 13th of December; on the 25th of the fame month, he fell in with the coaft of Barbary; and, on the 29th, with Cape de Verd. The 13th of March he paffed the line; the 5th of April he made the coaft of Brazil, in 30° N. lat. and entered the river de la Plata, where he miffed the Swan, and the pinnace; but, meeting them again, and taking out all their hands, and the provifions they had on board, he turned them adrift. On the 29th of May, he entered the port of St. Julian, to take in provifions.

After he had continued about two months in port St. Julian, lying within one degree of the Streights of Magellan, to make the neceffary preparations for paffing the Streights with fafety, on a fudden having carried the principal perfons engaged in the fervice to a defart ifland lying in the bay, he called a court-martial, where he opened his commiffion; by which the queen granted him the power of life and death, which was delivered to him with this remarkable expreffion from her own mouth: "We do account that he, Drake, who ftrikes at thee, does ftrike at us." He then laid open, with great eloquence, the caufe of the affembly; for though

his

his education had been slender, he was an excellent speaker, and proceeded to charge Mr. John Doughty, who had been second in command during the whole voyage, first, with plotting to murder him, and then to ruin the enterprize.

"I had," said he, "the first notice of this gentleman's intentions before he left England, but was in hopes his behaviour to him would have extinguished such dispositions, if there had been any truth in the information."

He then appealed for his behaviour to the whole assembly, and to the gentleman accused: he next exposed his practices from the time they left England, while he behaved towards him with all the kindness and cordiality of a brother; supporting his charge by producing papers under his own hand; on which Mr. Doughty made a full and free confession. After this, the captain, or, as he was then called, the general, quitted the place, telling the assembly he expected that they should pass a verdict upon him; for he would be no judge in his own cause.

Camden says he was tried by a jury. The accounts affirm, that the whole forty persons of which the court consisted, adjudged him to death, and gave this in writing under their hands and seals, leaving the time and manner of it to the general. Upon this, captain Drake, having maturely weighed the whole affair, gave Mr. Doughty his choice of three things. First, to be executed on the island where they were; secondly, to be set ashore on the main land; or, lastly, to be sent home to abide the justice of his country. After desiring till next day to consider of these, he declared, that he made the first his choice; and, having received the sacrament with the general, from the hands of Mr. Francis Fletcher, chaplain to the fleet, in the morning, and dined chearfully with the officers, of whom he severally took leave, as if he had been going a journey: dinner being ended, he walked very composedly to the place prepared for his execution; and submitting to his fate with astonishing fortitude and serenity, he was beheaded, in July 1578.

This is the most authentic account of his catastrophe; but as it was well known, that the earl of Leicester bore a mortal hatred to Doughty, for having accused him of poisoning Walter earl of Essex, it was credited by many at the time, and has been transmitted to us, by some historians, that Drake had secret orders from Leicester, then in power, to take him off, on some pretence or other, and that being both a skilful mariner and a man of great courage and conduct, Drake, jealous of his rising fame, readily consented to execute this secret, bloody commission. But as the imputation is not supported by any evidence, the most humane and candid method, in all such cases, is, to try the accusation by the general character of the accused. On this equitable system, Drake must stand acquitted, and his accusers be considered as calumniators.

This island had been the scene of another tragedy of the same kind, 58 years before, when Magellan caused John de Carthagena, who was joined in commission with him by the king of Spain, to be hanged for the like offence; and from hence it was called the island of *true justice*.

Drake left St. Julian on the 17th of August, on the 20th he entered the Streights of Magellan, and after a difficult navigation he passed them on the 25th of September, and found himself in the Great South-Sea. Here he met with such tempestuous weather, that he was forced back to the westward near 100 leagues, and the Marygold, captain Thomas, was lost. Near the 57th degree of south-latitude, he entered a bay, where he found a naked a naked people, ranging from one island to another in canoes, in search of provisions. Sailing northward from thence, on the 3d of October, he found three islands, in one of which was an extraordinary plenty of birds. On the 8th, he lost sight of the Elizabeth, captain John Winter, who returned through the Streights, and arrived safe in England, on the 2d of June 1579, being the first ship that ever made that passage homewards.

Captain Drake had now only his own ship, which he had new named the Hind, with which he arrived at Macao, on the 25th of November 1578; and from thence sailing along the coasts of Chili and Peru, he greatly annoyed the Spaniards, taking and destroying several ships, and frequently landing to seize on rich booties, till his crew were satiated with plunder; (the particulars of this cruize are to be found at large in Lediard's Naval History) when he boldly attempted to find a passage by North America, sailing to the latitude of 42 degrees; but then meeting with severe cold, and open shores covered with snow, he returned back to 38 degrees of latitude, and there put into a harbour in the north part of California, where he was kindly received by the Indian inhabitants, who were so highly pleased with him, that they offered to make him their king.

To this country, Drake gave the name of *New Albion*; and erecting a stone pillar, he placed an inscription thereon, with the name, style, and titles of queen Elizabeth, denoting his having taken possession of the country for his sovereign; to which was added his own name, and the date of this transaction; some of the queen's coin were likewise deposited under its base; and then, after careening his ship, he set sail for the Molucca islands. He chose this passage round, rather than to return by the Streights of Magellan; partly from the danger

danger of being attacked by the Spaniards, and partly from the lateness of the season, when dreadful storms and hurricanes were to be apprehended.

On the 13th of October, 1579, Drake fell in with certain islands, inhabited by the most barbarous people he had met with in all his voyage. On the 4th of November he had sight of the Moluccas; and, coming to the island of Ternate, was extremely well received by the king of that island, who seems to have been a wise and polite prince. On the 10th of December he made Celebes, where his ship struck upon a rock, on the 9th of January, 1580, from which she was got off with great difficulty, after being in the utmost peril for twenty-seven hours, and under the necessity of throwing over-board eight of her guns, and some valuable merchandize. Then touching at Java, where he received great civilities from one of the kings of the island, he continued his course for the Cape of Good Hope, and from thence to Rio Grande in Negroland; where taking in water, he set sail for England, and arrived safe at Plymouth, on the 25th of September, 1580; having sailed round the globe, in less than three years, to the great admiration of the people of those times.

Drake's success in this voyage, and the immense treasure he brought home with him, became the general topic of conversation, some highly commending, and others as loudly censuring him. In this uncertainty matters continued during the remainder of this year, and the spring of the next; when, at length, on the 4th of April, her Majesty going to Deptford, went on board Drake's ship; where, after dinner, she conferred the honour of knighthood on him, and declared her absolute approbation of all he had done. She also gave directions for the preservation of his ship, that it might remain a monument in honour of himself

and

a[ ] country. But this famous vessel, which, for many years, had been viewed with admiration at Deptford, being decayed, was at length broken up, and a chair made out of the planks was presented, by John Davies, Esq; to the university of Oxford, where it is still preserved.

In the year 1585, Sir Francis, now admiral Drake, was sent on an expedition against the Spanish West-India settlements, with a fleet of twenty-one sail, having on board 2000 land-forces, under the command of Christopher Carlisle. Taking the Cape Verd islands in their way, they landed at St. Jago, and taking the chief town of the same name, they sacked it, and carried off a considerable booty. From thence they proceeded to Hispaniola, and took St. Domingo, Carthagena, and St. Augustine; by which he exceeded the most sanguine hopes of his warmest friends. Yet the profits of this voyage were but moderate, Sir Francis's instructions being, rather to weaken the enemy, than to take prizes.

Two years after, he proceeded to Lisbon with a fleet of thirty sail; and, receiving intelligence of a considerable fleet assembled in the bay of Cadiz, intended to make part of the Spanish armada, he bravely entered that port, and burnt upwards of ten thousand tons of shipping: then, having advice of a large Caracca ship expected at the island of Tercera from the East-Indies, he sailed thither; and, though his men were in great want of provisions, he prevailed on them to go through those hardships for a few days; in which time the East-India ship arriving, he took and carried her home in triumph: this capture was of very great importance; for, besides the value of the treasure on board, estimated at 200,000 crowns, it gave the English merchants the first idea of the profitable traffic carried on with the East-Indies, and was the occasion of establishing the first East-India company.

The general applause bestowed on him, when he returned from this glorious expedition, was heightened into grateful admiration, when it was observed, what a laudable use he made of the wealth he had acquired from the enemies of his country.

In the year 1588, Sir Francis undertook to convey water to the town of Plymouth, for want of which, till then, it was greatly distressed; and performed it by bringing thither a stream from springs at the distance of eight miles, if the distance be measured in a strait line; but in the manner by which he conducted it, the course it runs is upwards of twenty miles.

This year also, he was appointed vice-admiral under lord Charles Howard of Effingham, high-admiral of England, and signalized himself in the engagements with the Spanish Armada: here he was as fortunate as ever, for he took a very large galleon, commanded by don Pedro de Valdez, who yielded without striking a blow at the bare mention of his name. This don Pedro remained above two years Sir Francis Drake's prisoner in England, and, when he was released, he paid him for himself and his two captains, a ransom of 3500*l*. In his ship were found upwards of 50,000 ducats, which he generously distributed among his sailors and soldiers. It must, however, be owned, that, through an oversight of his, the admiral ran a great hazard of being taken by the enemy; for Drake was appointed, the first night of the engagement, to carry lights in his ship for the direction of the English fleet; but, being in pursuit of some hulks belonging to the Hans-towns, he neglected it; which occasioned the admiral's following the Spanish lights, and in the morning he found himself in the centre of the enemy's fleet. But his succeeding services sufficiently

ficiently atoned for this oversight, the greatest execution done on the flying Spaniards being performed by his squadron. But of this boasted Armada, and its defeat, a more satisfactory account will be found in the life of the lord high admiral Howard.

In 1589, Sir Francis Drake was appointed admiral of the fleet sent to restore don Antonio, king of Portugal, and the command of the land-forces was given to Sir John Norris. But the fleet was scarce at sea before the commanders differed; on this occasion the general was earnest for landing at the Groyne, whereas the admiral and sea-officers were for sailing directly to Lisbon; in which, had their advice been taken, doubtless their enterprize had succeeded, and Don Antonio been restored; for the enemy made such good use of the time in fortifying Lisbon, that no impression could be made. Sir John, indeed, marched by land to Lisbon, and Sir Francis promised to sail up the river with his whole fleet; but, upon perceiving the consequences, he chose rather to break his word than hazard the queen's navy; for which he was highly reproached by Norris, and the miscarriage of the whole affair imputed to the failure in his promise. Yet Sir Francis fully justified himself on his return; for, he shewed the queen and council, that whatever was done there, for the credit of the nation, was performed solely by the fleet, and by his orders; in consequence of which, a large fleet, laden with naval stores from the Hans-towns, was taken, with a great quantity of ammunition and artillery on board: that his sailing up the river of Lisbon would have signified nothing to the taking the castle, which was two miles off; and that, without reducing it, there was no taking the city.

The war with Spain still continuing in 1595, and it being evident that nothing distressed the enemy so much as the losses they met with in the
West-

West-Indies, an offer was made to the queen by Sir John Hawkins and Sir Francis Drake, to set on foot a more effectual expedition to those parts than had hitherto been attempted; at the same time, they agreed to bear a great part of the expence, and to engage their friends to assist them. The queen readily listened to this proposal, and furnished a stout squadron of ships of war, on board one of which, the Garland, Sir John Hawkins, embarked. Their whole force consisted of twenty-seven ships and barks, having on board a land-force, consisting of 2500 men. The fleet was detained some time after it was ready, on the English coasts, by the arts of the Spaniards, who receiving intelligence of its strength and destination, gave out, that they were ready themselves to invade England; and to render this the more probable, they actually sent four gallies to make a descent on the coast of Cornwall. This had the desired effect, for the queen and the nation being thereby alarmed, thought it by no means adviseable to send so great a number of ships on so long a voyage, at that critical juncture. At last, this alarm blowing over, the fleet set sail; but when out at sea, the admirals differed: Drake and Baskerville, the commander of the land-forces, determined, against the advice of Hawkins, to attack the chief of the Canary Islands, instead of proceeding directly to Porto Rico, where the richest of the galleons lay at anchor: the failure of the design on the Canary Islands, shewed, that Hawkins was right, for they could not recover the time they lost there.

The day after the death of admiral Hawkins, in whose life will be found further particulars of the expedition, Sir Francis made his desperate attack on the shipping in the harbour of Porto Rico, in pursuance of a resolution taken by a council of war. This was performed with all imaginable courage,

rage, and with confiderable lofs to the Spaniards, but with little advantage to the Englifh, who, meeting with a ftronger refiftance and better fortifications than they expected, were obliged to fheer off. The admiral then fteered for the main, where he took the town of Rio de la Hache, which, (a church and a lady's houfe excepted) he burnt to the ground. After this, deftroying fome other villages, he proceeded to Santa Martha, which he alfo burned. Nombre de Dios, finally fhared the fame fate, the Spaniards refufing to ranfom thefe places; and in them an inconfiderable booty was taken. On the 29th of December, Sir Thomas Bafkerville, commander of the troops, marched with 750 men towards Panama, but returned on the 2d of January, finding the defign of reducing that place wholly impracticable: fo that the whole of this expedition was a feries of misfortunes. If they had gone at firft to Porto Rico, they had done the queen's bufinefs and their own: if, when they had intelligence of the Spanifh fuccours being landed there, they had proceeded directly to the Ifthmus, in order to have executed their defigns againft Panama, before their forces had been weakened by that defperate attack, they might poffibly have accomplifhed their firft intention; but grafping at too many things fpoiled all.

A very ftrong fenfe of this threw Sir Francis Drake into a deep melancholy; and brought on a bloody flux, the natural difeafe of the country, which put a period to his ufeful life. His body, according to the cuftom of the fea, was funk very near the place, where he firft laid the foundation of his fame and fortune. Such was the end of this great man. His death was lamented by the whole nation, but more efpecially by thofe of his native place, who had great reafons to love him from the circumftances of his private life, as well as to esteem him in his public character. He had been elected burgess for the town of Bossiney in Cornwall, in the parliament held the twenty-seventh of queen Elizabeth, and afterwards for Plymouth in Devonshire, in the thirty-fifth of the same reign. Having hitherto chiefly confined ourselves to his public transactions, it may not be unacceptable to add a few words concerning his person and his private character.

He was low of stature, but well set, had a broad open chest, his eyes large and clear, of a fair complexion, with a fresh chearful and engaging countenance: as navigation had been his whole study, he was a perfect master in every branch of it, especially astronomy, and the application of it to the nautical art. His voyage round the world is an incontestable proof of his courage, capacity, patience, and public spirit; since he performed every thing that could be expected from a man, who preferred the honour and profit of his country to his own private advantage: and it is apparent, that if Sir Francis Drake amassed a large fortune by continually exposing himself to labours and perils, which hardly any other man would have undergone, for the sake even of the greatest expectations, he was far from being governed by a narrow and private spirit: on the contrary, his notions were free and noble; and the nation stands indebted to him for many advantages which she at present enjoys, in arms, navigation, and commerce.

He is represented as having been choleric in his temper, and too fond of flattery; but to counterbalance these foibles, he was a steady friend, and very liberal to those who served under him: it is also observed, that in his prosperity he was always affable and easy of access.

This

This great man left no issue, and his landed estate, which was very considerable, descended to his nephew, Francis (the son of his brother Thomas) who was created a baronet in the reign of James I.

⁎ *Authorities.* Campbell's Lives of the Admirals. Biog. Britan. Rapin's Hist. of England.

The LIFE of

Sir JOHN HAWKINS.

[A. D. 1520, to 1598.]

Including Memoirs of Sir RICHARD HAWKINS, his Son, and of Sir MARTIN FROBISHER.

THE improvements made by the Spaniards in navigation towards the close of the fifteenth, and early in the sixteenth century, and the visible effects they had produced in aggrandizing that kingdom, excited a noble spirit of emulation in other nations to attempt discoveries by sea, in the then unknown regions of the globe; and in this design, no people manifested such a genius for bold and hazardous enterprises on the ocean as the English: but their ardour and indefatigable industry being checked by domestic troubles during the reigns of Henry VIII. Edward VI. and Mary, the plans which had been formed in private, for extending the maritime power and commerce of England,

could

could not be carried into execution with any prospect of national success, till the constitution itself, new modelled, with respect to its religious establishment, had acquired a proper degree of strength, and the government was in a capacity to prevent a revolution meditated and threatened by its foreign foes and domestic traitors.

The successful navigations, therefore, of our countrymen, which ended in permanent commercial settlements, began late in the sixteenth century, and their fortunate issue was owing to a variety of concurrent circumstances, which deserve our notice.

The private adventures of the merchants of Southampton, who had traded to the Brazils as early as 1540, had thrown a great light upon the nature of the profitable trade carried on by the Spaniards from the West-Indies, and the South-Seas, with Europe; and had laid open the sources of their immense wealth.

The accounts brought home by the sailors and masters of the merchant ships employed in carrying on the trade to Brazil, circulated through the west of England; and encouraged numbers to bring up their children to the sea, in hopes that some future rupture with Spain, or other favourable circumstances, might make the sea-service the channel to riches and honours: with this view, the study of navigation and cosmography was preferred to all others; and the event justified their expectations; for it is very remarkable, that the west of England proved a nursery of able mariners, and gave birth to most of those renowned naval officers, whose discoveries and victories extended the power, increased the commerce, and secured the independency of their country, in the glorious reign of Elizabeth.

Before

Before her time, the naval force of England was insufficient to protect adventurers, in any important foreign enterprise. But soon after her accession, our navy was put upon a respectable footing; not only by building ships in the royal yards, but by encouraging the merchants to build large trading vessels, which could be occasionally employed in the service of the crown.

The commmanders, in general, were men of equal bravery, skill and generosity: as the sailors shared the dangers, so they liberally divided with them, the spoils of war.

The manufactures newly established in England by the foreign protestants who had fled to England for refuge, furnished valuable commodities to enable us to carry on a beneficial barter with the natives of the new world; and some of these being received by them, with a degree of veneration, as if they had been presents from heaven, this was another circumstance, which tended to abate the ferocity, and to establish a friendly intercourse, even with savage nations.

And finally, the bad policy of Spain contributed in the highest degree to the establishment of the English in America; for the cruelties they had committed on the natives, had rendered their very name odious, in the southern hemisphere; the same bad policy likewise plunged them into a war with England; and if ever war could be considered as a national happiness, it certainly must be allowed to have been such for England at this period, when her merchants adventurers found their private interest combined with the public, which induced them to fit out fleets to undertake expeditions against Spain at their own expence. And our brave seamen, at the same time that they enriched themselves with the spoils of the Spanish settlements in America, defeated the designs of the enemies

mies of their country, whose deep-concerted plans threatened no less than the assassination of Elizabeth, and the total annihilation of the protestant religion and succession in England.

These historical anecdotes, we hope, will be considered as a proper introduction to the important maritime and commercial transactions in which Sir John Hawkins had so considerable a share. This gentleman was the second son of William Hawkins, Esq; who gained great reputation as a seaman, and acquired a competent fortune by trading to the coast of Brazil, being the first Englishman who established a friendly intercourse with the natives, a people represented by the Portugueze to have been so savage, that no other Europeans would venture to visit them. Young Hawkins, early in youth, discovered a strong inclination for the sea, and applied himself with great assiduity to the study of navigation; and at a proper age, he made several voyages to Spain, Portugal, and the Canaries, in the merchants service; it is likewise supposed, that he went with his father to the coast of Brazil; but this is only conjecture, for he was born at Plymouth in the year 1520, and we have reason to think his father quitted the sea, to retire and live upon his fortune, about the year 1536. In fact, we have no authentic memoirs of the first voyages of the son, upon his own account; but our historians take notice, that he was employed by queen Elizabeth, soon after her accession; and most of the celebrated admirals, who so eminently distinguished themselves in the service of their country, in the latter part of her reign, were brought up under him.

It was customary however in those days, for naval officers of great reputation, when they were not actually engaged by the crown, in any national service, to undertake commercial voyages by the
aid,

aid, and in conjunction with the merchants, for which they obtained permission from the queen, and generally some conditional privileges were annexed to their special licences upon these occasions. The plan of a voyage of this kind was proposed by captain John Hawkins, to a set of gentlemen and merchants in the spring of the year 1562, and a small squadron was soon after fitted out at their own expence, to establish a trade to the coast of Guinea for slaves, to be bartered at the Spanish West India islands for silver, sugar, hides, &c. Their whole force consisted of only two ships of 100 tons, and one bark of forty tons, with only one hundred men in all. With these he set sail in October for the coast of Guinea, and having by force or purchase acquired 300 negroe slaves, he steered his course for Hispaniola, where he exchanged them for the commodities already specified, on very advantageous terms, and returned safe, from this successful enterprise in September 1563. And thus was the foundation of our slave trade commenced, which considered on the principles of the law of nature must be deemed both inhuman and illicit; but viewed only in a commercial light the consequences of this voyage appear to have been highly beneficial to England; for when our North American settlements were established, the purchase of negroes for the cultivation of them became indispensably necessary, and though they might have been taken by force at first, they were afterwards as regularly contracted for as any other merchandize, and it should be remembered, that they frequently sold themselves, as they still continue to do.

In 1564, captain Hawkins undertook a second voyage, but with greater force, his own ship the Jesus, being of the burthen of 700 tons; the Solomon of 120; the Swallow of 100, and the Tyger

ger bark of 40. He sailed from Plymouth in October, and on his arrival at Guinea, he procured the number of negroes he wanted, and proceeded with them to the West Indies: he arrived at the island of Dominica on the 9th of March 1565, and this place being at that time very inconsiderable, he repaired to the island of Margaretta, where he was hospitably received by the Alcaide, and supplied with provisions; but the governor positively refused to permit him to traffic with the inhabitants, he likewise detained a pilot whom he had hired, and dispatched intelligence of his arrival to the governor of St. Domingo, who immediately issued orders, and caused them to be notified to all the Spanish subjects along the coasts, prohibiting every species of traffic with the English fleet. Thus disappointed, our brave adventurer made for the continent, and took in water and fresh provisions at Santa Fé, then cruizing along the coast, he cast anchor on the third of April, before the town of Burboroata, and sent a deputation on shore, to request the liberty of trading with the inhabitants, but after waiting fourteen days, the conditions annexed to the permission, were found to be such, as could by no means be complied with; for the duties imposed, were calculated so as to make it a losing contract for the English. Captain Hawkins exasperated at this ill usage, sent a detachment on shore consisting of 100 men completely armed to demand better terms, which they obtained, and he then traded with them on an equitable footing. The same refusal he met with at other places, and by the same spirited measure, he compelled the Spaniards to trade with him, and in the end made a prosperous voyage, and then returned home through the Gulph of Florida. Soon after his arrival in England, which was in September 1565; the queen

in

in commemoration of his opening the trade to the coasts of Guinea, granted him a patent to bear for his crest, a demi-moor, bound with a cord, and to do him the greater honour, clarienceux king at arms was commanded to wait upon him, in proper form with the patent.

Captain Hawkins was next employed on the government service, to convoy the English troops sent to the relief of the French protestants at Rochelle, and after his return from France, while he was lying with his squadron at Cat-water, waiting for further orders from the queen, the Spanish fleet, consisting of fifty sail, passed by without paying the honours of the flag to the English squadron, upon which Hawkins ordered a shot to be fired at the admiral's flag, which producing no effect, a second was fired, which went through it, and then the Spanish fleet came-to, and took in their colours; the admiral then sent off one of his principal officers in a boat to desire an explanation, but the captain would not suffer him to come on board, neither would he receive his message in person, it was therefore reported to him by one of his own inferior officers, by whom he sent to the Spaniard, to require him to inform his admiral, that as he had passed one of the queen's ports, and neglected the customary honours paid to her majesty, especially as he had so large a fleet under his command, it gave room to suspect some hostile design, wherefore he insisted on his departure in twelve hours, otherwise he should treat him as an enemy. This gallant behaviour brought the Spanish admiral himself to wait on captain Hawkins, in the same boat, and upon their meeting, the Spanish admiral desired to know if the two crowns were at war unknown to him? Captain Hawkins replied in the negative, but that possibly this affront might occasion one, for he was determined to send an express, to inform the queen what had passed. The Spaniard at first, did not apprehend the nature of the offence he had committed, but being at last fully convinced of his error, he genteely acknowledged it, and captain Hawkins as politely agreed to let it rest with them, after which they reciprocally entertained each other, on board their respective ships and on shore, and with the first fair wind, the Spanish fleet set sail for the coast of Flanders.

In the month of October of the same year, 1567, captain Hawkins sailed on a third trading voyage to the coast of Guinea and the West Indies, in his old ship the Jesus, accompanied by the Minion, and four other ships, one of which was commanded by captain, afterwards admiral Drake. On their arrival at Guinea, they took on board about 500 negroes, and then pursued their voyage to the Spanish settlements in America. *Rio de la Hacha* was the first place where he attempted to trade, but being refused, he landed his men and took possession of the town, and then an accommodation took place, and he met with such success, that he disposed of great part of his negroes; with the remainder he sailed for Carthagena, and there completed his commercial transactions; but on his return home, he met with stormy weather on the coast of Florida, which obliged him to put into the harbour of *St. John de Ulloa*, in the bay of Mexico, on the 16th of September, 1568. The Spanish inhabitants, imagining his squadron was part of the fleet of their own nation expected from Spain, readily came on board, and were greatly terrified when they discovered their mistake; but captain Hawkins entertained them with great civility, and to dispel their fears, assured them, that he only came there by stress of weather, and wanted nothing but provisions, nor did he he attempt any thing againſt twelve merchant ſhips richly laden, then lying in the port; for his own ſecurity however, he detained two perſons of rank, as hoſtages, till the return of an expreſs ſent to Mexico, with an account of his arrival. The next day the Spaniſh fleet appeared, having on board the viceroy newly appointed, and on his voyage to his government; in this delicate ſituation captain Hawkins was at a loſs how to act, for as England was not at war with Spain, he was apprehenſive of his ſovereign's diſpleaſure, if he ſhould prevent their entrance into the harbour, eſpecially as the ſtorms continued, and they muſt have periſhed; at the ſame time he had ſtrong ſuſpicions, that ſome treachery would be practiſed againſt him, when the Spaniſh fleet was ſecure in their own port, and that he ſhould be overpowered by numbers. He therefore took the precaution to inſiſt on ſuch conditions from the viceroy, before he would admit his fleet into the harbour, as were beſt calculated to guard the Engliſh againſt any latent perfidy on the part of the inhabitants of the town, from whom every thing was to be dreaded, with the aſſiſtance of their fleet. With this view he required, that the Engliſh fleet ſhould be ſupplied with proviſions on their paying for them; that hoſtages for keeping the peace ſhould be given by both parties, and that the iſland, with the cannon on the fortifications ſhould be put into the hands of his people during their ſtay. The viceroy at firſt rejected theſe propoſals with diſdain, but upon being told that captain Hawkins conſidered himſelf as the repreſentative of the queen of England, and therefore of a rank equal to his, he vouchſafed to negociate the matter with him in perſon, and ſolemnly promiſed to fulfil the agreement in every particular.

The

The treaty thus concluded, the Spanish fleet entered the harbour on the 26th, and as it had been agreed, the canal of the port being narrow, that the fleets of the two nations should be ranged on each side, this arrangement took up two days, during which the greatest harmony seemed to prevail between the English and the Spanish officers. Yet a conspiracy at this time was forming at land, to attack the English, no less than 1000 men being mustered on shore, and it was agreed that the people of the town should support the operations of the fleet. Accordingly, on the morning of the 24th, the English observed unusual manœuvres on board the Spanish ships; their small arms were shifted from one ship to another, and their ordnance pointed at the English fleet; a greater number of men than usual likewise appeared upon the decks; and several other circumstances contributing to alarm captain Hawkins, he sent to the viceroy, to know the meaning of all these extraordinary motions: when, in order to carry on the base deception, the viceroy, to all outward appearance, gave all possible satisfaction to the English commander, and assured him, on his parole of honour, that if the inhabitants of the place had any secret designs, and should attempt any violence against the English fleet, he would protect and assist them. But captain Hawkins, from a variety of circumstances, had reason to doubt the sincerity of the viceroy, and therefore he ordered his people to stand upon their defence; soon after, suspecting that a considerable land force was concealed in a ship which lay next to the Minion, he sent to the viceroy, to demand a categorical answer, who, unable any longer to conceal his treachery, detained the messenger, and ordered a trumpet to be sounded, which was the signal for falling upon the English.

Captain

Captain Hawkins was at dinner when he heard the trumpet, and in the same instant, Don Augustine de Villa Neuva, a Spaniard, whom he had treated with great respect and civility, felt in his sleeve for a dagger, which he had concealed, having engaged to assassinate Hawkins, but one John Chamberlayne, who waited at table, perceived his motion in time to stop his hand and arrest him: he was directly secured in the steward's room, and Hawkins flew upon deck, where he perceived the Spanish troops boarding the Minion from the vessel wherein they had been concealed, upon which he exclaimed with great ardour, "God and Saint "George fall upon these traitors, and rescue the "Minion: I trust in God the day shall be ours." His crew thereupon boarded the Minion, drove out the Spaniards, and fired a shot into the vice-admiral, which it is imagined, passed through the powder-room, for three hundred Spaniards on board were blown up into the air. Another shot set fire to the Spanish admiral, which continued burning half an hour. But this dreadful havock was unhappily retaliated upon the English on shore, who were all cut off except three, who swam to the English ships. Hawkins, though overpowered, continued the engagement with undaunted resolution, even after the ordnance of the fort had sunk his small ships, at the utmost peril of his life, for his ship was already greatly disabled, when, having drank success to his men, encouraging them to ply their guns briskly, a shot from a demi-culverin struck the cup he had just put out of his hand, carried that, and a cooper's plane, which lay near the main-mast, overboard, and went out through the opposite side of the ship. Upon which Hawkins only re-animated his men, by telling them "to fear nothing, for God who had preserved "him from that shot, would also deliver them all

Vol. II.   I   "from

"from those traitors and villains the Spaniards." At length, the masts and rigging of the Jesus being so shattered by the artillery of the fort, that it was impossible to bring her off, it was resolved to place her as a screen to the Minion till night, and then it was proposed to take out her provisions, necessaries, &c. and abandon her; but soon after, two Spanish fire-ships bearing down upon the Minion, the crew consulting their own safety, without waiting for orders from their officers, hove away from the Jesus, with so much precipitation, that it was with great difficulty Hawkins was taken on board; as for his people, they were obliged to take to their boats, and row after the Minion, which had got under sail; some reached her, but others fell victims to the savage barbarity of the Spaniards.

The Spanish fleet suffered greatly in the action; the admiral and vice-admiral were rendered unfit for service, and four other ships were totally destroyed; they lost likewise about 500 men, and this was all the reward they had, for their infamous conduct. Of the English squadron, which consisted of five sail, none but the Minion and the Judith escaped, and the latter, a bark of 50 tons, separated from the Minion in the night, soon after the engagement was over; and we have no further account of her. As for the Minion she was crowded with men, having on board all the wounded they could bring off, and great part of the crew of the Jesus; and some of the men, who had escaped in boats from the ships that were sunk. Captain Hawkins now took the command of the Minion, and it does not appear whether this was the ship before under Drake; all we know is, that he returned home in her. They remained out at sea, in want of provisions and water, for their numerous complement of men, till the 8th of October, when they

they entered a creek in the bay of Mexico, in search of refreshments. This was near the mouth of the river Tampico, and here fortunately for those who remained on board, upwards of an hundred of the men requested to be put on shore, preferring the uncertain fate to which they exposed themselves, to the apparent risk of perishing for want of necessaries for such numbers, before the ship could reach any friendly port.

These unhappy people however, endured every species of human misery; a few were killed, and others wounded by the Indians upon their march up the country; but when the affrighted savages found they were not Spaniards, they treated them kindly, and directed them to the port of Tampico. Here they divided, and the major part unfortunately marched westward, and fell into the hands of the governors of different Spanish settlements, by whom they were inhumanly treated, and sold to slavery; some were burnt, and others tortured by the Inquisition, and of sixty-five persons, we have no certain account of the return of any to England, except Job Hortop, gunner of the Jesus, who, after twelve years imprisonment by the Inquisition, found means to obtain his liberty and got safe to England in 1590, after having suffered incredible hardships for twenty-three years.

Captain Hawkins, with the rest of the crew, consisting likewise of about 100 men, sailed thro' the gulph of Florida, the latter end of October, and after running the hazard of being seized at a Spanish port, which they were obliged to enter for provisions, they got safe to Vigo, where they met with some English ships, from them they received full supplies of every necessary for their voyage, and on the 25th of January, 1570, they arrived safe in England, which was all the consolation they had after this unsuccessful dismal enterprise, for as to Hawkins, he suffered greatly in his fortune by the loss of his merchandise, and the inferior officers and men saved nothing but their lives.

To indemnify our brave commander for the fatigues and hardships he had endured, the queen promoted him to an honourable office at home, admirably suited to his capacity, a circumstance which is but seldom attended to, in the disposal of the public employments; he was made treasurer of the navy; in virtue of this post, he had the chief direction of the royal docks, and he took care to keep the navy upon a respectable footing, more ships being built and repaired after he came into this office, than had ever been known in England before. It was likewise part of his duty to take the command of any squadrons fitted out for the purpose of clearing the narrow seas of pirates; and upon these occasions he exerted himself so effectually, that the merchants thanked him in a body, for the protection and security given to commercial navigation, in 1575.

From this time to the year 1588, we have nothing memorable transmitted to us concerning him, except an ugly accident which happened to him, as he was walking in the Strand: a lunatic mistaking him for Sir Christopher Hatton, the queen's vice-chamberlain, suddenly stabbed him in the back; the wound did not prove mortal, but was so dangerous, that there were little hopes of his recovery for some time. This desperate wretch was committed to the Tower, where he killed his keeper with a billet brought to him for firing, and being tried and condemned for this murder, he was executed in the Strand, near the place where he had wounded captain Hawkins; who was providentially preserved to share the glory of that great day, when the Spanish Armada was defeated: he served under the lord high admiral Howard in the rank of rear-admiral, and he chaced the flying Spaniards with such intrepidity and success, that the queen in person publicly applauded his conduct, before the whole court, and conferred on him the honour of knighthood.

The war continuing with Spain, a grand expedition was meditated soon after the destruction of the Armada, to annoy the coasts of Spain, and at the same time, if possible, to defray the expences of the enterprise, and reward the valour of the subjects engaged in it, by intercepting the plate fleet. A fleet of ten ships of the line was fitted out for these purposes, and divided into two squadrons of five sail, with instructions to act in concert, but each squadron had a separate commander; and upon this occasion Sir Martin Frobisher was judged the properest person to be joined in commission with Sir John Hawkins. Very great expectations were formed of the success of this expedition from the known valour and abilities of the two admirals, for they were rivals in naval reputation.

Sir Martin Frobisher was born in Yorkshire, and was put apprentice by his parents, who were of low degree, to the master of a coasting vessel, and having discovered great talents for navigation, joined to a bold enterprising genius, and undaunted courage, he was distinguished early in life as an able seaman, and, but by what means we know not, he procured recommendations to Ambrose Dudley, earl of Warwick, who with other persons of rank and fortune, patronised an enterprise he had long meditated, which was to discover a north-west passage to the East Indies: being provided with three small vessels at the expence of his patrons, he sailed from Deptford in the summer of the year 1576, and in about five weeks he
found

found himself in 61 degrees of north latitude, where he discovered high points of land covered with snow, but not being able to approach the shore on account of the quantity of ice, and the impossibility of casting anchor from the extraordinary depth of the water; he entered his observations in his journal, and gave the title of *Queen Elizabeth's Foreland*, to the eastern promontory of the coast.

In the month of August he sailed into the Streights, lying a little to the northward of Cape Farewell and West Greenland, in 63 degrees of latitude, these he named *Frobisher's Streights*, and they still continue to be so called. His endeavours however, to open an intercourse with the natives on the coasts proved unsuccessful; the Indians seizing his men and his boats; and according to some accounts, either by storms, or hostilities, he lost two of his vessels, which obliged him to make for England, where he arrived safe in October; and though the chief object of the voyage was not accomplished, yet the discovery of the situation of these places, proved highly beneficial to future navigators.

Frobisher made two voyages to these parts in 1577 and 1578, and with great perseverance and bravery attempted to approach nearer to the North Pole; but being the first adventurer, as it frequently happens, his observations served rather as instructions to his successors, than as splendid monuments of his own great reputation; and 'tis probable that his unpolished manners might prevent the good fortune he had promised himself in these enterprises, for he was a very severe commander, rigid in his discipline, and more dreaded than beloved by his men. With this cast of temper, his success was more signal in engagements with an enemy, than in attempts to traffic, or to establish

blish a friendly communication with the inhospitable natives of North America. Accordingly, he performed wonders against the Spanish Armada, was knighted on the recommendation of the lord admiral in 1588, and in 1590, he was sent with Sir John Hawkins on the expedition, to which we now return. The king of Spain gaining early intelligence of this armament, and of its destination, at first proposed to oppose it with a more formidable fleet; but his council wisely judging that Elizabeth, who had a strong navy at this time, would speedily reinforce the admirals, if she found it requisite, that plan was laid aside, and a more prudent measure adopted; which was to keep his ships in their harbours, and to send expresses over land to India, to order the Plate-fleet to remain in port, instead of sailing that year. Thus circumstanced, the admirals were obliged to remain inactive for seven months, cruizing off the Azores, without taking a single ship. At last, determined to attempt some signal action, they attacked the Island of Fayal; but the governor being well provided with every necessary to support a long siege, they were obliged to retire with some loss and little reputation; and soon after, they were ordered home, where they were but coolly received by the people, who are struck only with brilliant acts; but the intentions of the court being in a great measure answered, by obliging the Spanish fleets to remain in their harbours, and preventing the arrival of the plate fleet in Spain, which occasioned bankruptcies amongst her merchants, the court considered them in the light of faithful servants, and they were highly esteemed by their sovereign.

The last and the most arduous enterprize, in which Sir John Hawkins was engaged, proved fatal to himself. In the life of Sir Francis Drake, we have given an account of the armament fitted out in the year 1595, to attack the Spanish settlements in the West-Indies; and we have marked the operations of the fleet under the joint command of Hawkins and Drake, till they made an unsuccessful attack on the chief of the Canary Islands. Sir John Hawkins, being the oldest commander, was not a little chagrined at having his advice overruled; and his resentment against Drake and Baskerville was increased, when he found, that while they were employed in this fruitless attempt, the Spaniards had time to put their chief places in the West-Indies in a proper state of defence. With much chagrin therefore, he sailed for Dominica, where the seamen and the troops, by some mismanagement, wasted more time in taking in provisions and other refreshment, and in preparing their pinnaces, which were designed for sailing closer to the harbour of Porto Rico, than the men of war could approach. In the interval, the Spaniards sent five large frigates well manned, to bring off the galleon; these, on their way, fell in with the rear of the division of the fleet under Sir John Hawkins, who had sailed from Dominica for Porto Rico, in the evening of the 30th of October. The Spaniards took the Francis, a bark of 135 tons, and having tortured some of the crew into a confession, that all the English force was bent against Porto Rico, the Spanish admiral crouded all his sail, and made the best of his way, without attempting to engage Sir John Hawkins, though he had a superior squadron, and by this prudent conduct he saved the place. As for Hawkins, he foresaw the inevitable consequences of the repeated delays of the English fleet, and of the capture of the Francis, which augmenting his chagrin, threw him into a fever, and put a period to his valuable life on the 21st of November 1595, when they had just made the island of Porto Rico. The unfortunate issue of the desperate attack on on Porto Rico, and its similar fatal effect on Sir Francis Drake, the reader will naturally recur to in the life of that admiral.

The great character Sir John Hawkins acquired, was tarnished by the mean passion of avarice; and it is much to be feared, that it had too great an influence on some parts of his public conduct. However, his great abilities in the naval department, both at land and at sea, extenuated his defects: he was no less than forty-eight years commander at sea, and twenty-two years treasurer of the navy, for the regulation of which he established many excellent orders; and he was both the author and the patron of several useful inventions and improvements in the art of navigation. Lastly, in conjunction with his brother William, he contributed to the great increase of sailors, by promoting commercial navigation; for they were owners of thirty sail, says Dr. Campbell, of goodly ships.

He likewise bred up his son Richard to the sea, and had the happiness of seeing him knighted, two years before he died, for his signal services. Sir Richard Hawkins accompanied his father in most of his expeditions, and upon all occasions proved that he inherited his father's valour. In the engagement with the Armada, he commanded the Swallow, a frigate, which was closely attacked, and suffered more than any ship in the English fleet. In 1590, under the command of his father and Sir Martin Frobisher, he exerted himself in a signal manner on the coasts of Spain; and in 1593, he fitted out two large ships at his own expence, having first procured a commission from the queen, to annoy the Spaniards in South-America: he had likewise a further design of sailing round the globe, that he might share the glory of Drake and Cavendish: with this view, he passed the Streights of Magellan with only one ship, in the spring of the year 1594,

and

and cruized along the coasts of Patagonia, which have lately been the object of curiosity, and the subject of general conversation. In 48 degrees of southern latitude, he discovered a fair and promising country, situated in a very temperate climate, and to particular places he gave different names; but the land collectively, he called HAWKINS's MAIDEN LAND, assigning as a reason, that he had discovered it at his own expence, under the auspices of a maiden queen. After taking some valuable prizes in the South-Seas, and once, bravely disengaging himself from an attempt made by Don Bertrand de Castro to take him, it would seem strange that he did not return home, if it did not appear, that with his valour, he inherited his father's foible, an inordinate love of money, which detained him in those parts, to make more valuable captures, till in the end, he himself was taken with all his treasure by the Spanish admiral, after a desperate engagement, in the course of which he received several dangerous wounds: he surrendered on a promise, that the whole crew should have a free passage to England as soon as possible; but the Spaniards, with their usual perfidy, sent him to Seville, and afterwards to Madrid, retaining him a prisoner in Spain, till the peace between that country and England was negociating in 1600; and though the treaty was broke off, he then obtained his release, and returned home; after which, he passed the remainder of his days in retirement: he died suddenly of an apoplectic fit, in an outer chamber, while he was attending on the privy-council; but upon what business, or in what year this event happened, we are left in the dark, by the writers of his life. He left an account of his voyage, to the time of his being taken, part of which was put to press by himself, and the whole manuscript was printed and published after his decease, in one volume, folio, intitled,

intitled, " The Observations of Sir Richard Hawkins, in his voyage to the South-Seas;" but it is imperfect, the author having designed to complete it, in a second part.

It now remains, that we should conclude the memoirs of this respectable *naval triumvirate*, by completing our account of Sir Martin Frobisher.

In the year 1592, he commanded a squadron, fitted out at the expence of Sir Walter Raleigh and his friends, with instructions to watch the arrival of the Plate-fleet on the coast of Spain; and though his whole armament consisted of only three ships, he burnt one galleon, richly laden, and brought home another.

In 1594, the queen sent him to the assistance of Henry IV. of France, against his rebellious subjects the Leaguers, and the Spaniards, who had gained possession of part of *Bretagne*; and had fortified themselves in a very strong manner at *Croyzon* near *Brest*. Admiral Frobisher commanded four ships of the line, with which he blocked up the port; at the same time, Sir John Norris, with 3000 infantry, attacked the place by land, which however would not have been carried, if the admiral had not landed his sailors to reinforce the general: the sailors made a desperate attack, and took it by storm; but their brave admiral received a musket-ball in his side, and by the mismanagement of the surgeon, the wound proved mortal, in a few days after his arrival at Plymouth.

⁎ *Authorities.* Lediard's Naval History. Campbell's Lives of the Admirals. Baker's Chronicle. Hume's History of England.

THE LIFE OF WILLIAM CECIL,

Lord BURLEIGH,

[A.D. 1520, to 1598.]

Including Memoirs of Sir NICHOLAS BACON, Sir NICHOLAS THROGMORTON, and THOMAS HOWARD, Duke of Norfolk.

WE are now to refume the thread of Britifh hiftory, which we fhall find regularly connected with the principal incidents of the life of this great ftatefman, who had the chief guidance of the reins of government forty years; frequent changes of adminiftration, the bane of modern politics, being in thofe days unknown.

William Cecil was the fon of Richard Cecil, Efq; of Burleigh, in the county of Northampton, principal officer of the robes in the reign of Henry VIII. and in great favour with the king. His mother was the daughter and heirefs of William Hickington, Efq; of Bourn, in the county of Lincoln: at which place he was born in the year 1520.

The firft rudiments of his education he received at the grammar-fchools of Grantham and Stamford, and difcovering an ardent thirft for knowledge, his father determined to qualify him for the law; with this

this view, he sent him to St. John's college, Cambridge, where his close application to his studies, assisted by an uncommon genius, soon acquired him considerable reputation, but at the expence of his health, for he contracted a humour in his legs, from his long sittings, which laid the foundation of that tormenting disease, the gout, afterwards, a disagreeable companion to him, for life.

In his nineteenth year, he had completed his university education, and was therefore removed by his father to Gray's-inn, London, then the most eminent of the inns of court. Here his proficiency in the law was as rapid, as his general learning at the university. And while he was thus laudably employed, an accident happened which introduced him to the notice of his sovereign, and diverted his attention, in some measure from the law, to the attainment of courtly accomplishments.

In the latter end of the reign of Henry VIII. Mr. Cecil went to court, on a visit to his father, and in the presence-chamber he met two priests, chaplains to O'Neale, a famous Irish chief, who was negociating the affairs of his country with the king. With these priests, who were bigotted papists, young Cecil fell into conversation upon theological topics; a warm dispute ensued, which was carried on in Latin, and managed with so much wit and sound argument on the part of Cecil, an advocate for the reformed religion, that the chaplains seeing themselves foiled by a youth, broke from him in rage. Upon this, it was reported to the king, that young Cecil had confuted both O'Neale's chaplains; and his Majesty thereupon ordered him into his presence, and was so delighted with the pertinent answers he gave to several intricate questions, that he directed his father to find out a place for him at court; but as it happened there was no vacancy. The old gentleman therefore, asked for the reversion of the Custos Brevium Office in the Common Pleas; which the king willingly granted.

About this time, Mr. Cecil married Mary Cheeke, sister to Sir John Cheeke, by whom he had his first son, Thomas. This lady died in less than two years after her marriage. Five years after, he married Mildred Cooke, a daughter of Sir Anthony Cooke, one of the tutors to Edward VI. a lady of great merit, and uncommon learning.

Upon the accession of Edward VI. he was promoted at court, for Sir John Cheeke recommended him to the lord protector, the king's uncle, who made him master of the requests, and soon after he came to the possession of his office of Custos Brevium; these acquisitions, and the fortune of his second wife, enabled him to make a distinguished figure amongst the courtiers.

Mr. Cecil attended the protector Somerset in his expedition to Scotland, and was at the battle of Musselburgh, where he had a narrow escape, his life being saved by the generous interposition of one of his friends, who pushed him out of the level of a cannon, and had his arm instantly shattered to pieces by the ball, which would otherwise have destroyed Cecil.

In 1548, he grew into great favour with the young king, which Somerset observing, he advanced him to the office of secretary of state; but the following year, a party being formed against the protector, he was involved in the misfortunes of his patron, and was committed to the Tower, where he remained a prisoner three months. But to recompense him for this temporary disgrace, the king conferred on him the honour of knighthood, soon after his release; and in October 1551, he was sworn of the privy-council. The following year, party disputes ran very high at court; and though Sir William Cecil acted with great caution,

endea-

endeavouring, on the one hand, to avoid involving himself in the fate of his falling patron, and on the other, not to court the duke of Northumberland, the rising favourite, in an unbecoming, servile manner, yet his enemies accused him of promoting the ruin of Somerset. But the aspersion is grounded solely on his cool reply to the duke, when he told him, he was apprehensive of some evil design against him. "If you are not in fault, said Cecil, you may trust to your innocence; if you are, I have nothing to say, but to lament you."

In 1553, Sir William Cecil undertook the liquidation of the crown debts, and having proposed ways and means which were agreed to by the council, he was, for this eminent service, made chancellor of the noble order of the garter; and about this time, the people began to form great expectations of him, on account of his attention to the commercial affairs of the nation; for the promotion of which, he patronized every rational scheme proposed to him.

At the council-board, he strenuously opposed the resolution for changing the succession to the crown, in favour of Lady Jane Grey, and refused to sign the instrument for that purpose, as a privy-counsellor, but he witnessed it as the act and deed of the king: but on his Majesty's demise, he refused to draw up the proclamation, declaring Lady Jane's title, neither would he write a letter, on the duke of Northumberland's solicitation, to acknowledge her right, and to treat Mary as illegitimate. This discretion paved the way to his future advancement. For queen Mary, soon after her accession, granted Sir William Cecil a general pardon; and, on chusing her counsellors, she said, if he would change his religion, he should be her secretary and counsellor: to which he nobly answered; "he was taught and bound to serve God first, and next the queen.

queen: but if her service should put him out of God's service, he hoped her Majesty would give him leave to chuse an everlasting, rather than a momentary service: that she had been his so gracious lady as he would ever serve and pray for her in his heart; and with his body and goods be as ready to serve in her defence as any of her loyal subjects; but hoped she would please to grant him leave to use his conscience to himself, and serve her at large as a private man, rather than to be her greatest counsellor." Yet the queen still treated him very graciously, and forebore either to hear his enemies, who were many, or to disgrace him; for, in the second year of her reign, he was sent to Brussels, with the lord Paget, to bring over cardinal Pole.

During the remainder of this reign, Sir William Cecil continued in a private station, only attending his duty in parliament, as knight of the shire for the county of Lincoln; and though in parliament, he frequently opposed the measures of administration, yet he was held in such respect by the queen's ministers, and particularly by cardinal Pole, that he was never molested either for his religious or political sentiments, though he openly avowed both, with manly freedom.

When queen Elizabeth succeeded to the throne, " Sir William Cecil, for his truth and tried service to her, was worthily called and honourably advanced by her Majesty to be her secretary of state and a privy-counsellor; and was the first sworn of any counsellor she had, at Hatfield, where she resided at her first coming to the crown."

In the first parliament holden in the beginning of the queen's reign, great difficulties arose in reforming and altering religion, and for the better satisfaction of the parliament, by Sir William's advice, a conference was held in Westminster church,

by

by the old and new bishops, and other learned men, upon some questions and points devised principally by himself touching the exercise of religion; which produced a happy coalition, and that form of worship, which has ever since been the establishment of the church of England.

His next care was, to remedy the abuses in the coinage; for this purpose, he called in all the base money, and ordered a new coinage, and put the gold and silver on the noble standard it has ever since continued.

In the beginning of the year 1560, he was made master of the wards, upon the death of Sir Thomas Parry; and the same year he was sent to Scotland in conjunction with Dr. Wotton, to negotiate a treaty of peace with the bishop of Valence and the count de Randan, between England, Scotland, and France; they executed their commission successfully, but the French count absolutely refused to ratify it, though the above-named ambassadors, vested with full powers, had signed it.

The influence of Sir William Cecil increased every day at the council-board; and assured of the queen's support, who besides the high esteem in which she held his political abilities, was under considerable obligations to him, for giving her intelligence of all the motions of her enemies in the late reign; he now began to oppose the earl of Leicester, and that nobleman, jealous of his rising reputation, as earnestly endeavoured to ruin Cecil. This contest between two such considerable men, produced a powerful division at court, but as yet Leicester's party prevailed; and these being in league with the popish zealots, some of whom Elizabeth had allowed to retain their seats in council, they accused him to the queen of having written, or patronized a book, found upon his table, containing scandalous reflections on the whole body of the

the nobility; and when this, and some other dark intrigues failed, they basely plotted against his life, hiring assassins to take him off, from whom he narrowly escaped, at one time, by going down the back stairs, on a hint that a villain waited for him at the foot of the great stairs of the palace. At another, by the failure of the cruel resolution of the assassin, who being alone with him in his chamber, with a poignard in his hand, had not the power to perpetrate the horrid crime.

Notwithstanding his great discernment, and his wary conduct, he would most probably have fallen a victim to the inveterate malice of the popish party, and the envy of Leicester, if he had not been firmly supported by Francis Russel, earl of Bedford, and Sir Nicholas Bacon: of the latter, whose cool judgment, whose knowledge of the law, and whose high station, all combined to protect Cecil, we shall here introduce concise memoirs.

Sir Nicholas Bacon first distinguished himself in the reign of Henry VIII. by presenting a plan to that prince, of a seminary for the education of youth, of rank and family, in order to qualify them for the public service. The outlines of the plan were, that they should study in a college, the elements of natural and political law, and the institution of government; then they were to be divided into classes; and some, being distinguished by superior talents and address, were to be sent abroad under our ambassadors, while others were to write the history of our foreign negociations, and treaties, and of domestic national events, at home. But, though this noble design was not carried into execution, it remains a perpetual memorial of the extensive views of its author, for the honour and happiness of his country. Mr. Bacon's highest promotion in the law, (for which he had been educated) in the reign of Henry VIII. was
the

the post of attorney to the court of wards, which he held under his successor. In the reign of Mary, to avoid being involved in the troubles of the times, he resided abroad, and had the honour to correspond privately with the princess Elizabeth, who on her accession, nominated him to be one of the eight privy-counsellors, in the protestant interest, to be added to the old council, whom for political reasons she did not choose to remove suddenly. To this honour, her Majesty added that of knighthood; and soon after, Heath, archbishop of York, and lord chancellor of England, having refused to comply with the queen's orders, respecting the reformation of religion, the seals were taken from him, and given to Sir Nicholas Bacon, with the title only of lord keeper, but with the full powers of chancellor.

As he came into office by the protestant interest, so he firmly supported all his friends, embarked in the same cause; and in this view, he favoured the succession of the house of Suffolk, in opposition to the claim of Mary queen of Scots; and as this succession, in case of Elizabeth's death without issue, was the principal object of the secret cabals at court, he rendered himself extremely obnoxious to the earl of Leicester, the patron of the Scotch or Popish interest. But, regardless of menaces or intrigues, he boldly adhered to his friends, and he and Sir William Cecil may be truly said to have been the reciprocal deliverers of each other. Sir Nicholas Bacon performed the first good office to Cecil, as we have already seen; and when Leicester had prevailed so far with the queen, that she forbad Bacon the court, and ordered him to confine himself solely to the business of his tribunal, Cecil prevented the further progress of her Majesty's displeasure, and restored him to her favour, on condition

dition he should not give his opinion any more about the succession.

Sir Nicholas Bacon enjoyed his office with an unsullied character, and the highest reputation, for the wisdom and equity of his decrees, upwards of twenty years, when he grew extremely corpulent, and was suddenly taken off by the effects of a violent cold, to the great grief of the queen and the whole nation, in the year 1579, and in the 69th year of his age.

Sallies of wit and repartee were the fire of conversation in his time; we must not therefore omit two, which have been preserved in all the memoirs of this great man. The one by the queen, respecting his corpulency, her Majesty said, " the soul of Sir Nicholas Bacon lodged well." At another time, the queen honouring him with a visit at his house at St. Alban's, her Majesty observed, that the house was too little for him. " No, madam," answered Sir Nicholas, " but your Majesty has made me too great for my house."

Having given this short account of Cecil's best friend, it may not be improper to sketch the character of the person employed by Leicester, as the chief agent of his practices against him.

This was Sir Nicholas Throgmorton, a gentleman descended from an ancient family in Warwickshire, and educated in foreign parts. From early youth he manifested an inclination for political studies, and before he was thirty years of age he was esteemed an accomplished courtier; his knowledge of the true interests of his country, led him to oppose the marriage of queen Mary with Philip of Spain, in parliament; and his attachment at that time to the protestant cause, engaged him in secret measures for the support of Wyat's rebellion, which being discovered, he was indicted for high treason; but he pleaded his own cause so ably, that

that neither the strength of the evidence, nor the influence of the ministry, could prevail against him, for the jury acquitted him; for which offence, they were prosecuted by the attorney-general in the star-chamber.

Queen Elizabeth, who was a ready discerner of merit, called him to court in the first year of her reign, and employed his talents in the department wherein she knew he chiefly excelled: she sent him on various special embassies to France and Scotland, his knowledge of the political state of Europe, and of men and manners, having acquired him the reputation of being one of the ablest negociators of his time. But the same talents, under the influence of ambition, carried him deep into court intrigues at home, and made him sacrifice his honour to support his interest with the reigning favourite. It is no wonder therefore, that he became a principal in Leicester's faction, and involved himself in troubles on his account; particularly in the year 1569, when Leicester espoused the proposal made to him by the earl of Murray, regent of Scotland, of marrying the queen of Scots to the duke of Norfolk; Throgmorton, upon Leicester's confession of the whole scheme to Elizabeth, was taken into custody; but finding, by this instance of perfidy, that he had mistaken Leicester's true character, he made some concessions to Cecil, went over to his interest; and it is imagined, betrayed some important secrets, which rendered him so obnoxious to Leicester, that he only kept upon good terms with him to outward appearance, the better to accomplish his design of taking him off, in the manner related, in the life of Leicester.

About the time of Sir Nicholas Throgmorton's death, which happened in 1571, the queen began to be jealous of Leicester's high spirit and towering ambition; and probably, being conscious of her unjustifiable

unjuſtifiable partiality in his favour, ſhe prudently advanced Cecil in honours and confidence, as a check upon her own paſſions, and the deep deſigns of her favourite.

Be this as it may, certain it is, that ſhe never conferred particular marks of diſtinction on any of her ſubjects, but upon the moſt urgent occaſions, and from political motives; and ſhe now raiſed Sir William Cecil to the dignity of a peer, by the ſtyle and title of baron lord Burleigh; and his enemies obſerving the high degree of eſtimation in which he was held by the queen, contended who ſhould be firſt reconciled to him. Lord Burleigh further recommended himſelf to her Majeſty, by his aſſiduity in watching all the motions of Mary queen of Scots, whoſe friends were for the moſt part the ſecret enemies of Elizabeth, and the abettors of all the popiſh plots to dethrone, or to aſſaſſinate her.

The unfortunate queen of the Scots, from the time that ſhe was detained priſoner in England, thought every meaſure juſtifiable, which had a tendency to reſtore her to the throne of Scotland; to ſtrengthen her claim to the ſucceſſion of that of England; to gratify her perſonal reſentment againſt Elizabeth; or to promote the re-eſtabliſhment of the Romiſh religion in both kingdoms.

To one or other of theſe objects, ſhe continually ſacrificed her reputation; and ſhe was ſo eager in the purſuit of them, that ſhe placed her confidence frequently, in the very perſons who were placed about her, to betray her. Conſpiracy upon conſpiracy was diſcovered by lord Burleigh's agents; and at length, the deſign of marrying the duke of Norfolk completed her ruin.

This nobleman was the eldeſt ſon of Henry earl of Surrey, whoſe memoirs the reader will find in the firſt volume of this work. Queen Mary reſtored

stored him in blood, and he succeeded to the title of duke of Norfolk on the death of his grandfather. When Elizabeth came to the throne, she made him a knight of the garter, and bestowed on him many other marks of her royal favour; but his ambitious design of succeeding to the throne of England, being avowed by Leicester, he was taken into custody, and from that moment, Elizabeth regarded him with a jealous eye; yet, upon his going over to Cecil's party, and promising to drop all intercourse with the queen of Scots, he was released.

But no tie of honour or gratitude could keep him within the bounds of his duty, for he renewed his correspondence with Mary, entered into a contract of marriage, exchanged vows with her, transmitted money to her friends in Scotland to support her cause there, and took such unguarded measures at home, to release the royal captive, that the spies employed by Burleigh, soon procured sufficient grounds to accuse him to the privy-council of high treason; upon which he was committed to the Tower, the second time, and was brought to his trial in January 1572, the earl of Shrewsbury being appointed high steward upon the occasion; and upon the fullest evidence, he was found guilty; but so greatly was he beloved by his brother peers, that they all lamented the impossibility of saving him, the lord high steward bursting into tears when he pronounced the fatal sentence; and it is certain, that the peers who condemned him solicited his pardon, which occasioned a suspension of his execution for five months; but unfortunately, in the interval, Mary and her friends were more active than ever, in their attempts to take off queen Elizabeth; the parliament therefore addressed her Majesty on the expediency of executing the sentence against the duke of Norfolk, and the necessity of bringing on the trial of Mary. In compliance with the

the addresses of both houses, Norfolk suffered on the 2d of June; and died greatly regretted by the people, being a nobleman of great merit, who had cultivated popularity, by his affability and liberality, and whose crime was rather considered as the effect of his high rank, being the first peer of the realm, and perhaps led to believe, as there were no princes of the blood, that his aspiring to the crown was not so criminal, as to be construed into high treason, for his enemies acquit him of being privy to any designs on the queen's life: these base plots Mary artfully concealed from him, while she held forth the lure of one crown in possession, and another in reversion.

The execution of the duke of Norfolk, effectually put a stop to the intrigues of all ambitious adventurers, who had entertained any hopes of marrying the unfortunate queen of Scots; and therefore, this obstacle being removed, every conciliatory measure was tried: Elizabeth even condescended to treat with her, for her enlargement; and dispatched lord Burleigh, and Sir Thomas Mildmay, chancellor of the Exchequer, a privy-counsellor, remarkable for his great moderation, his popularity, and his wisdom, to negociate the conditions of a reconciliation. Mary was, at this time, confined at Chatsworth, in Derbyshire (now the seat of the duke of Devonshire) but all the arguments and intreaties of these great men, were lost upon this devoted woman, who with a firmness which would have done honour to a better cause, adhered to the party she had espoused, and resolved to merit the crown of martyrdom from the Roman pontiff; for, upon no consideration could she be prevailed upon to break off her connections and correspondence with the English, the Irish, and the Scotch papists, who were declared enemies to Elizabeth, and were continually forming plans to destroy

destroy the happy constitution in church and state, now firmly established, and gloriously maintained by the wisdom of her councils, and the valour of her fleets and armies.

Yet Elizabeth, though she thought it highly expedient for her own security, to detain her in custody, shewed no inclination to proceed to violent measures against her, in the course of fifteen years, from the time of Norfolk's execution, when the parliament addressed her Majesty to proceed capitally against her.

In fact, she relied so entirely on the vigilance, the policy, and the general influence of lord Burleigh, whom, upon the death of the marquiss of Winchester, in 1572, she raised to the office of lord high treasurer, that she gave herself little or no concern about the queen of the Scots, till such daring attempts were made against her royal person, that she began to think she should fall a victim to her own, and Burleigh's moderation; and therefore, upon the conviction of Babington, on whose trial it appeared that he was countenanced by Mary, and her party, she was more closely confined, and at length removed to Fotheringay-castle, in Northamptonshire, in order to take her trial, a commission being issued out for that purpose, by the advice of the privy-council, in the month of October 1586.

It is a difficult matter to determine whether Mary was guilty or not, as an accomplice, in any direct attempt, against the life of Elizabeth; and charity should incline us to believe her own dying words upon this tender point; for though the commissioners, before whom she was tried, unanimously found her guilty of having been privy to Babington's conspiracy, yet the whole charge rested chiefly on the evidences of Nau and Curle, her two secretaries, who had deserted her in her misfortunes, and had been countenanced by the English ministry to betray her.

Indeed, it would have shewn more temper and sounder policy to have proceeded against her, on the heavy accusations brought against her by her own subjects, particularly her being accessary to the murder of lord Darnley, her second husband; and they were certainly competent to try her on this charge, as lord Darnley was an English subject.

However, from the high rank, consummate knowledge of the laws, and the great number of the commissioners, being no less than forty-two of the chief persons in the kingdom, including five of the judges, the majority of our historians decide, that she had an impartial trial, and was clearly convicted of "conspiring the destruction of the queen, the realm of England, and the protestant religion." Thuanus, the celebrated French historian, likewise observes, that, "though there were several popish lords in the commission, even these found her guilty of the impeachment."

The discovery of the correspondence between Mary and Babington, was effected by the policy of Sir Francis Walsingham; but the bringing the royal criminal to condign punishment, required a degree of firmness and resolution suited to the crisis; and nothing but a consciousness of the rectitude of the measure, of the ascendency he had gained over the queen, and of the popularity he had acquired by his public virtues and his private beneficent character, could have supported Cecil, under that load of censure which fell upon him from all quarters, as the chief cause of Mary's execution.

But, being now fully convinced, that the safety of his sovereign and of his country, depended on cutting off the hopes of the popish faction, by making a sacrifice of their chief, the only branch of the royal blood devoted to their cause, the sentence

tence pronounced against Mary was executed, near four months after her trial: she suffered in the great hall of Fotheringay-castle, on the 8th of February 1587, in the 46th year of her age. She met death with noble fortitude, and with pious resignation; and it may be truly said, that the last moments of her life, did her more honour than all her preceding years.

Queen Elizabeth, apprehensive that this execution would excite great clamours against her in all the popish courts of Europe, artfully endeavoured to throw the blame of it upon Davison, one of the secretaries of state, to whose department it belonged to get the warrants signed, after the condemnation of criminals; who, accordingly, presented the warrant for the execution of Mary to the queen, soon after sentence was passed, and her Majesty signed it, without hesitation; but she afterwards declared, that she had charged him not to part with it, nor even to let any person know she had signed it.

Davison however, from hints dropped by the queen at sundry times, which shewed her secret desire to have her taken off, thought it his duty, to inform the privy-council, that the warrant lay in his office signed; and some of the lords, knowing that the queen had reproached the council in private, for their dilatoriness in this affair, made a motion at the board, that orders should be given to Davison to forward the warrant to Fotheringay-castle, without the queen's knowledge, which was agreed to, and the execution followed; for which Elizabeth thought proper to prosecute Davison, as her own immediate servant, in the star-chamber, where he was fined 10,000 *l*. and sentenced to imprisonment during the queen's pleasure, for having disobeyed her Majesty's secret orders.

As for lord Burleigh, being convinced in his own mind, that Davison had acted the very part the queen wished, though she denied it to the world, he remonstrated with great freedom, against the disgrace of Davison, in a letter to the queen, still extant.

One of the chief objects of the mighty preparations made in Spain in the course of this year, for invading England, was to release Mary, and to replace her on the throne of Scotland; but by the assiduity and great abilities of lord Burleigh, the whole expedition failed for this year, as we have related in the life of Sir Francis Drake.

The following year however, the Spaniards resolved upon ample vengeance; and the thunder of the vatican was fulminated in aid of the Spanish arms. Excommunications, anathemas, denunciations of the wrath of heaven, and every other popish engine of terror, was made use of, to shake the allegiance of the English, and to terrify them into defection from their renowned sovereign. But lord Burleigh had taken advantage of ten years of peace, to put the nation in such a posture of defence, as to be able to resist the attempts of the most formidable enemy. The navy had been considerably improved and augmented, and the seamen kept in practice, by the frequent naval expeditions, sent out in quest of discoveries, under the great admirals, whose lives we have already given. The army likewise was well disciplined, and had gained experience in several campaigns in Holland and in Ireland. And so exact was his intelligence, in foreign parts, that, to use the words of Lloyd, " he could write to a friend in Ireland, what the king of Spain could do for two years together, and what he could not do."

The defeat of the Spanish Armada, having delivered the nation from all further apprehensions of a revolution in religion, and the queen from the personal dangers to which she had been continually exposed, the plots for assassinating her Majesty, having for their ultimate object, the subjection of the realm to the see of Rome; universal joy and transport prevailed among all orders and ranks of people.

But the inexpressible satisfaction which Burleigh must have felt, on this final happy issue of all his political manœuvres at home and abroad, was chequered with an adverse stroke of fortune, in his family, which cast a gloom of melancholy over his remaining days. In the beginning of the year 1589, he lost his second wife, a lady distinguished by her rare talents, being no less celebrated for her piety and learning, than for those domestic virtues which rendered her the ornament and example of her sex. This affliction was the more severely felt, from their long and happy union, lady Burleigh having been the faithful companion of her husband upwards of forty-three years. She was the daughter of Sir Anthony Cooke, and had been educated with lady Jane Grey, from whom she imbibed a taste for the learned languages, in which she was well skilled; and when her lord's prosperity placed her in a situation to act agreeably to her disposition, she was a constant patroness of learned men; and, among other instances of her benevolence, she founded two perpetual fellowships in St. John's-college, Cambridge.

It was now, that almost exhausted with incessant application to public business, and rendered infirm, by that most painful distemper the gout, this great statesman earnestly solicited leave to resign all his employments; but the queen, who knew the value of such an able senator, and steady counsellor, whose wisdom increased with his grey hairs, would by no means consent to it: but to console him for his great loss, she paid him frequent visits, and took every opportunity to do him honour in the eyes of the people, than which nothing could be better calculated to soothe and flatter declining age, and to excite it to fresh exertions of zeal in the public service. Accordingly, we find, the good old man very active, upon sundry occasions, during the last ten years of his useful life. In 1591, the queen founded the university of Dublin, by the advice of lord Burleigh, by whom the plan of education was drawn up; and in 1593, he had the management or direction of every branch of administration, filling the dangerous post of prime minister, and acquitting himself of all its painful and extensive duties with as much ability, accuracy, and dispatch, as if he had been in the prime of life.

" To him all ranks of people addressed themselves, to the very last. The bishops and clergy for encouragement, protection, and preferment: the puritans, (who were persecuted against his opinion in council) for favourable treatment and relief from the oppressions of the prelates, and of the ecclesiastical courts: fugitives in foreign countries for pardon, which he granted, in consideration of the intelligence they procured him of the designs of the popes, and of the king of Spain, against his country. The lieutenants of counties for instructions and advice: the admirals for fleets and supplies; in a word, the interests of the state abroad, and its domestic tranquillity at home, were provided for, and preserved to the latest hour of his life.

" At length, his dissolution approached by slow and easy gradations; and in fact, his disease, properly speaking, was nothing more than the decay of old age, hastened by incessant labour, and fatigue of mind and body.

"His death was not sudden, nor his pain in sickness great; for he continued languishing two or three months, yet went abroad to take the air in his coach all that time; retiring from the court, sometimes to his house at Theobald's, and sometimes at London. His greatest apparent infirmity, was the weakness of his stomach. It was also thought his mind was troubled, that he could not effect a peace for his country, which he earnestly desired, seeking to leave it as he had long kept it.

"About ten or twelve days before he died, he grew weak, and so driven to keep his bed, complaining only of a pain in his breast; which was thought to be the humour of the gout, wherewith he was so long possessed, falling to that place, without any ague, fever, or sign of distemper; and that pain not great nor continual, but by fits; and so continued till within one night before his death. He expired on the 4th of August, 1598.

"Now might one see all the world mourning; the queen, for an old and true servant; the council, for a wise and grave counsellor; the court, for their honourable benefactor; his country, and commonwealth, trembling as it were at one blow, to have their head stricken off; the people, widows, and wards, lamenting to lose their protector; religion, her patron; justice, her true minister; and peace, her upholder. His children bewailing the loss of such a father, his friends of such a friend, and his servants of such a master; all men rather bewailing his loss, than hoping ever to find such another. Yea, his very enemies, who in his lifetime could not abide him, did now both sorrow for his death, and wish him alive again.

"He was the oldest, the gravest, and greatest statesman of Christendom; for there was, before his death, never a counsellor left alive in Europe, that were counsellors when he was first made.

As to his person, it is thus described, by his cotemporaries. "He was rather well proportioned than tall, being of the middle size, very straight and upright of body and legs, and, until age and his infirmity of the gout surprised him, very active and nimble of body."

After such an ample account of the most important transactions in the life of this great man, in his public capacity, we must be excused in deviating from the conduct of some modern compilers, who have swelled his memoirs, with long details of his private concerns, and tedious repetitions, of characters drawn of him by various authors.

Indeed, some of them have given nothing else, but an extract from an ancient manuscript in the library of the earl of Exeter, published by Arthur Collins, Esq; in 1732. And, among the rest, the editor of the first edition of the British Plutarch fell into this error; and reprinted a kind of diary or journal, of the private life of Cecil, instead of recording the great public transactions of the statesman.

Yet that we may not be accused of any deficiency, in this most valuable article, we have subjoined the best summary extant of lord Burleigh's general character, drawn by that able historian, the learned Camden, who survived him, many years, but who flourished with him in the reign of Elizabeth.

"Having lived long enough to nature, and long enough to his own glory, but not long enough to his country, he resigned his soul to God with so much peace and tranquillity, that the greatest enemy he had, freely declared, that he envied him nothing, but that his sun went down with so much lustre; whereas, generally, public ministers are not blessed with such calm and fortunate periods."

"Certainly

"Certainly he was a most excellent man; for he was so liberally furnished by nature (to say nothing of his presence and aspect, which had a commanding sweetness in them) and so polished and adorned with learning and education, that every way, for honesty, gravity, temperance, industry, and justice, he was a most accomplished person."

He had also, an easy and flowing eloquence, which consisted not in a pomp and ostentation of words, but in a masculine plainness and significancy of sense. He was master of a prudence formed upon experience, and regulated by temper and moderation: his loyalty was true, and would endure the touch, and was only exceeded by his piety, which indeed was eminently great.

To sum up all in a word, the queen was happy in so great a counsellor, and the state of England for ever indebted to him for his sage and prudent counsel.

I shall forbear too lavish a commendation of him; but this I may venture to affirm with truth, that he was one of those few, who lived and died with equal glory. Such a man, as while others regard with admiration, I, after the ancient manner, am rather inclined to contemplate with the sacred applause of silent veneration."

Lord Burleigh left two sons, Thomas, the eldest, by his first wife, who was created earl of Exeter by James I. which title continues in the same family at this time.

The youngest, by his second wife, was Sir Robert Cecil, afterwards earl of Salisbury, who succeeded him in all his offices. And this title likewise continues in the family.

₊ *Authorities.* Life of Cecil by Collins, 1732. Lloyd's State Worthies. Salmon's Chronological Historian. Biog. Britan. Walpole's Catalogue of Royal and Noble Authors.

The Life of ROBERT DEVEREUX, EARL of ESSEX.

[A. D. 1567, to 1601.]

ROBERT DEVEREUX, was the eldest son of Walter, the first earl of Essex, by Lettitia, the daughter of Sir Francis Knolles, who was related to queen Elizabeth. He was born in the year 1567, at Netherwood, his father's seat, in Herefordshire.

In his tender years, he gave no tokens of a bright genius; but, on the contrary, he was so backward in his learning, that his father died with a very cold conceit of his abilities; which, some thought, proceeded from his great affection for his younger son, Walter Devereux, who, it seems, had quicker and more livelier parts in his childhood. However, when he breathed his last in Ireland, he recommended his son Robert, then in the tenth year of his age, to the protection of Thomas Radcliffe, earl of Sussex; and to the care of lord Burleigh, whom he appointed his guardian.

Mr. Waterhouse, then secretary for Ireland, a person equally favoured by his father and Sir Henry Sidney, lord-deputy of Ireland, had the immediate direction of his person and estate, which, though not a little injured by his father's public spirit, was,

was, however, very considerable; and the regard shewn for his concerns, by the most powerful persons at court, was so remarkable, that Mr. Waterhouse made no difficulty of affirming, there was not, at that time, any man so strong in friends as the little earl of Essex.

In 1578, when he was about twelve years of age, he was sent to the university of Cambridge by lord Burleigh, who placed him in Trinity-college, under the care of Dr. Whitgift, the master, afterwards archbishop of Canterbury. Here he first began to apply himself to learning, with uncommon assiduity: so that in a short time, he surpassed all the young noblemen of his age in the university.

In 1582, having taken the degree of master of arts, he soon after left Cambridge, and retired to his own house at Lambsie, in South-Wales, where he spent some time in privacy and retirement; and was so far from having any thing of the eagerness or impetuosity natural to youth, that he grew fond of his rural retreat; so that it was with difficulty, he was prevailed upon to leave it.

His first appearance at court, at least as a candidate for royal favour, was in the seventeenth year of his age: however, when he came thither, it is certain, he could not have hoped, or even wished, a better reception. He brought with him, with other powerful recommendations, a fine person, a polite address, and an affability which procured him many friends.

Besides these qualifications, which, together with his high rank, and the intercession of his friends, recommended him to the notice of the queen, it must not be forgot, that his mother, who was her Majesty's cousin, not long after his father's death, had married the famous earl of Leicester, the queen's favourite. At first however, the young earl of Essex shewed a strong reluctance to make any use of of Leicester's interest, being disgusted at his mother's second marriage; but in the end, by the persuasion of his best friends, he was so far reconciled to Leicester, that, towards the close of the year 1585, he accompanied him, with many others of the nobility, to Holland; where we find him the next year in the field, with the title of general of the horse; and, in this quality, he gave the highest proofs of personal courage, in the battle of Zutphen; and, for his gallant behaviour upon this occasion, the earl of Leicester conferred upon him the honour of a knight-banneret in his camp.

On his return to England, it very quickly appeared, that the queen not only approved, but was desirous also of rewarding, his services; and his step-father, the earl of Leicester, being advanced to the office of lord-steward of her Majesty's household, in 1587, the earl of Essex succeeded him as master of the horse.

The following year, when her Majesty thought fit to assemble the army at Tilbury, for the defence of the kingdom, in case the Spaniards had landed, and gave the command of it, under herself, to Leicester, she created the earl of Essex general of the horse: so that, from this time, he was considered as the rising favourite; and in this opinion of him, the people were soon confirmed, by the queen's conferring on him, shortly after, the most noble order of the garter.

The earl of Leicester's death, which happened the same year, placed this new favourite on the pinnacle of prosperity, he had now no rival near the throne; but, on the contrary, the chief person in power, lord Burleigh, was his patron.

From this time, the queen shewed a decisive partiality in his favour, which, joined to his rapid promotions, affected his better judgement, obscured his reason, and made him give way to the impetuous

tuous sallies of pride, vanity, and arrogance, the effects of which discovered themselves occasionally in rude behaviour to the queen, who was pleased with the following incident, which gave a check to his presumption.

Sir Charles Blount (afterwards earl of Devonshire) a very handsome youth, having distinguished himself at a tilting-match, her Majesty sent him a chess-queen of gold enamelled, which he tied upon his arm with a crimson ribbon. Essex perceiving it, fired with jealousy, cried out, with affected disdain, "now I perceive, every fool must have a favour." This affront was justly resented by Sir Charles, who thereupon challenged Essex: they fought in Marybone-park, and the earl was disarmed, and wounded in the thigh. The queen was so far from being displeased at the disgrace that had befallen her favourite, who in affronting Sir Charles, had called in question her judgement, that she swore a round oath, that it was fit that some one or other should take him down, otherwise there would be no ruling him. However, she reconciled the rivals, who to their honour continued good friends as long as they lived.

In the beginning of the year 1589, Sir John Norris and Sir Francis Drake, undertook an expedition for restoring Don Antonio to the crown of Portugal; which the earl beheld as an action too glorious for others to perform, while he was only a spectator. He, therefore, followed the fleet and army to Spain, and, having joined them at Corunna, prosecuted the rest of the expedition with great vigilance and valour; which was not attended with much success, and it exposed him to the queen's displeasure, for he went without her Majesty's leave. At his return, however, he soon recovered her good graces; nor was it long before this was testified to the world, by his obtaining

new

new marks of favour, in grants of a very considerable value; a circumstance in which his credit with the queen seemed much superior to that of all her other favourites.

About this time, he ran a new hazard of the queen's favour, by a private, and, as it was then conceived, inconsiderate match with Frances, the only daughter of Sir Francis Walsingham, and the widow of Sir Philip Sidney; which her Majesty apprehended to be, in some measure, derogatory to the honour of the house of Essex; and, though, for the present, this business was passed by, yet it is thought that it was not soon forgotten.

In 1591, Henry IV. of France, having demanded fresh assistance from the queen, though he had already a body of her troops in his service, she was pleased to send the earl of Essex, with four thousand men, a small train of artillery, and a competent fleet, into Normandy; where it was proposed that he should join the French army, in order to undertake the siege of Rouen. The French king, however, either through want of power, the distraction of his affairs, or some other cause, neglected to perform the conditions upon which the succours were sent, though Essex made a long and hazardous journey to his camp, at that monarch's request, in order to concert measures for giving the queen satisfaction.

Upon his return from this journey, which proved of little consequence, Essex, to keep up the spirits of his officers, conferred the honour of knighthood upon many of them:——A circumstance with which the queen was much offended. He likewise made excursions from his camp to the very walls of Rouen and exposed his person very freely in these skirmishes, and came off unhurt, but he was much blamed for his rashness, his younger
brother,

brother, Walter Devereux, then in the flower of his age, being slain in one of these mad exploits.

He went to England soon after, to give an account of the state of things to the queen; and then returned to take the command of his troops: the siege of Rouen being formed, and the French king expressing a great desire to become master of it.

This winter service harrassing the troops exceedingly, provoked Essex not a little, who solicited king Henry for leave to proceed in his manner, promising to make a breach with his own artillery, and then to storm the place with the English troops, which the king refused, being unwilling to let the English take and plunder one of the richest towns in his dominions.

Essex, still more displeased at this, and resolving not to continue in a place where no reputation could be acquired, challenged the governor of Rouen, Mr. Villars; and, upon his refusing to fight, he left the command of the English troops to Sir Roger Williams, an officer of great courage and experience, and then embarked for England, where his presence was become very necessary, his enemies having represented his behaviour in a very different light to the queen.

The next mention made of him by respectable historians, relates to his being present in the parliament which began at Westminster in February, 1595; in which session, chiefly through his interest, Sir Thomas Perrot, (the son of the unfortunate Sir John Perrot) who had married his sister, was restored in blood.

About this time the queen raised him to the dignity of an efficient privy-counsellor, which in our day, is styled, a cabinet-counsellor.

He met, however, in this, and in the succeeding years, with various causes of chagrin; partly
from

from the loftiness of his own temper, and partly from the artifices of those who envied his greatness.

A dangerous and treasonable book, written abroad by a jesuit, was published under the name of Doleman, with a view to create dissention in England about the succession to the crown. This book, as the whole design of it was most villainous, so, from a superior spirit of malice, it was dedicated to the earl of Essex, on purpose to give him trouble; in which it had its effect; but his great popularity at this time, raised him so many friends, that in the end, the artifice of his enemies was discovered, and both they and the book fell into that contempt they so justly merited.

Essex was ambitious of military fame, and uneasy without it; this made him solicit the queen for the command of the land forces sent out with the fleet, under Sir Francis Drake and Sir John Hawkins, against the Spanish colonies in 1594, but the queen absolutely refused him, and upon this occasion manifested a personal interest in his safety, which exposed her to defamatory censures. She told him, " She loved him and her realm too " much to hazard his person in any lesser action " than that which should import her crown and " state; and therefore willed him to be content;" and in order to make him so, though she was generally very parsimonious, she gave him a warrant for 4000 *l.* adding these remarkable words, " Look " to thyself, good Essex, and be wise to thyself, " without giving thy enemies advantage, and my " hand shall be readier to help thee than any other."

Thus disappointed of going abroad, Essex employed his talents at home in cultivating the queen's good graces and the favour of the people, and he happily succeeded in both, to which an alarming conspiracy against the queen discovered by him, greatly contributed. Roderigo Lopez, a Portuguese Jew, of whose medical abilities and integrity queen Elizabeth entertained so high an opinion, that she made him her domestic physician, had been bribed by the agents of Spain to poison the queen; but by the activity and vigilance of Essex, and of his dependants, who frequented the palace, and were familiar with the royal household, the whole diabolical plan was traced and detected. Lopez, and two other Portuguese subjects, were condemned and executed for high treason, and Essex was highly extolled by the whole nation. And after this affair, the queen could not decently deny him those military honours he had so long solicited in vain.

Accordingly, in 1596, when the Spaniards laid siege to Calais, and the discharges of their artillery were heard at Greenwich, an army was hastily raised, and marched to Dover, the command of which was given to the earl of Essex, the queen intending to have embarked these troops for the assistance of the French: which, however, they wisely declined, being willing rather to let the Spaniards keep Calais for a short time, than to see it rescued from them by the English, who would, presuming on their old rights, probably keep it for ever.

But the queen taking advantage of the disposition which appeared in her people, to contribute, as far as in them lay, to keep the war at a distance, and to prevent the Spaniards from meditating a second invasion, ordered a fleet to be equipped for attacking Cadiz, best part of the expences being borne by the principal persons engaged in that enterprize.

The command of the army and of the fleet for this expedition was intrusted to the earl of Essex, and lord Howard, then lord high admiral of England,

land, with joint and equal authority: the fleet, for its number of ships, and for the land soldiers and mariners aboard, being the most considerable that in those times had been seen at sea.

Amongst other persons of distinction, who served on this expedition were, lord Thomas Howard, Sir Walter Raleigh; Sir Francis Vere, a veteran general, and who had acquired immortal fame in several campaigns in Holland and Flanders: Sir George Carew, and Sir Conyers Clifford, and these were nominated to be a council of war to the commanders in chief, upon any emergency. The English fleet consisted of 150 sail, and they were joined by a Dutch fleet, consisting of 24 ships of the line, under the command of admiral Vanderwood.

On the first of June they sailed from Plymouth, but were forced to put back by a contrary wind; which changing, they took the first opportunity of putting again to sea. On the 18th of the same month, they arrived at Cape St. Vincent, where they met with an Irish bark, which informed them that the port of Cadiz was full of rich merchant ships, and that they had no notice whatever of the sailing of the English fleet, or that such an expedition was so much as intended.

After this welcome news they pursued their voyage, and, on the 20th, in the morning, they anchored near St. Sebastian's, on the west side of the island of Cadiz, where the admiral would have had the forces landed, in order to their immediately attacking the town; which Essex caused to be attempted, but found it to be impracticable; and, upon the advice of Sir Walter Raleigh, desisted.

It was then proposed by the earl to begin with attacking the fleet, which was a very hazardous enterprize, but, at last, agreed to by the lord-admiral;

admiral; on which Essex, when he received the news, threw his hat into the sea for joy. The next day, this gallant resolution was executed with all imaginable bravery, and, in point of service, none did better, or hazarded his person more, than the earl of Essex, who, in his own ship, the Due Repulse, went to the assistance of Sir Walter Raleigh, and offered, if it had been necessary, to have seconded him in boarding the St. Philip. The Spaniards behaved very gallanty, so long as there were any hopes; and, when there were none, set fire to their ships and retired.

The earl of Essex then landed 800 men at the port of Puntall; and having first taken proper measures for destroying the bridge, he attacked the place with so much fury, that it was quickly taken; and, the next day the citadel surrendered upon capitulation, by which a great ransom was stipulated for the town. An offer was then made of two millions of ducats to spare the ships, and more might have been obtained; but the lord high-admiral said, He came there to consume, and not to compound: when the Spaniards were informed of this, they resolved to have the burning of their own fleet, which they accordingly set on fire; and their loss was computed at twenty millions.

The earl was very desirous of keeping Cadiz, which he offered to have done with a very small garrison; but the council differed from him in opinion: so that, having plundered the island and demolished the forts, they embarked on the fifth of July, and bore away for the port of Faro, a bishop's see in Portugal, which they plundered and destroyed, and a very valuable library belonging to Jerom Osorius, a celebrated Portuguese prelate, who died in 1580, fell to the share of the earl of Essex, who, generously gave it to the Bodleian library,

library, founded by Sir Thomas Bodley the following year, 1597.

They then proceeded to Cape St. Vincent, and, being driven by a brisk wind out to sea, it fell under consideration, whether they should not sail for the Azores, in hopes of intercepting the plate fleet, which was carried in the negative; and the earl's proposal, with two of her majesty's ships, and ten others, to make this attempt, likewise was rejected, which Camden attributes to the desire of some of the officers, who had made large booties, to get their treasure safe on shore. They looked in, however, at Corunna, and the earl would have proceeded to St. Andreo and St. Sebastian; but others thinking they had done enough, the whole fleet returned prosperously to Plymouth on the 8th and 10th of August following.

The earl of Essex was so much disgusted at the other officers, for refusing to concur in the enterprizes he had proposed, that after his return, he drew up and dispersed an account of this expedition, in which he freely censured the conduct of his brother officers, not sparing even the lord-high admiral himself: this produced a recrimination, in which Essex was charged with want of cool judgment, and intemperate rashness. His adversaries likewise being men of approved valour, and long experience, he created a number of powerful enemies by this indiscreet step, and they never forgave him.

The party against him was daily strengthened, by all who envied his greatness, and the first measure they took, was, to make the queen jealous of his popularity; on this account, they told her majesty, that it would not be at all expedient for her service to receive such as he recommended to civil employments; and this they carried so far as to make even his approbation destructive to mens fortunes

fortunes whom themselves they had encouraged and recommended. A thing hardly to be credited, if we had not the highest evidence to prove it.

It was a natural consequence, that the earl should behave to those he took to be the authors of such counsels with visible marks of anger and discontent; and this conduct of his, made him frequently upon bad terms even with the queen herself, who was a princess very jealous of her authority, and, in cases of this nature, bore but very indifferently with any expostulations. However, as well out of her natural kindness to him, as from a desire of shewing a just acknowledgment for his late service, she was pleased to appoint him master of the ordnance by patent, in the year 1597.

This seems to have had a good effect, in quieting the mind, and raising the spirits of the discontented Essex, who, upon a report that the Spaniards were forming a new fleet at Ferrol and Corunna, for the invasion of Ireland at least, if not England, readily offered his service to the queen, and chearfully declared, as Camden assures us, that he would either defeat this new armada, which had threatened England for a year together, or perish in the attempt. The queen, well pleased with this proposal, gave it all the countenance that could be desired, and caused a considerable fleet, though not so considerable as the action required, to be equipped for this service; and the earl of Essex was appointed general, admiral, and commander in chief.

We may guess at the interest which the earl had in the success of this voyage by the number of his friends who engaged therein as volunteers; particularly, the earls of Rutland and Southampton, and the lords Cromwell and Rich. And his secret enemies observing his influence over the queen, could not refuse to serve under him in this expedition.

dition. His sanguine hopes, however, were, in some measure disappointed; for, sailing about the ninth of July, 1597, from Plymouth, they met, at sixty leagues distance, with so rough a storm, and of four days continuance, that they were obliged to put back to Plymouth, where they remained wind-bound for a month; in which time a great part of their provisions was consumed.

While the fleet was thus laid up, the earl of Essex and Sir Walter Raleigh set out post for the court, in order to receive fresh instructions. The proposals made by Essex, even after this disappointment, were very bold and great; but, as Camden seems to insinuate, very difficult and dangerous, if not impracticable; so that the queen would not countenance his projects, but rather left the direction of the expedition to the commanders in chief, according as the season and circumstances might encourage or permit.

The fleet being refitted, and victualled, Essex put all the land-forces on shore, and disbanded them by the queen's express command, except 1000 veterans, the regiment belonging to Sir Francis Vere, who went on the expedition. On the 17th of August, the fleet sailed a second time from Plymouth, having now two points in view, the one to burn the Spanish fleet in their own harbours, the other to intercept the homeward-bound Plate-fleet, expected to touch as usual, about this time, at the Azores.

Essex therefore made the best of his way for these islands; but first he took care to inform Sir Walter Raleigh, who commanded one division of the fleet, that he himself intended to attack Fayal, one of those islands. By some accident the squadrons separated, and Raleigh arriving first, and justly apprehending that the smallest delay might have prevented their design, very gallantly attacked, and
very

very happily succeeded, in making himself master of the island, before the arrival of Essex with the rest of the fleet.

But Essex, jealous of Raleigh, expressed great displeasure at his conduct, and construing it into a design to rob him of the honour of the conquest, he cashiered the captains who served under Raleigh, and would have shewn his resentment to the admiral himself, if lord Thomas Howard had not prevailed on Raleigh to make some concessions to the earl, as his superior in command, which produced a temporary reconciliation between them.

The Spanish fleet, the grand object of the expedition, got safe into the port of Angra, owing to the misconduct of one of the pilots, who dissuaded Essex from staying at Graciosa, where the whole fleet always touched; alledging, that the haven was unsafe, which occasioned a separation of the English fleet, into different divisions, with a view of intercepting the Spaniards; and thus they passed unseen, except by Sir William Monson, a naval officer of distinguished reputation, who had signalized himself in almost every engagement against the Spaniards, and was but ill-requited for his great services, in the reign of James I. This brave officer's station happened to be most remote from the Spanish fleet, yet he was the only commander who observed them, and gave the proper signals for a general chace, but without effect. However, the earl of Essex fell in with three rich Spanish merchant-men from the Havannah; the value of whose cargoes, according to Sir William Monson's account of this voyage, more than defrayed the expences of the whole armament.

Essex, greatly chagrined at the escape of the Plate-fleet, resolved to attempt some enterprise of consequence, that might keep up his popularity. With this view, he took the town of Villa Franca

by

by surprise, and pillaged it, after which he set sail for England; and, on his passage, he had certainly fell in with a formidable fleet of Spanish men of war, destined to make a second attempt to invade England, if a violent storm had not prevented it, and greatly damaged the English fleet. But the same storm proved still more fatal to the enemy, who lost eighteen capital ships; and the rest being dispersed, this projected invasion failed.

The earl of Essex immediately began to shew evident signs of deep displeasure, he retired to his house at Wanstead, and, under pretence of sickness, absented himself from the service of parliament, then sitting. Camden reports, that his dissatisfaction arose from the lord admiral's being created earl of Nottingham in his absence, with some particular clauses in the preamble of his patent, which, as they were highly honourable for that noble peer, Essex conceived threw some disparagement upon himself. And, by way of satisfaction, he was created earl marshal of England, in December, 1597.

Another cause of disgust was, the appointment of Sir Robert Cecil, in his absence, to the office of secretary of state: this gentleman was a secret enemy to Essex, and restrained only from opposing him to the utmost, by the advice of his father, the good old lord treasurer Burleigh. And, as if Elizabeth meant to apologize to her favourite for every step she took contrary to his inclinations, she made Essex a present of seven thousand pounds, to reconcile him to the promotion of Sir Robert Cecil, with whom he appears to have been upon good terms, soon after; for Sir Robert being sent on an embassy to France, he undertook the discharge of the duties of his office, during his absence; but on Cecil's return in May 1598, with an account of a peace being concluded between Henry IV. of France,

France, and Philip II. of Spain, a peace between England and Spain was propofed, which caufed violent difputes in the council about the expediency of that meafure, which was very earneftly, as well as eloquently preffed by the old and wife lord treafurer Burleigh; and as warmly decried by the earl of Effex. The treafurer, at length, grew into a great heat; infomuch that he told the earl, that he feemed to be intent upon nothing but blood and flaughter. Effex explained himfelf upon this, that the blood and flaughter of the queen's enemies might be very lawfully his intention: that he was not againft a folid, but a fpecious and precarious peace; that the Spaniards were a fubtle and ambitious people, who had contrived to do England more mifchief in time of peace than of war; and, that, as to an enemy, whofe hands it was impoffible to bind by treaty, it was better not to tie up our own. The treafurer at laft produced a prayerbook, in which he fhewed Effex this paffage, "Men of blood fhall not live out half their days."

Effex, in vindication of his own opinion, drew up an APOLOGY, (which he addreffed to his learned friend Mr. Anthony Bacon) "againft thofe who jealoufly and malicioufly tax him to be the only hinderer of the peace and quiet of his country:" this piece, is a lafting memorial of his great abilities, both as a ftatefman, and a writer; but being printed and publifhed, it gave great offence to the queen, who abhorred nothing fo much, as fubmitting any political meafure to the notice, and confequently to the ftrictures of the people.

To add to his misfortune, death deprived him of his great patron the lord Burleigh; and now his enemies, freed from all reftraint, began to form a powerful party againft him. But he ftill had fuch an afcendency over the queen, that if he had kept within the bounds of decent refpect to his fovereign, all their attempts to disgrace him would have been abortive.

By the death of the lord-treasurer Burleigh, the chancellorship of the university of Cambridge became vacant; upon which, that learned body chose the earl of Essex in his room. Upon this account he went down to pay them a visit, was entertained at Queen's-college with great magnificence; and, as a proof of their affection, the room in which he slept was, long after, distinguished by the name of Essex-chamber. We may account this one of the last instances of this great man's felicity, for he was now advanced too high to sit at ease; and those who wished for his honours and his employments, watched every opportunity to accomplish his fall.

In this situation of his affairs, unfortunately, instead of controuling his high and stubborn spirit, he suffered his passions to get the better of his reason, when his advice was not followed, he assumed the tone of a dictator; and if this failed him, he then affected to treat his opponents with supercilious contempt. In a dispute with the queen, concerning the choice of a proper person to be sent out governor of Ireland, towards the end of the year 1598, unable to prevail upon her Majesty to relinquish her own nomination of Sir William Knollys, the earl's uncle, in opposition to his recommendation of Sir George Carew, he had the insolence to turn his back upon her Majesty; who, taking fire at this unmanly resentment, instantly gave him a violent blow on the cheek; at the same time, bidding him go and be hanged.

The exasperated earl, losing all presence of mind, committed a second error, as unmanly as the first, for he put his hand to his sword; upon which the lord high admiral rushed in between him and the queen, and Essex withdrew, swearing bitterly, that he neither could, nor would put up with such an affront;

affront; but those, who make him guilty of a third mistake still grosser than all the rest, seem to have been as mad as himself. They add, that he said he would not have taken it from Henry VIII. himself. Assuredly, a great general might have been excused for resenting a blow from a royal master, which he ought to have overlooked from the hand of a royal mistress, who had loaded him with favours.

His ruin may be dated from this event, for Elizabeth, naturally jealous of her authority, and alarmed at the impetuosity of his temper, though she appeared to be reconciled to him, from a motive of prudence, no longer placed the same unlimited confidence in him.

An event happened much about this time, which shewed the sentiments the enemies of England had of the earl, and ought therefore to have endeared him to such as had a real affection for their country: one Edward Squire was seized and imprisoned for treason, and his case came out to be this; he had been a groom in the queen's stables, went afterwards to sea with Sir Francis Drake, was taken prisoner and carried to Spain, where he was persuaded by a jesuit to undertake poisoning the earl of Essex, and afterwards queen Elizabeth: for performing which, he had poison given him in a bladder. He found means to rub this, as he was directed, upon the pommel of the queen's saddle; got himself afterwards recommended to serve on board the earl's ship in the island voyage, where, in like manner, he poisoned both the arms of his great chair; yet no effect followed in either case. Upon this, the Spanish jesuit, suspecting the man and not his drug, caused information to be given in England against Squire, who, finding himself betrayed by his confessor, opened the whole scene, and plainly acknowledged his endeavours to dispatch both the queen and the earl; for which he was deservedly executed.

The miseries of Ireland continued all this time, or rather increased; and, when proposals were made, in the queen's council, for sending over a new governor, with certain restrictions, Essex took occasion of shewing, that nothing had been hitherto so expensive as an ill-timed frugality; and, that the Irish rebels had been the only gainers by the restraint put upon the English deputies. Those who hated the earl, were not displeased when they found him in this disposition, and, at length, in their turn, took occasion from his objections, to suggest, that the total reduction of that island was to be expected from none but himself; which, at first, he declined: but perceiving that he could enjoy little quiet or comfort at home; that it was with difficulty he maintained his credit; and that, by disappointing the expectations of his friends, he should gradually lose them, he consented to accept the fatal post of lord lieutenant of Ireland, and agreed to go over to that kingdom, which had been the grave of his father's fortunes, and, which his best friends foresaw, would prove the gulph of his own. It is true indeed that he had a great army granted him, that due care was taken for the payment of it; that his powers were very ample, and his appointments very great; but these were obtained with many struggles, and notice was taken of every thing he promised, or seemed to promise, in order to obtain them; and, when all things were regulated, he was so far from going with alacrity, as to a place which he had sought, and to a command which he meditated for the sake of greater things, that he seemed rather to look upon it as a banishment, and as a place assigned him to retreat from his sovereign's present displeasure, rather than a potent government bestowed upon him by her favour.

The

The truth of this is apparent, from an epistle of his to the queen, written after his appointment to the government of Ireland, and before his embarkation for that kingdom. It is preserved in the Harleian MSS. at the Museum, from which, the following copy was taken:

"To the Queen.

"From a mind delighting in sorrow; from spirits wasted with passion; from a heart torn in pieces with care, grief, and travail, from a man that hateth himself, and all things else that keep him alive; what service can your Majesty expect, since any service past, deserves no more than banishment and proscription to the cursedest of all islands? It is your rebels pride and succession must give me leave to ransom myself out of this hateful prison, out of my loathed body; which, if it happen so, your Majesty shall have no cause to mislike the fashion of my death, since the course of my life could never please you.

"Happy he could finish forth his fate
"In some unhaunted desert, most obscure
"From all society, from love and hate
"Of worldly folk; then should he sleep secure;
"Then wake again, and yield God ever praise;
"Content with hips, and haws, and brambleberry;
"In contemplation passing out his days,
"And change of holy thoughts to make him merry:
"Who, when he dies, his tomb may be a bush,
"Where harmless Robin dwells, with gentle Thrush.

Your Majesty's exiled servant,
ROBERT ESSEX."

On the 12th of March, 1599, his commission for lord lieutenant passed the great-seal; and, on the twenty-seventh of the same month, about two in the afternoon, he set out from Seething-lane, and passing through the city in a plain habit, accompanied by many of the nobility, he was attended by vast crowds of people out of town; and it was observed, with a view, perhaps, to prepare the world to have a bad opinion of his conduct, that the weather was exceeding fair when he took horse, but, by that time he came to Islington, there was a heavy storm of rain, attended with thunder and lightning. The like bad weather he met with at sea, so that he did not arrive at Dublin, or take upon him his charge, before the fifteenth of April, 1599.

He found things in that country in a state very different from what he expected, and perceived that there was nothing to be done, at least to any purpose, till he was well acquainted with the country in which he was to act. He found, likewise, that the new-raised men he had brought over were altogether unfit for action, till they were seasoned to the country, and well acquainted with discipline. These considerations hindered him from marching directly to Ulster, lest the earl of Tyrone should take any advantage of his weakness; and the council desiring that he would suppress some disorders in Munster, he thought that a fair occasion of exercising his new troops, and did it effectually.

On his return to Dublin, he wrote a letter to the queen, containing a free and full representation of the state of things in that country; which most admirable performance, pointing out all the steps that were afterwards taken, and by which his successor made an end of the war, remains upon record in Ireland. This letter he sent over to the queen by his secretary, in hopes, that from thence, she might

might have derived a just notion of the state of things in that island; but it produced no such effect: on the contrary, the queen was exceedingly provoked that he had not marched into Ulster, in order to attack Tyrone, and repeated her orders upon that head in very strong terms. Before these arrived, however, Sir Henry Harrington, with some of the fresh troops, had been worsted by an inferior number of the O'Brians; which so provoked Essex, that he cashiered all the officers, and decimated the private men.

When he received the queen's orders, and was on the point of marching into Ulster, he was prevailed upon to enter the county of Ophelie, to reduce the O'Connors and the O'Moores; which he performed; but his troops were so harrassed and diminished thereby, that, with the advice and consent of the council of Ireland, he wrote home for a recruit of two thousand men. In the midst of these crosses in Ireland, an army was suddenly raised in England, under the command of the earl of Nottingham; no-body well knowing why: but, in reality, from the suggestions of the earl's enemies to the queen, that he rather meditated an invasion on his native country, than the reduction of the Irish rebels.

At length, Essex, intending to proceed directly to Ulster, sent orders to Sir Conyers Clifford, who commanded in Connaught, to march towards the enemy on that side, that Tyrone might be obliged to divide his forces; which was executed, but with such ill fortune, that the English, being surprised, were defeated, with the loss of their commander in chief, together with Sir Alexander Ratcliffe, and one hundred and forty men.

But this fresh disappointment, did not prevent his march against Tyrone, as soon as the reinforcement from England arrived. His army, even with

with this augmentation, was considerably inferior to that of Tyrone; and, to add to his distress, a general dislike to the service prevailed among his troops, so that many deserted, and others counterfeited sickness; the season also was too far advanced for him to be able to bring on a decisive action with the enemy, who, possessed of all the strong holds, and advantageous situations for encampment, seemed resolved to harrass the English troops, by fatiguing marches and countermarches, and to avoid a battle by every stratagem of war.

Thus circumstanced, he accepted the proposal of a conference with Tyrone, who sent an express to him for that purpose by a special messenger. The generals, according to the agreement, met alone, at some distance from their camps, which were formed on the opposite banks of a river.

The earl of Tyrone, as a mark of respect and submission to the lord-lieutenant, advanced from his side of the ford of Ballyclynch into the river, saddle deep; and being then within hearing, he conferred with Essex, who remained on the opposite bank. This interview happened on the 8th of September, and a truce was concluded to the first of May, to be ratified however afresh every six weeks, and to be broke off by either party, on giving fourteen days notice from the expiration of any of the intermediate periods: the policy of Essex, in this reserved condition, is evident; for all he wanted, was to gain time to repair to England, to counter-act the designs of his enemies; and in case the queen should blame him for treating with Tyrone, he had it in his power to declare, that he could renew the war, if her Majesty thought proper, in a few days.

However, his artifice not only failed of its effect, but appeared to the queen to be such an unwarrantable stretch of power in a subject, that she readily listened to the suggestions of the earl of Nottingham, Sir Robert Cecil, and Sir Walter Raleigh, who all persuaded her, that this treaty concealed a treasonable design to invade England with the assistance of Tyrone's army, joined to his own forces; and as these ministers had the chief administration of public affairs, and had constantly opposed Essex, it is not at all surprising that their personal fears should have made them suspect too much, especially as Essex had openly declared he would use every means in his power to remove them from the queen's person and councils for ever. Yet some of our most respectable historians, seem to think, that unlawful connections took place between Tyrone and Essex at their private meeting; and from not permitting any of their attendants to be present, a presumptive proof of treason is adduced. Be this as it may, it is certain, that he took a step immediately after the treaty with Tyrone, which merited severe chastisement from his sovereign, for he quitted the supreme command with which she had invested him, and leaving the affairs of Ireland in an unsettled desperate state, repaired privately to England against the consent of his privy council there, and at the very instant he had received instructions from the privy council at home, to act with more vigour against the rebels in that kingdom.

He arrived in England, before the ministry or the queen had the slightest notice, or even any suspicion of his rash design; and by riding night and day, he reached the court before any intelligence could be conveyed to his enemies. His eagerness to see the queen before she could consult her ministers upon his return, was so great, that without staying to change his dress, in the dirty condition he was in, he entered the queen's bed-chamber, who was but juſt riſen, and was ſitting with her hair about her face: the earl inſtantly fell on his knees at her feet, kiſſed her hand, and intreated a private conference, which we may preſume turned upon the neceſſity of his preſence, to wipe off the aſperſions caſt on him by his enemies, and it is certain he ſo far prevailed, before the queen had time to reflect on his unprecedented conduct, that he withdrew with viſible marks of ſatisfaction, and was heard to ſay, though he had met with ſtorms abroad, he had found a ſweet calm at home.

But as ſoon as the news of his reception at court reached the ears of the lord high admiral, and Sir Robert Cecil, now lord treaſurer, they repaired to court, and moſt probably aſcribed the earl's ſecret journey to England, to diſloyal and factious motives, for when Eſſex returned to her majeſty in the afternoon, he found the ſtorm gathering againſt him, for ſhe not only received him with great coolneſs, but ordered him to be confined to his houſe, and to ſubmit his conduct in Ireland, as well as his deſertion of his high ſtation, to the examination of the privy council; the reſult of which was, his commitment to the cuſtody of the lord keeper Egerton, and all intercourſe was cut off between him and his friends, even by letters, nor was the counteſs of Eſſex permitted to ſee him.

At this time, it is probable, the queen would have been appeaſed, if he had aſked pardon and returned to Ireland; nor is it ſuſpected, that his enemies had any worſe deſign againſt him, than that of keeping him at a diſtance from court. But his pride was too deeply wounded; and though he behaved with great humility to appearance; yet he

He was so struck with the queen's change of behaviour, and the manifest advantage his enemies had gained over him, by his own rashness, that it threw him into a dangerous illness; upon which the queen relented; she even went so far, as to send messages to him, and assured him, if it could have been done, consistent with her honour, she would have visited him; and his disorder proceeding from grief and vexation, her majesty's kindness restored him to health, after he had been in a weak and languishing condition near three months.

But a new and most singular incident, brought upon him a return of the queen's indignation, soon after his recovery. An history of the first part of the reign of Henry IV. containing the deposition of Richard II. was published by Dr. Hayward, an author of repute, dedicated to the earl of Essex, and a remarkable expression in the dedication served to alarm the natural jealousy of Elizabeth, and to confirm the reports she had heard of his treasonable intentions. "He is styled the present "judge, and future hope of the English nation." For which the author was fined and imprisoned.

But in the summer of the year 1600, Essex recovered his liberty; and, in the autumn following, he made Mr. Cuffe, who had been his secretary in Ireland, his chief confident, who laboured to persuade him, that submission would never do him any good; that the queen was in the hands of a faction, who were his enemies; and, that the only way to restore his fortune, was to find the means, at any rate, to obtain an audience, in which he might be able to represent his own case. The earl heard this dangerous advice without consenting to it, till he found there was no hopes of getting his farm of the sweet wines renewed; then, it is said, that, giving loose to his passion, he let fall many vehement expressions; and, amongst the rest, this fatal reflection, " that the queen grew old and cankered, and " that her mind was as crooked as her carcase." Camden says, that this was aggravated by some of the court ladies, whom he had disappointed in their intrigues. His enemies, who had exact intelligence of all he proposed, having provided effectually against the execution of his designs, hurried him upon his fate, by a message sent on the evening of the seventh of February, 1601, requiring him to attend the council, which he declined. He then gave out that they sought his life, kept a watch in Essex house all night, and summoned his friends, for his defence, the next morning.

The queen being informed of the great resort of people of all ranks to the earl, sent the lord-keeper Egerton, the earl of Worcester, Sir Francis Knollys and the lord-chief-justice Popham, to know his grievances; whom, after a short and ineffectual conference, he confined; and then, attended by the earls of Rutland and Southampton, the lord Sands, the lord Monteagle, and about two hundred gentlemen, he went into the city, where the earl of Bedford, the lord Cromwell, and some other gentlemen, joined him; but his dependance on the populace failed him; and Sir Robert Cecil prevailing upon his brother, the lord Burleigh, to go with Sir Gilbert Dethick, then king at arms, and proclaim Essex and his adherents traitors, in the principal streets, the earl found it impossible to return to his house by land; and, therefore, he sent Sir Ferdinando Gorges before, to release the chief justice, who, for his own sake, thought fit to extend that order to the rest of the privy-counsellors; and then with his principal

at-

attendants, he returned in boats to Essex-house; which was quickly invested by the earl of Nottingham, lord-admiral, with a great force; to whom, after many disputes, and some blood spilt, he and his associates at last surrendered.

Essex was carried that night to the archbishop of Canterbury's palace at Lambeth, with the earl of Southampton, and the next day they were sent to the Tower.

Great pains were now taken to draw from him very large and full confessions; which was the more easy, as he was truly and sincerely pious; and, after he was once persuaded, that his project was of a treasonable nature, he made a point of conscience to disclose all he knew, though it was highly prejudicial to his friends, and could do no good to himself; and, indeed, he did not appear either to design or desire it.

On the 19th of February, the earl of Essex, and his friend the earl of Southampton were brought to their trial before twenty-five peers, who unanimously found them guilty of high treason; and indeed the overt-acts were so manifest, that the warmest friends of the unhappy Essex were astonished at his persisting in his innocence, instead of throwing himself on the mercy of the queen, and soliciting the recommendation of his judges. When sentence was pronounced by lord Buckhurst, appointed lord high steward for this occasion, the earl of Southampton, received it as a man sensible of the heinous crime of which he had been guilty; his behaviour was serene and submissive; he intreated the good offices of his brother peers, in such pathetic terms, that he excited the compassion of all the spectators; and it is highly probable he owed his pardon to their lordships, for he had laboured under the queen's displea-

displeasure, before this last offence, on account of his marrying without her majesty's consent.

The earl of Essex acted a very different part, he said in a haughty strain, that he was prepared to die, and though he would not wish to have it represented to the queen that he despised her clemency, yet he desired it might be understood, that he should not solicit it by any mean submissions.

However, it is certain, that he relaxed, as to his obstinate denial of his guilt, shortly after his condemnation, and made an ample confession in the Tower of the conspiracy, to Ashton his chaplain, and was reconciled to Sir Robert Cecil, whom he had justly considered as his greatest enemy. Sir Robert possessed the political talents of his father, but not his integrity, so that his talents were sometimes abused, and particularly in the case of the earl of Essex, whose ruin he occasioned, by artful tricks of state; such as procuring him to be appointed lord-lieutenant of Ireland, and then sending him instructions which he knew he could not follow, for want of a sufficient force; at the same time, availing himself of his absence, he misrepresented all his actions to the queen; and by these means hurried him into those criminal excesses, which proved fatal to him. Cecil is even accused of having taken a base unwarrantable step to determine Essex to quit Ireland precipitately, which was the foundation of his disgrace, by stopping all the ships bound from England for Ireland, except one, which sailed direct for Dublin, and by his orders carried over and spread a false report of the queen's death: an event which he knew would make Essex desert his station.

The earl now cast a blemish on his character, independant of his public conduct, which turned the tide of his popularity, and made his death much less lamented than might have been expected, as he had been such a favourite with all orders of men. He unnecessarily gave up his friends, delivering in his own hand-writing a detail of his connections, which proved fatal to several who had not the least apprehension of being thus betrayed by the very man, who had seduced them into a treasonable correspondence with him. Amongst others, the lord Montjoy, resident in France, was recalled and committed to the Tower; nor is it at all improbable that the high spirit of Essex, suggested to him, after he was sensible of his guilt, this method of saving his own life, as less degrading than that of soliciting for mercy: the discovery of the whole plot, he might consider as a service, which intitled him to a pardon as a matter of right, not of concession.

However this be, it was natural for Elizabeth to feel some reluctance to sign the warrant for taking off the head of a nobleman, who had been her professed favourite, who notwithstanding all his vices, had done the nation signal service upon various occasions, and had so lately been the ornament of her court; in which he was respected for every amiable accomplishment; she accordingly appeared irresolute, but after waiting a few days, in expectation he would sue for a pardon, she was exasperated at his pride, and her own getting the better of any remaining affection for him, she signed the warrant, and ordered his execution, complying only with his wish, in permitting it to be as private as possible. A scaffold was therefore prepared in the inner court of the Tower, and he was beheaded on the 25th of February 1601, only a few of the aldermen, and some noblemen of the court, being present, by the express command of the queen; it was thought however, extremely indecent,

ndecent, that Sir Walter Raleigh, his avowed enemy, was of the number, and it created such a murmur, that he was obliged to withdraw.

The behaviour of Essex in his last moments was truly penitent and devout, and though at the point of being cut off in the flower of his age, he did not express any solicitude for life, or fear of death; but unfortunately, he must have suffered great mortal pain, for the executioner gave him three blows of the axe, before he severed the head from the body.

Thus fell the gallant Earl of Essex, whose military glory, loyalty to his sovereign, (the treason for which he suffered excepted) zeal for the true interest and prosperity of his country, and many eminent virtues, would have rendered him one of the brightest characters in the records of fame; if ambition, self-conceit, and impetuosity of temper, which are but too frequently the companions of rapid prosperity in the early stages of life, had not triumphed over fortitude, reason and integrity.

His royal mistress did not long survive this domestic calamity, and the ill state of health which came upon her after the death of the countess of Nottingham, has by most historians been attributed to a confession made by the countess on her death-bed to the queen concerning Essex; the particulars of this interview and secret, will be found in the succeeding life of the earl of Nottingham, which follows next in order, as his lordship, after the fall of Essex, was the queen's principal confident, and in fact, her first minister of state.

The earl of Essex was a liberal patron of learned men, and several small tracts written by him, have likewise obtained him a place, in the

ingenious

ingenious Mr. Walpole's catalogue of Royal and Noble Authors, who bestows very great encomiums on a state of Ireland, drawn up by the earl and transmitted to the queen; styling it a masterly composition, in which the abilities of a great general and statesman are conspicuous, as well as the talents of a fine writer.

⁎ *Authorities.* Camden's Annals. Baker's Chronicle. Winstanley's English Worthies. Birch's Memoirs of the Reign of Queen Elizabeth. Hume's History of England.

The Life of CHARLES HOWARD, EARL of NOTTINGHAM, AND LORD HIGH ADMIRAL of ENGLAND.

Including an Account of the laſt Illneſs and Death of QUEEN ELIZABETH.

[A. D. 1536, to 1603.]

THE glorious catalogue of immortal patriots, whoſe valour, wiſdom and integrity ſupported the dignity, and preſerved the independency of the realm of England, at a criſis, when the moſt formidable power of Europe, aided by the Roman pontiffs, and the ſecret enemies of our happy conſtitution meditated her ruin; is now to be cloſed with conciſe memoirs of the illuſtrious admiral, who had the command of the Engliſh fleet in that great and victorious engagement, which happily decided the fate of this country, and fixed the ſtandard of religious and civil liberty, on a ſure and permanent baſis.

Charles Howard was the ſon of Thomas Howard, created baron of Effingham in Surry, by queen Mary in 1554, and raiſed to the dignity of lord high admiral, in which office he was continued by queen

queen Elizabeth, till age and infirmities rendered him unfit for that active department, and then he was made lord-privy-seal, in which station he died in 1572. This, his only son was born in 1536, and in his early youth, having discovered an inclination for the sea service, his father bred him up under him, and took him out with him upon some cruising voyages, in the reign of Mary. In the second year of Elizabeth, by his father's interest with the queen, he was appointed ambassador extraordinary, to compliment Charles IX. of France on his accession to the throne of that kingdom; and this his first promotion was considered as a signal instance of the queen's favour, as he was then not quite twenty-three years of age. The next account we have of him is in the year 1569, he was made general of the horse, under the earl of Sussex, warden of the northern marches, on occasion of the insurrection, headed by the earls of Westmoreland and Northumberland, in favour of Mary queen of the Scots; in this service he greatly signalized himself, and greatly contributed to the suppression of the rebellion, having obliged the earl of Westmoreland to fly, and take refuge in Scotland, before the arrival of the earl of Warwick, who bringing a considerable reinforcement from the midland counties, to the assistance of the earl of Sussex, lord Charles Howard, and Sir George Bowes, completed the victory over the rebels, which they had partly accomplished.

In 1570, the command of a fleet of ten ships of the line was given to lord Charles Howard, with instructions to receive the Imperial and Spanish fleets, which were to convoy the emperor's sister, Anne of Austria to the coast of Spain, at their entrance into, and to escort them through the British channel. Upon this occasion, our gallant commander bravely maintained the privileges of the

the British flag, by obliging the fleets, consisting of one hundred and fifty sail, to pay him the compliment of striking their colours in the English seas, after which he obeyed his instructions, and shewed every mark of honour and curtesy to the princess and her attendants. The following year, he was chosen knight of the shire for the county of Surry, but he did not sit long in the house of commons, for in 1572, his father dying, he succeeded to his title, and took his seat in the house of peers; and from this time, the queen constantly honoured him with her royal favour, and by degrees raised him to the highest and most honourable employments in the government. Soon after his father's death her majesty made him lord chamberlain of the houshold, and in 1573, he was installed a knight of the most noble order of the garter. From this period to the year 1585, lord Effingham led the life of a courtier, and enjoyed not only the smiles of his royal mistress, but the affections of the people, by whom he was greatly esteemed for his affability, hospitality and other social virtues; it therefore gave the nation entire satisfaction, and more especially the seamen, when upon the death of the earl of Lincoln, in the course of that year, lord Effingham was constituted lord high admiral of England.

This very extensive department required a man of great abilities and cool judgment, nor could he have succeeded to it at a time when the exertion of such talents was more wanted; for Philip II. of Spain was now meditating his grand design of subverting the protestant religion in Europe, as the first step to which, England was to be invaded and conquered, in resentment for the assistance queen Elizabeth had given to the United Provinces, after their revolt from the Spanish government. The immense preparations for this important

tant enterprise, had been carried on with the utmost precaution and secrecy, but they could not escape the notice of the vigilant Walsingham, who as early as the year 1584, had discovered the base plots of the king of Spain and the duke of Guise, against the person of the queen, which were to facilitate the conquest of the kingdom. But soon after she had appointed lord Effingham to be lord high admiral, the designs of the Spanish court were openly avowed; and the election of a protestant princess to fill the throne of England, being deemed in the popish countries null and void; the jesuits encouraged Philip II. boldly to assert a claim to the imperial crown of England, derived by genealogical descent from John of Ghent, duke of Lancaster, the fourth son of Edward III. No bar to his title remained in the popish account, Elizabeth having been deposed by the bulls of pope Pius V. and Gregory XIII. except the nearer affinity to the royal blood, of Mary queen of the Scots, who was easily persuaded formally to assign over her right to the crown of England in favour of the king of Spain, as the only means of restoring popery in this nation. The whole project being brought to light, by means of a letter from the king of Spain to pope Gregory XIII. a copy of which was obtained by a Venetian priest, who transmitted it to Walsingham, the lord high admiral sent Sir Francis Drake to Cadiz, to interrupt and retard the preparations, which service he performed in the manner mentioned in his life. In the mean time, the lord high admiral was assiduous in augmenting the royal navy, which only ten years before this æra, was in so low a state, that it consisted of no more than 24 ships, the largest of which was of the burthen of 100 tons, and the smallest under 60. In 1585, it had only received the addition of three ships, and the total number

number of seamen fit to be employed in the service of the crown, amounted to no more than 14,295 effective men. On this emergency therefore, it was necessary to adopt the most vigorous measures, and, owing to the wise regulations of the lord admiral, whose popularity daily increased, the queen soon saw herself in possession of a formidable naval armament. Every commercial town in England was required to furnish a certain number of ships specified by the lord admiral, and proportioned to their abilities; but the zeal of the queen's subjects, in most parts, exceeded the stipulated demand; the city of London, in particular, fitting out double the number required as its quota. The principal nobility and gentry likewise formed associations in all parts of the kingdom, and produced forty-three ships completely armed, manned and victualled ready to put to sea.

In the lives of secretary Walsingham, and admiral Drake, we have amply related, by what means the king of Spain was disabled from carrying his grand design into execution, till the year 1588, though it had been in agitation upwards of three years. However all impediments being got over, the Spanish fleet, proudly called, The INVINCIBLE ARMADA, set sail from the port of Lisbon, on the third of June, 1588, but was forced back by a violent storm, and obliged to take shelter at the Groyne, which had been the station of general rendezvous for the different squadrons, as they were fitted out. The whole fleet consisted of 92 galleons, or large ships of the line; 4 galliasses; 30 frigates; 30 transports with cavalry, and 4 gallies.

The force on board consisted of 19290 regular troops, 8350 marines, and 2080 galley slaves, provided with 2630 pieces of ordnance. This formidable armament, which exceeded every thing that had been known in modern times, was under the command of the Duke de Medina Sidonia, admiral in chief; Don Juan Martinez de Ricaldo, a naval officer of great abilities, and experienced mariner, was vice admiral, and almoſt every noble family in Spain, had ſome relation embarked as a volunteer on this expedition. But ſtill further to inſure ſucceſs, Philip ordered the duke of Parma to provide tranſports to carry over an army of 25000 men from the Netherlands to England. The duke punctually obeyed theſe orders, and quartered his army in the neighbourhood of Gravelines, Dunkirk and Nieuport. Dunkirk has been from time immemorial, an aſylum for fugitives from England, who ſullied with crimes of various dyes are permitted to find ſecurity for their perſons, and to carry on a deſpicable kind of commerce for their ſupport in this den of thieves. Here the duke of Parma picked up 700 deſperadoes, chiefly Iriſh and Scotch papiſts, who enliſted under his banners, to conquer England.

To oppoſe this mighty armament, the lord high admiral of England ſailed with a ſtrong ſquadron to the Weſt, where he was joined by the vice-admiral Sir Francis Drake; and lord Henry Seymour, ſecond ſon to the duke of Somerſet, with another ſquadron, cruiſed along the coaſts of Flanders, to prevent the embarkation of the troops under the duke of Parma. The preparations made by land have been mentioned in the life of the earl of Leiceſter. We ſhall therefore only give an account in this place of the operations of the fleets.

About the 12th of July, the Spaniſh Armada ſet ſail a ſecond time for England, and after a tempeſtuous paſſage, they appeared on the 19th off the weſtern ſhore; and ſpread a general alarm and conſternation all along the coaſts, which was greatly increaſed by obſerving, that moſt of the

Spaniſh

Spanish galleons were of such an enormous size, that they seemed like floating castles in comparison to the English, and their upper works were almost cannon proof, being three feet thick. The first design meditated by the Spanish admiral, was to attempt burning the English fleet in their harbours, for he had no idea, they would venture to put to sea, to face his *Invincible Armada*; but being discovered off the Lizard, by one Fleming a Scotch pirate; this man, with great loyalty, crowded all the sail of his light pinnace, and bore away for Plymouth, the station of the English admiral, and the rendezvous of the different squadrons now out on cruizes to watch the motions of the Spaniards. Fleming arrived in time to enable the lord admiral to take what measures he thought proper, without being surprized by the enemy. Lord Effingham hereupon, resolved to get the ships under his command out of the harbour without loss of time, and to encourage the sailors, he worked himself, and personally gave orders to the other officers, which so encouraged the men, that on the morning of the 20th of July, he got clear of the port, and descried the Spanish fleet, which must have made a most formidable appearance, and have appalled any other but his brave seamen; for he had but thirty sail of the line with him. Our admiral suffered them to pass without seeming to take any notice of them, that having the advantage of the wind, he might bear down upon their rear and attack them. They moved very flowly along, though with all their sail out, being extremely heavy and unweildy, so that scarce one of them answered to the helm. A circumstance greatly in favour of the English admiral, who with his light vessels, if he had been worsted in his attempt upon the Spanish rear, could have retreated with ease, and it would have been impossible to have pursued him

him with these heavy ships. Lord Effingham however, took care to send a special messenger to the queen, to inform her Majesty of the arrival of the enemy, of the superiority of their fleet, and of his design, notwithstanding this disadvantage, to fall upon their rear; likewise to desire her to make the proper dispositions by land, in case the Spaniards should succeed so far as to set their troops on shore; and to give orders for all the other squadrons and ships in her Majesty's service, to join him with all possible expedition. Having taken these prudent precautions, the lord-admiral resolved to make a vigorous attack on the enemy, with a view of preparing them for a general engagement, and to take off the terror which the sight of the large Spanish galleons had impressed on the minds of the English seamen. He therefore gave chace to this formidable fleet, and soon fell in with the rear division, commanded by Don Ricaldo; a skirmish ensued, in which the English had the advantage; and it fully answered our admiral's purpose, who perceiving that the Spanish admiral in the center, and Don Alphonso de Levya commander of the van, were endeavouring to incircle his little fleet; he made a signal for a retreat, which was soon made in excellent order; and this trial convinced both his officers and his men, how easily they could manage their own ships, and either attack or retire from the heavy-floating castles of the enemy: but our historians and biographers, who assert that this was a general engagement, and mention Drake, Hawkins, and Frobisher as parties concerned in it, are guilty of a capital error; for these latter commanders were at different stations when this first blow was struck, and they brought the lord-admiral the forty ships which formed their squadrons, only on the 22d, when his lordship was still continuing a kind of running fight with the Spaniards,

niards, firing at their large ships as opportunity served of sailing up to them, and then retreating with the same expedition.

The Spaniards, however, being greatly worsted in different attacks, and finding the English fleet more numerous and powerful, than it had been represented, on a sudden tacked about, and made for the coast of Calais. The lord-admiral then called a council of war, and after conferring the honour of knighthood on vice-admiral Drake, Hawkins, Frobisher, and three other principal officers, he proposed to pursue the Spanish fleet; and he was further induced to advise this measure, by the prospect of being joined by the squadrons under lord Henry Seymour and Sir William Winter, stationed off the Flemish coast. The council concurring in opinion with the lord-admiral, the English fleet gave chace to the Spaniards, and on the 27th, the other squadrons joined them, in the Streights of Calais; and then their whole force consisted of one hundred and forty sail. Yet still it was inferior to the Armada, which now lay at anchor off Calais, and disposed in such order, that lord Effingham saw there were no hopes of separating the fleet, and attacking different divisions, as he had proposed; unless some stratagem could be devised to throw the whole fleet in disorder: his great capacity, however, supplied him with the happiest expedient for this purpose. He converted eight of his worst barks into fire-ships, and these, under the conduct of two experienced captains, were convoyed about midnight to the Spanish fleet, and being properly filled with combustibles, and their sails set, they were fired by the crews of the two ships that convoyed them, who then took to their boats; these barks went into the center of the Spanish fleet, and threw the whole into the utmost dismay and confusion. Some fell foul of each other, after

cutting

cutting their cables, others got up their anchors, and put to sea to avoid the flames, which had caught the rigging of several ships; and as soon as the dawn appeared, the English fell upon them in this dispersed state, and took or destroyed twelve of their largest ships. This was the first introduction of the use of fire-ships in the English navy. The Spaniards now laying aside the thoughts of invasion and conquest, endeavoured to make their escape through the Streights of Dover, but adverse winds drove them on the coast of Zealand, where the Spanish admiral narrowly escaped shipwreck. After this, a council of war was held, and it was determined to retreat entirely, by sailing round the north-part of our island; but here, a second storm dispersed them, and the admiral, with twenty-five sail, steered his course for the Bay of Biscay, leaving the rest of his Invincible Armada to the violence of the tempest, and the mercy of the English. Upwards of thirty of their best ships perished on the Irish coast, others were driven on shore in the Orkney Islands, and several were taken by those brave admirals Hawkins, Drake, and Frobisher: in fine, out of the whole fleet, consisting of one hundred and thirty sail, only fifty-four got safe to Spain, and those in a shattered condition; it is likewise computed that they lost 25000 men in this fatal expedition, among whom were so many volunteers of distinguished rank, that most of the noble families in Spain went into mourning, after the return of the remains of the fleet. As for the English admiral, after he had cleared the channel of the Spaniards, he returned triumphant to the Downs; and then repairing to London, joined in the joyful acclamations and thanksgivings of the whole nation upon this great deliverance from impending destruction. The queen repaired publicly to the cathedral of St. Paul's, and there with great solemnity

solemnity and devotion expressed her gratitude to God, for his great mercy in rescuing her from the manifold secret plots and open violence of her enemies. Soon after, she ordered two medals to be struck in commemoration of this signal victory; and as the inventive genius, cool judgment, and active valour of the lord high admiral, had greatly contributed to the success of the day, her Majesty acknowledged his signal merit in the most honourable manner for him before the whole court, and rewarded him with a pension for life: Fleming, the pirate, was pardoned at his intercession, and an annual gratification was allowed him for the intelligence he had given to the lord-admiral of the arrival of the Spanish fleet.

The next important service performed by the lord-admiral was against Cadiz, which was taken by the English fleet and the land-forces under the earl of Essex in August 1596, to the incredible loss of Spain; for besides two rich galleons, thirteen men of war, and one hundred pieces of brass cannon, fell into the hands of the English, and the lord-admiral refused a ransom of two millions of ducats for the merchant-ships in Port-Real, his instructions being to burn them, because a second invasion of England had been meditated.

Upon lord Effingham's return, the queen, who had been generally partial to the earl of Essex, attributed the conquest of Cadiz chiefly to the admiral: in honour of the glorious expedition she created him earl of Nottingham; and in the patent, the reason assigned for conferring this new dignity, was his signal services in the taking of Cadiz: this gave birth to the quarrel between the admiral and Essex, which ended only with the death of the latter.

In 1599, the nation was alarmed with another projected invasion from Spain; and Essex being in Ireland, the queen, to manifest her intire confidence in the earl of Nottingham, made him sole commander of her fleets and armies, with the addition of a new title, that of lord lieutenant-general of all England; by which he was invested with more ample powers than had ever been granted to any subject: but this extraordinary commission expired with the occasion that gave birth to it. The dread of an invasion subsiding in six weeks, the earl of Nottingham resigned it into the queen's hands; however, he became her chief minister soon after; and by the death of the earl of Essex, sole administrator of the government. But, in order to secure this high station, it is strongly suspected, that the earl of Nottingham aggravated every act of rashness committed by the earl of Essex, and fomented the quarrel between that unhappy nobleman and his royal mistress, till by the unkindness of the one, the other was driven to desperation and rebellion.

From the moment that Essex surrendered to the earl of Nottingham, the queen, who had been uncommonly terrified by so daring an insurrection in the heart of the capital, was extravagant in her praises of the lord-admiral; she said publicly, that he was born to be the Saviour of his Country. Thus raised to the summit of a statesman's ambition, we have but too much reason to believe, that fearing a relapse on the part of the queen, in favour of his great rival, he intercepted the token sent from the unfortunate Essex as the last application for mercy.

On these well-grounded suspicions, the earl stands accused of an act of cruel policy, which throws a baleful shade over the bright character of this Saviour of his Country, and even leaves a stain upon his loyalty; for a man of his abilities could not but be aware of the fatal consequences to the queen, if ever this secret reached her royal ear.

For many years after the event, the following remarkable anecdote was discredited by our best historians; but later discoveries, which have thrown more light upon the court intrigues in the last years of the reign of Elizabeth, have left little room to doubt the truth of it, as it is here related.

The earl of Essex, soon after his return from the successful expedition against Cadiz, grew extremely jealous of being supplanted in the royal favour; and being confirmed in his apprehensions by the new peerage conferred on the lord-admiral, he resolved to secure himself against any fatal reverse of fortune, while the queen's attachment to him remained. In this disposition, having obtained a private audience, he took occasion to regret, that her Majesty's service should so frequently oblige him to be absent from her person; by which he was exposed to all those ill-offices, which his enemies, in the course of their constant attendance on her, had it in their power to do him, by misrepresentations of his conduct, and false accusations, while he was at a remote distance from court; perhaps not even in the kingdom: her Majesty, it is said, being greatly moved at his pathetic remonstrance, took a ring from her finger; desired him to keep it as a pledge of her affection; and assured him, that whatever prejudices she might be induced to entertain against him; or whatever disgrace he might happen to fall into, if he sent her that ring, she should instantly call to mind her former affection for him, and grant him his request, whatever it might be. The reader will be pleased to recollect that Henry VIII. had acted in the very same manner in the case of archbishop Cranmer; and he will further observe, that in many instances, Elizabeth affected to imitate the manners of her father. This is a circumstance which has escaped the notice of our historians, in their warm contests upon the credibility of this story; but highly presumptive in favour of its authenticity. After sentence of death had been passed upon the unfortunate Essex, it is a well-known fact, that he requested the favour of a visit from the countess of Nottingham, at that time principal lady of the bed-chamber to the queen; to what purpose, but to give her this ring, and to charge her to deliver it to her Majesty, and to enforce his prayer for pardon, by her intercession? The countess was prevailed upon by her husband to keep the ring, and to stifle the commission she had undertaken; and the queen, who hourly expected this last appeal from her fallen favourite, found various excuses to delay signing the warrant for his execution, till female resentment at his supposed pride and obstinacy, made her listen to the political motives urged by Cecil, and she consented to his death.

Towards the close of the year 1602, the countess of Nottingham was seized with her last illness, and finding her dissolution fast approaching, she sent a special messenger to intreat a private visit from the queen, alledging that she had something of importance to impart to her Majesty, which troubled her conscience; the queen complying with her earnest request; as soon as the attendants withdrew, the countess revealed the fatal secret, and at the same time implored the queen's pardon; who, astonished at the foul deed, burst forth into a violent passion of rage, shook the dying countess in her bed, and exclaiming with great vehemence, "God " may forgive you, but I cannot;" she broke from her, and the countess expired soon after.

As fo the distracted queen, a deep melancholy and incessant grief succeeded to rage; and from this time her health visibly declined: still, however, she affected to conceal it, and she caused her inauguration day, the 17th of November, to be observed with the usual magnificence and rejoicings. But the courtiers, according to custom, began already to pay their court to the rising Sun, the young king of Scotland, her presumptive heir; this did not escape her notice, and she was heard to lament, in bitter terms, that she was neglected, betrayed, and deserted. And, when she found the very same ministers advising her to sign the pardon of the earl of Tyrone, who had urged her to put Essex to death, she could not forbear making a just comparison between the guilt of an arch-rebel, who had desolated great part of Ireland, and the single act of mad desperation committed by Essex, for which these statesmen had made her forget and cancel all his great services to her and his country. Her grief, upon this occasion, could not be concealed; and as if she had been determined not to out-live the disgrace of being duped by her servants, she now neglected the care of her health, removing from Westminster to her palace of Non-Such at Sheene, in very tempestuous weather, on the last day of January, 1603. Here she daily grew worse, and the privy-council sat in London, deliberating on the measures for securing the peaceable succession of James I. with this view, they thought it most adviseable, that the queen, in her life-time should absolutely nominate him to succeed her; and though the earl of Nottingham and Sir Robert Cecil knew how painful this task would be to her, and that in fact, it was by no means necessary, the whole council being of one mind; yet they, together with the lord-keeper Buckhurst, undertook the disagreeable office. The queen, before she left Westminster, had declared to the lord-admiral, now likewise earl-marshal of England, that the crown ought to go to her next heir. But the

the jealous Scots, and the English ministers, who wished to stand high in favour with James, did not think this declaration sufficient. The three deputies from the council, found the queen almost speechless; but she had strength enough to repeat the meaning of her former declaration to the lord-admiral. " I have filled," said she, " a royal throne, and I desire to have a royal successor." The Stuart party, not yet satisfied, wrote to Sir Robert Cecil to press the dying queen to be more explicit. Being therefore importuned again, on the same subject, she seemed to resent it; and with tokens of vexation, at their affected ignorance—she uttered these her last words upon this subject: " I desire that a king should succeed me, and who should that king be, but my nearest kinsman, the king of Scotland?" Her Majesty continued languishing, in a most deplorable condition, near two months, and for ten days together she sat up dressed, upon cushions and carpets, and would not be put to bed, till she was compelled; and after this refreshment she seemed easier, but continued to lay on her side without speaking or taking notice of any of her attendants. At times, she would however join in prayers with Whitgift, archbishop of Canterbury, who was constantly in waiting. On the 23d of March she was quite speechless, but composed; and at night she fell into a sleep, which lasted five hours, when she waked only to breathe her last, seemingly with little pain or sensibility. Thus, in the 70th year of her age, and the 45th of her glorious reign, at about two in the morning of the 24th of March, 1603, was England deprived of a sovereign, who raised the splendor of the British throne, who laid the foundation of the extensive commerce of England in after-ages, who by her magnanimity, penetration, and vigilance, preserved England, Scotland, and Ireland from becoming provinces

provinces to Spain, and againſt whom no accuſation can be brought to diminiſh a peerleſs character, but that ſhe ſuffered the royal prerogative to infringe on the rights of the people; yet, let it be remembered, that it was at ſuch critical junctures, as thoſe, when ancient Rome ſubmitted to the rigorous adminiſtration of dictators.

In a word, the beſt character that can be given of this great queen, will be found in the ſtory of her life, even as it is written by foreigners of acknowledged literary abilities, who have written her hiſtory under the diſadvantage of being Roman catholics, and the ſubjects of deſpotic princes. Such, among others, was the preſident de Thou, commonly called Thuanus, to whom the reader is referred.

The remaining memoirs of the earl of Nottingham, hardly merit our notice; it may therefore ſuffice to obſerve, that his zeal in the affair of the ſucceſſion, procured him the honour of officiating as high-ſteward at the coronation of James I. that he was ſent on a ſplendid embaſſy to Spain, to conclude a treaty of friendſhip with that crown, in which he had been very inſtrumental; that he reſigned his office of high-admiral for a penſion, to Villiers duke of Buckingham, and retired into the country, where he died in 1624.

*** *Authorities.* Salmon's Chronol. Hiſtorian. Hume's Hiſtory of England. Birch's Negociations and Memoirs of the Reign of Elizabeth. Campbell's Lives of the Admirals. Thuanus's General Hiſtory from 1545 to 1607. Carte's edit.

SUPPLEMENT.

The lives of the most eminent persons, who were distinguished chiefly by their public characters and the high stations they held under queen Elizabeth, are contained in the preceding pages; it remains now, to trace the progress of the human understanding in Britain, during, and for about twenty years after, this glorious æra of our history; the age of Elizabeth having given birth to a few celebrated men of uncommon genius, whose memoirs could not be blended with the civil history of the times. Besides, some of them, though they flourished under Elizabeth, survived her many years: on which account, we have assigned them a distinct department, as not belonging entirely to the annals of either Elizabeth or James I.

So great was the attention of the people to the revival and extension of commerce, to the encouragement of navigation, and to the fixing of manufactures in the kingdom, (brought from foreign countries) that the mechanical and useful arts, were greatly preferred to the polite and liberal, in the reign of Elizabeth: we have therefore only to mention, that painting still continued to be of foreign growth, though England produced two persons. who are noticed as men of some eminence, Nicholas Hilliard, a limner, jeweller and goldsmith; whose natural inclination for painting, led him to copy after Holbein, while he was an apprentice as a jeweller and goldsmith: he confined himself chiefly to portraits, and was excellent in miniature: this artist was born in 1547, and died in St. Martin's in the Fields in 1619. Isaac Olliver, another miniature painter, was his pupil, and the virtuosi give his performances the preference; he died in Blackfriars two years before his master.

Engraving, as a branch of the mechanic arts, met with great encouragement in the reign of Elizabeth, and by the indefatigable industry of the celebrated *Vertue* in our times, some capital performances, and a list of the artists of repute in this branch, have been restored; an account of which, the reader will find at large in Mr. Walpole's Anecdotes of Painting in England, Vol. II.

Music was likewise at a low ebb, though Elizabeth endeavoured to revive a taste both for vocal and instrumental, setting the example by her own performances; but history and poetry received considerable improvements from the immortal pens of Buchanan, Spenser, Shakespeare, and Camden. Of whom, we shall give concise memoirs, in chronological order.

The LIFE of
GEORGE BUCHANAN.

[A. D. 1506, to 1582.]

THIS celebrated historian, and Latin poet, was a native of Scotland; of whose family we have little or no account, except that his grandfather was a person concerned in trade, by whose failure, his father and mother were reduced to distressed circumstances. George Buchanan was born in the Shire of Lenox, in 1506; and his father dying while he was very young, the care of his education

education devolved on his mother, who was left almoſt unprovided for, with five ſons and three daughters; but by the kind aſſiſtance of her brother, Mr. James Herriot, ſhe was enabled to ſend George to ſchool, where his inclination for learning recommended him to the further patronage and diſtinguiſhed attention of his uncle, at whoſe expence he was ſent to Paris, the univerſity in that city, being then eſteemed the beſt in Europe. But the death of Mr. Herriot, after he had been two years at Paris, depriving him of the means of purſuing his ſtudies, he was obliged to return to Scotland: it is obſerved, however, that if this alteration had not happened, his bad ſtate of health alone, would have forced him to leave Paris.

About the year 1524, having a deſire to acquire ſome knowledge of military affairs, he made a campaign with the French auxiliaries, who came over to Scotland under the command of John duke of Albany, to aſſiſt in carrying on the war againſt England, the French and the Scots being in alliance againſt Henry VIII. but the fatigues he underwent were too much for his delicate conſtitution; and this martial experiment occaſioned him a ſevere fit of illneſs, which confined him to his bed during the enſuing winter.

In the ſpring however, he was ſo well recovered, that he went to the univerſity of St. Andrew's to learn logic, under the famous Mr. John Mair, with whom he went a ſecond time to Paris; there he embraced the tenets of Luther, which began to prevail in France about this time. After ſtruggling for near two years, againſt the miſeries of indigent circumſtances, his great merit procured him admiſſion into the college of St. Barbe, where he became profeſſor of grammar, which he taught near three years, and acquired by it a decent ſubſiſtence. At length, one of his pupils, Gilbert Kennedy, earl of

Caſſels,

Cassels, a young Scotch nobleman, admiring the conversation, and esteeming the literary abilities of his countryman, engaged him solely as his tutor and companion, and they remained five years in France, after which they returned together to Scotland. The death of the earl of Cassels, in 1534, left Mr. Buchanan once more without a patron: thus circumstanced, he was preparing to return to France, when James V. sent for him, and made him preceptor to his natural son, James Stuart, afterwards the famous earl of Murray, chosen regent of Scotland, when queen Mary was deposed. But his evil genius again interposed to thwart his fortune, for having written a satirical, but elegant Latin poem, intitled, *Somnium*, in which the ignorance and laziness of the Franciscan friars was severely lashed; the pious fraternity were so highly exasperated, that they accused him of atheism and heresy. This proof of their malice answered no other purpose, but to animate our young poet to fresh exertions of his vein for satire; and the irregular lives of the friars having furnished sufficient grounds, he was highly pleased to find in his royal patron, an encourager of his design. A conspiracy against James V. was discovered at this time, and the Franciscans were suspected by the king to have been privy to it; upon which he commanded Buchanan to write a poem against them. It should seem however, as if the poet was apprehensive of the consequences to himself, of carrying matters too far, for he wrote a sketch of his poem, susceptible of a double interpretation. But the king, being displeased at this evasion of his orders, positively enjoined him to lash their vices, without disguise or reserve, which gave occasion to the celebrated Latin poem of our author, intitled, FRANCISCANUS. All the religious orders in Scotland now took the alarm, and vowed destruction to the man,

man, who had the infolence to expofe them to the fcorn and derifion of the laity; and though the king was highly pleafed with the performance, it is faid, he had the bafenefs to confent to have him put to death, in confideration of a confiderable fum of money raifed by the ecclefiaftics, and depofited in the hands of that perfecuting bigot, Cardinal Beatoun, for this infamous purpofe: Buchanan received private intelligence, that the Francifcans had a defign upon his life, though of what nature his friends could not exactly inform him; but it foon appeared, that they intended to have him burnt as a heretic: for being accufed of this capital crime, he was arrefted and imprifoned in the beginning of the year 1539; fortunately, however, he watched his opportunity, and while his keepers were afleep, got out of his chamber-window, and made his efcape to England undifcovered. There, finding that Henry VIII. had fet on foot a bloody perfecution againft both papifts and heretics, who did not conform to the fix articles, he went to Paris, where he hoped to find an afylum from the vengeance of his enemies; but unfortunately cardinal Beatoun had been fent on an embaffy from Scotland to the court of France, and was juft arrived; Buchanan therefore thought it moft advifeable to retire to Bourdeaux, having received an invitation from Andrew Govea (better known by his Latin name Andreas Govianus) a celebrated profeffor of the civil law, who had been invited from his native country Portugal, to prefide at the head of a college newly founded in that city. Here Buchanan taught the claffics, rhetoric, hiftory, and poetry, in the public fchools for his fubfiftence, near three years, and at his leifure hours he compofed four tragedies, *Jeptha*, *Alceftes*, *Baptifta*, and a tranflation of the *Medea* of *Euripides*. He wrote them in compliance with the rules of the fchools, a new fable being required

from

from the profeſſors every year; and inſtead of the trifling allegories uſually furniſhed upon theſe occaſions in the French univerſities, by which the taſte of their youth for rational entertainment had been vitiated, he introduced regular dramatic pieces, founded on hiſtorical facts, and thus engaged the ſtudents to imitate the ancients. Such an improvement as this could not eſcape the notice of the moſt eminent men in France, who highly approved it, and Buchanan's reputation was circulated throughout the whole kingdom, to the no ſmall mortification of the haughty cardinal Beatoun, who wrote to the archbiſhop of Bourdeaux, informing him, that Buchanan was a profeſſed heretic, and requeſting that he might be apprehended: but the cardinal's letters, falling into the hands of his friends, he was delivered from this ſnare; and his patron, Andreas Govianus, being ſoon after ordered home by the king of Portugal, and commanded to bring with him ſome learned men capable of teaching philoſophy and claſſical learning, in the univerſity he had juſt founded at Cambria, Buchanan embraced this opportunity of avoiding the meditated vengeance of Beatoun and his clergy. While Govianus lived, Buchanan and the other learned men, who had followed him to Portugal, met with all ſuitable encouragement; but after his death, the natural averſion of the Portugueſe to foreigners, overcame their deſire of improvement, and theſe profeſſors were extremely ill-uſed. Our author's poem againſt the Franciſcans, his eating meat in Lent, and his having advanced in private converſation with ſome Portugueſe youth, that he thought St. Auſtin's doctrines were more favourable to the reformed, than to the Romiſh religion, were made the grounds of an accuſation of hereſy; in conſequence of which, he was ſeized and thrown into the priſon of the inquiſition in the year 1549;
but

but the hopes of converting a man of his great reputation in the learned world, procured him the indulgence of a removal to a monastery, to be instructed in the mysteries of the holy Roman Catholic faith by the Monks, who, by his own account, treated him with great civility. It was during this confinement that he translated the Psalms of David into elegant Latin verse.

In 1551, by the interest of some of his pupils of distinction, the king ordered, that he should be set at liberty; and to indemnify him for his imprisonment, he now supplied him liberally with money for his current expences, and promised him preferment. But Buchanan, having no opinion of Portuguese faith, and having already experienced their treachery, obtained a passport to return to England, and embarked on board a ship then in the harbour of Lisbon, taking in a cargo for London. The confusion that prevailed in the councils of Edward VI. during his minority, did not seem to promise any great encouragement to literature: Buchanan therefore returned again to France in 1552, as he had nothing to apprehend in that country, his old enemy cardinal Beatoun having been assassinated by the Leslies in Scotland, in 1548. Our author was now famous all over Europe, for his great learning, but more particularly for the elegance and correctness of his Latin poetry, a specimen of which he had presented to the renowned Charles V. emperor of Germany, in a small complimentary poem, while he resided at Bourdeaux; and copies of it had been dispersed in Spain and Germany by order of his Imperial Majesty. The principal nobility of France, therefore, thought it an honour to protect and encourage him upon his return to Paris; and this gave him an opportunity of publishing his tragedy of Jephtha in the most advantageous manner; Charles de Cossi, marshal of France, permiting

ing him the honour to dedicate it to him: Buchanan, in return, made so just an eulogium on the character of that great man, that the marshal, highly pleased with this well-judged compliment, gave him an invitation to settle in Piedmont, with genteel appointments, in quality of preceptor to his son. Buchanan accepted the offer, and passed five years very agreeably with this youth, employing the hours of recess from his charge, in the study of the Scriptures and polemical authors, with a view of forming his own opinion, on the controversies which at this time involved all Europe in religious feuds.

In 1563, Buchanan returned to Scotland, and joined the reformed church of that kingdom. In the beginning of 1565, he made another excursion to France; but the following year, he was ordered home by Mary queen of the Scots, to be preceptor to her son, James VI. as soon as that prince should be of a proper age to be put under his care, and in the mean time, in order to fix him in his own country, she made him principal of St. Leonard's college in the university of St. Andrew, where he presided four years; and at his leisure hours, he collected together all his poems, except such as were in the hands of his friends, of which he had kept no copies. When the civil dissentions broke forth between queen Mary and her subjects, he joined the party in opposition to the queen, and became a favourite of the earl of Murray, chosen regent of Scotland, by whose order he wrote a piece, intitled, *The Detection*, containing very severe reflections on the character and conduct of Mary; for which his memory has been aspersed, as a writer, by all popish historians, and by those, who have undertaken the more than Herculean labour of endeavouring to exculpate that weak and vicious woman. The states of Scotland, however, approved of Mary's choice of Buchanan, to be preceptor to the young king,

for

for they confirmed him in this office; and when it was remarked some years after, that he had made his Majesty a pedant, Buchanan used to reply, "it was the best he could make of him." When we review his character as the sovereign of three kingdoms, we shall be enabled to form a judgment of his preceptor's sarcasm.

In 1568, Buchanan was chosen one of the commissioners, who were sent to England to accuse queen Mary of the heinous crime of being privy to the murder of her husband lord Darnley; and upon his return, he had the revenues of the abbey of Crofs Raguel assigned to him for life, he was made moderator of the church of Scotland, though a layman; director of the chancery; one of the lords of the council; and finally, lord privy-seal. Besides all these promotions and emoluments, it is said, queen Elizabeth allowed him a pension of one hundred pounds yearly.

Being now entirely at his ease, he employed the remaining thirteen years of his life chiefly in literary pursuits; and from the time he was first employed in the public service of his country, he directed his studies to those important subjects, politics and history. His two last performances of this kind, were his celebrated tract, *De Jure Regni apud Scotos*; and his History of Scotland; both of them by impartial judges are esteemed as masterly productions, but favouring too much the principles of democratic government, they could not be acceptable in a monarchy; accordingly, they were both condemned by the states; and on the publication of the history, the author was cited to appear before the lords of the privy-council, to be responsible for some bold political truths, said to be of a dangerous tendency; but he died before the day appointed for his appearance. The king was likewise highly incensed at some passages, which struck at the root of the royal prerogative; and this being told to Buchanan during his illness, he said, with the cool indifference of a stoic philosopher, "that his Majesty's anger gave him little or no concern, as he was shortly going to a place where there were few kings."

We are told likewise, that a short time before he expired, he called for his servant, enquired how much money he had belonging to him; and finding it insufficient for his burial, he ordered him to distribute it amongst the poor. Upon which the servant desired to know, who, in that case, would defray the expences of his funeral. To this Buchanan replied, "That he was very indifferent about that; for if he was once dead, if they would not bury him, they might let him lie where he was, or throw his corpse where they pleased." And persisting in his resolution, the magistracy of Edinburgh were obliged to bury him at the public expence.

Various characters have been given of this admired writer; and both his private life, and his public opinions, have been grosly misrepresented by popish authors, insomuch, that they have not scrupled publishing the most notorious falshoods respecting both. Independent of these, he has been too lavishly praised, and too rigidly censured by British writers of eminence, according to the influence of their own political tenets: but, upon the whole, we are enabled to collect from four very respectable authorities, one foreign, and the others his countrymen, that he was one of the brightest ornaments of the learned world in his day: as a Latin poet, none excelled him: as an historian, he united the force and brevity of Salust, with the elegance and perspicuity of Livy: he may be reckoned, the greatest and best of our modern authors: his history is written with such beauty of style, easiness of expression, and exactness in all parts, that no service or honour like it, could have been done to the Scottish nation, had he ended so noble a work as he begun, and carried it on only to the death of James V. but being unhappily engaged in a faction, and resentments working violently upon him, he suffered himself to be so strangely biassed, that in the relation he gives of many of the transactions of his own time, he may rather pass for a satyrist than an historian. These are the sentiments of Thuanus, Crawford, and Mackenzie. Guthrie's authority, in this case, is so little to be relied on, that his severe censures of our author do not merit any attention; but from the latest and most respectable of all his critics, Dr. Robertson, we must quote a summary of his character, as a writer, drawn up with cool, deliberate reflection, and a spirit of candor, which marks the goodness of the writer's heart.

" The happy genius of Buchanan, equally form-
" ed to excel in prose and in verse, more various,
" more original, and more elegant, than that of
" almost any other modern, who has written in
" Latin, reflects, with regard to this particular,
" the greatest lustre on his country." With respect to his history, the doctor observes, " if his
" accuracy and impartiality had been, in any de-
" gree, equal to the elegance of his taste, and to
" the purity and vigour of his style, his history
" might be placed on a level with the most admired
" compositions of the ancients. But, instead of
" rejecting the improbable tales of chronical wri-
" ters, he was at the utmost pains to adorn them,
" and hath cloathed, with all the beauties and
" graces of fiction, those legends which formerly
" had only its wildness and extravagance."

Buchanan died at Edinburgh, in February 1582, and the first complete edition of all his works, collected

collected together in two volumes, folio, was not published in that city till 1704. A second edition, which is the last, appeared in 1715.

⁎ *Authorities.* Buchanan, *in vita propria poëmatus prefixa.* Thuanus's General History. Sir James Melvil's Memoirs, Lond. edit. 1752. Mackenzie's Lives and Characters of Scotch Writers. Dr. Robertson's History of Scotland.

The LIFE of

EDMUND SPENSER.

[A. D. 1572, to 1598.]

EDMUND SPENSER was born in London, and educated at Pembroke-hall in Cambridge, where he took the degree of bachelor of arts in 1572, and of master of arts in 1576. The accounts of the birth and family of this great man are but obscure and imperfect, and at his first setting out into life, his fortune and interest seem to have been very inconsiderable. After he had continued some time at college, and had laid that foundation of learning, which, joined to his natural genius, qualified him to rise to so great reputation as a poet, he stood for a fellowship, in competition with Mr. Andrews, a gentleman in holy orders, and afterwards lord bishop of Winchester, in which he was unsuccessful. This disappointment, joined with the narrowness of his circumstances, forced him to

EDMUND SPENSER.

...it the university; and we find him next residing ...the house of a friend in the north, where he fell ...with his Rosalind, whom he finely celebrates ...pastoral poems, and of whose cruelty he hath ...pathetic complaints. It is probable, that about this time, Spenser's genius began first to distinguish itself; for, The Shepherd's Calendar, which is so full of his unprosperous passion for Rosalind, was amongst the first of his works of note, and the supposition is strengthened, by the consideration of poetry's being frequently the off-spring of love and retirement. This work he addressed, by a short dedication, to the Mæcenas of his age, the immortal Sir Philip Sidney; a gentleman then in the highest reputation, who for wit and gallantry, was the most popular of all the courtiers of his age; and, as he was himself a writer, excelling in the fabulous or inventive part of poetry; it is no wonder he was struck with our author's genius, and became sensible of his merit. A story is told of him by Mr. Hughes, which does great honour to the humanity and penetration of Sidney, and to the excellent genius of Spenser. It is said that our poet was a stranger to this gentleman, when he began to write his Fairy Queen, and that he took occasion to go to Leicester-house, and introduce himself, by sending in to him a copy of the ninth canto of the first book of that poem. Sidney was much surprised with the description of despair in that canto, and is said to have shewn an unusual kind of transport on the discovery of so new and uncommon a genius. After he had read some stanzas, he turned to his steward, and bid him give the person who brought those verses fifty pounds; but upon reading the next stanza, he ordered the sum to be doubled. The steward was no less surprised than his master, and thought it

his

his duty to make some delay in executing so sudden and lavish a bounty; but upon reading one stanza more, Sidney raised the gratuity to two hundred pounds, and commanded the steward to give it immediately, lest as he read further he might be tempted to give away his whole estate. From this time he admitted the author to his acquaintance and conversation, and prepared the way for his being known and received at court. Though this seemed a promising omen, to be thus introduced to court, yet he did not instantly reap any advantage from it. He was indeed created poet laureat to queen Elizabeth, but he for some time wore a barren laurel, and possessed the place without the pension. Lord-treasurer Burleigh, who considered the mechanic and useful arts as more important in a rising commercial state, than the polite, is accused of intercepting the queen's favours to this unhappy, great genius. As misfortunes have the strongest influence on elegant and polished minds, so it was no wonder that Spenser was much depressed by the cold reception he met with from the great.

These discouragements greatly sunk our author's spirits, and accordingly we find him pouring out his heart, in complaints of so injurious and undeserved a treatment; which, probably, would have been less unfortunate to him, if his noble patron, Sir Philip Sidney, by his employments abroad, and the share he had in the Low-Country wars, had not been obliged to be frequently, and for a long time together absent from court. In a poem, called, The Ruins of Time, which was written some time after Sidney's death, the author seems to allude to the discouragements just mentioned, in the following stanza:

" O grief

"O grief of griefs, O gall of all good hearts!
 "To see that virtue should despised be,
"Of such as first were rais'd for virtue's parts,
 "And now broad-spreading, like an aged tree,
 "Let none shoot up that nigh them planted be;
"O let not those, of whom the muse is scorned,
"Alive, or dead, be by the muse adorned."

These lines are certainly meant to reflect on Burleigh for neglecting him, and the lord-treasurer afterwards conceived a hatred towards him for the satire he apprehended was levelled at him, in Mother Hubbard's Tale. In this poem, the author has, in the most lively manner, pointed out the misfortune of depending on court-favours: in the following beautiful lines.

"Full little knowest thou, that hast not try'd,
"What hell it is in suing long to bide,
"To lose good days, that might be better spent,
"To waste long nights in pensive discontent;
"To speed to day, to be put back to-morrow,
"To feed in hope, to pine with fear and sorrow;
"To have thy prince's grace, yet want her peers,
"To have thy asking, yet wait many years.
"To fret thy soul with crosses, and with care,
"To eat thy heart, through comfortless despair;
"To fawn, to crouch, to wait, to ride, to run,
"To spend, to give, to want, to be undone."

As this was very much the author's case, it probably was this particular passage in that poem which gave offence; for as Hughes very elegantly observes, even the sighs of a miserable man, are sometimes resented as an affront, by him who is the occasion of them. There is a story, related by some as a matter of fact commonly reported at that time, which reflects upon the character of Burleigh; but it is discredited by Dr. Birch, and other judicious historians and critics, because the same circumstances are recorded to have happened to a poet of inferior merit, and the poetical petition here given as Spenser's composition, is ascribed to the inferior bard.

It is said, that upon his presenting some poems to the queen, she ordered him a gratuity of one hundred pounds; but the lord-treasurer Burleigh objecting to it, said, with some scorn, of the poet, of whose merit he was totally ignorant, "What, all this for a song?" The queen replied, "Then give him what is reason." Spenser for some time waited, but had the mortification to find himself disappointed of her Majesty's bounty. Upon this he took an opportunity to present a paper to queen Elizabeth, in the manner of a petition, in which he reminded her of the order she had given, in the following lines:

> "I was promis'd on a time
> "To have reason for my rhyme,
> "From that time, unto this season,
> "I receiv'd nor rhyme, nor reason.

This paper produced the intended effect, and the queen, after sharply reproving the treasurer, immediately directed the payment of the hundred pounds she had first ordered. In the year 1579, he was sent abroad by the earl of Leicester, as appears by a copy of Latin verses, dated from Leicester-house, and addressed to his friend Mr. Hervey; but Mr. Hughes has not been able to determine in what service he was employed.

When the lord Grey of Wilton was chosen deputy of Ireland, Spenser was recommended to be his secretary. This drew him over to another kingdom, and settled him in a scene of life very different from what he had formerly known, but, that he understood, and discharged his employment with skill and capacity, appears sufficiently by his discourse on the state of Ireland, in which there are many solid and judicious remarks, that shew him no less qualified for the business of the state, than for the entertainment of the muses. His life was now freed from the difficulties under which it had hitherto struggled: but the lord Grey being recalled in 1582, Spenser returned with him to England, where he seems to have continued till the untimely death of his gallant patron Sir Philip Sidney, in 1586; with which catastrophe he was deeply affected. His services to the crown, in his station of secretary to the lord-deputy, were recompensed by a grant from queen Elizabeth of three thousand acres of land in the county of Cork. This induced him to reside in Ireland. His house was at Kilcolman, and the river Mulla, which he has, more than once, so finely introduced in his poems, ran through his grounds. Much about this time he contracted an intimate friendship with the great and learned Sir Walter Raleigh, who was then a captain under the lord Grey. His elegant poem, called, Colin Clout's come home again, in which Sir Walter Raleigh is described under the name of the Shepherd of the Ocean, is a beautiful memorial of this friendship, which took its rise from a similarity of taste in the polite arts, and which he agreeably describes, with a softness and delicacy peculiar to him. Sir Walter afterwards fixed him in the esteem of queen Elizabeth, through whose recommendations her Majesty read his writings.

He now fell in love a second time, with a merchant's daughter, in which, says Mr. Cooper, author of The Muse's Library, he was more successful than in his first amour. He wrote upon this occasion a beautiful epithalamium, which he presented to the lady on the bridal-day, and it has consigned that day and her, to immortality. In this pleasant, easy situation, our excellent poet finished the celebrated poem of The Fairy Queen, which was begun and continued at different intervals of time, and of which he at first published only the three first books; to these were added three more, in a following edition, but the six last books (excepting the two cantos on mutability) were unfortunately lost by his servant, whom he had in haste sent before him to England; for though he passed his life for some time very serenely here, yet a train of misfortunes still pursued him, and in the rebellion of the earl of Desmond he was plundered and deprived of his estate. This distress forced him to return to England, where, for want of such a noble patron as Sir Philip Sidney, he was plunged into new calamities. It is said by Mr. Hughes, that Spenser survived his patron about twelve years, and died the same year with his powerful enemy the lord Burleigh, 1598. He was buried, says he, in Westminster-Abbey, near the famous Geoffery Chaucer, as he had desired; his obsequies were attended by the poets of that time, and others, who paid the last honours to his memory. Several copies of verses were thrown into his grave, with the pens that wrote them, and his monument was erected at the charge of Robert Devereux, the unfortunate earl of Essex.

This is the account given by the editor of his works, of the death of Spenser, but there is some reason to believe that he spoke only upon imagination, as he has produced no authority to support his opinion, and in a work of great reputation, we find a different relation delivered upon probable grounds. The ingenious Mr. Drummond of Hawthronden, a noble wit of Scotland, had an intimate correspondence with all the literati of his time who resided at London, particularly the famous

mous Ben Jonson, who had so high an opinion of Mr. Drummond's abilities, that he took a journey into Scotland in order to converse with him, and stayed some time at his house at Hawthronden. After Ben Jonson departed, Mr. Drummond, careful to retain what passed between them, wrote down the heads of their conversation; which he published amongst his poems and History of the Five James's, kings of Scotland. Amongst other particulars there is this: "Ben Jonson told me that Spenser's goods were robbed by the Irish in Desmond's rebellion, his house and a little child of his burnt, and he and his wife nearly escaped; that he afterwards died in King-street, Dublin, by absolute want of bread; and, that he refused twenty pieces sent him by the earl of Essex, and gave this answer to the person who brought them, "That he was sure he had no time to spend them." In the inscription on his tomb in Westminster-Abbey, it is said he was born in the year 1510, and died in 1596; Camden says 1598: but in regard to his birth, both the dates must be wrong, for it is by no means probable he was born so early as 1510, if we may judge by the remarkable circumstance of his standing for a fellowship in competition with Mr. Andrews, who was not born, according to Hughes, till 1555. Besides, if this account of his birth be true, he must have been sixty years old when he first published his Shepherd's Calendar, an age not very proper for love; and in this case it is no wonder that the beautiful Rosalind slighted his addresses; and he must have been seventy years old when he entered into business under lord Grey, who was created deputy of Ireland in 1580: for which reasons we may fairly conclude, that the inscription is false, probably through the error of the sculptor, who had the care of repairing the monument in after-times. The original inscription was in Latin, and had this remarkable memorial *immatura morte*, which would have been highly improper if he had been born in 1510, and lived to 1598.

We have very few anecdotes of the private life of this great poet, and this must be a mortification to all lovers of the muses, as he was the greatest ornament of his profession, in the age in which he lived. No writer ever found a nearer way to the heart, and his verses have a peculiar happiness of recommending the author to our friendship, as well as raising our admiration; one cannot read him without fancying one's-self transported into fairy-land, and there conversing with the graces in that enchanted region. In elegance of thinking and fertility of imagination, few of our English authors have approached him, and no writers ever possessed equal power to awake the spirit of poetry in others. Cowley owns that he derived inspiration from him: the celebrated Mr. James Thomson, the author of the Seasons, justly esteemed one of our best descriptive poets, used to say, that he formed himself upon Spenser; and how closely he pursued his model, and how nobly he has imitated him, whoever reads his Castle of Indolence with taste, will readily confess. Mr. Addison, in his Characters of the English poets, addressed to Mr. Sacheverel, thus speaks of Spenser:

" Old Spenser next, warm'd with poetic rage,
" In ancient tales amus'd a barbarous age;
" An age, that yet uncultivate and rude,
" Where'er the poet's fancy led, pursu'd
" 'Thro' pathless fields, and unfrequented floods,
" To dens of dragons, and enchanted woods.
" But now the mystic tale, that pleas'd of yore,
" Can charm an understanding age no more;
" The long-spun allegories, fulsome grow,
" While the dull moral lies too plain below.
" We

"We view well pleased at distance, all the sights,
"Of arms, and palfries, battles, fields, and fights,
"And damsels in distress, and courteous knights.
"But when we look too near, the shades decay,
"And all the pleasing landscape fades away."

It is agreed on all hands, that the distresses of our author helped to shorten his days; and indeed, when his extraordinary merit is considered, he had the hardest measure of any of our poets. It appears from different accounts, that he was of an amiable, sweet disposition, humane and generous in his nature. Besides the Fairy Queen, we find he had written several other pieces, of which we can only trace out the titles; the works being lost. Amongst these, the most considerable were nine comedies, in imitation of the comedies of his admired Ariosto, inscribed with the names of the nine muses. The rest which we find mentioned in his letters, and those of his friends, are his Dying Pelican, his Pageants, Stommata, Dudleyana, The Canticles paraphrased, Ecclesiastes, Seven Psalms, House of our Lord, Sacrifice of a Sinner, Purgatory, A Seven Night's Slumber, The Court of Cupid and Hell of Lovers. It is likewise said he had written a treatise in prose, called, The English poet; as for the epithalamium, Thamesis, and his Dreams, both mentioned by himself in one of his letters, Mr. Hughes thinks they are still preserved, though under different names. It appears from what is said of the Dreams, by his friend Mr. Hervey, that they were in imitation of Petrarch's Visions.

The works of Spenser will never perish; though he has introduced unnecessarily, many obsolete terms into them, there is a flow of poetry, an elegance of sentiment, a fund of imagination, and an enchanting enthusiasm, which will secure him the applauses of posterity, while any lovers of poetry remain.

remain. We find but little account of the family which Spenser left behind him, only that in a few particulars of his life, prefixed to the last folio edition of his works, it is said, that his great-grandson, Hugolin Spenser, after the restoration of king Charles II. was invested by the court of claims with so much of the lands as could be found to have been his ancestor's. There is another remarkable passage, of which, says Hughes, I can give the reader much better assurance: that a person came over from Ireland, in king William's time, to solicit the same affair, and brought with him letters of recommendation, as a descendant of Spenser. His name procured him a favourable reception, and he applied particularly to Mr. Congreve, by whom he was generously recommended to the favour of the earl of Halifax, then at the head of the treasury; by whose means he obtained his suit. This man was somewhat advanced in years, and might be the person before-mentioned, who had possibly recovered only some part of his estate at first, or had been disturbed in the possession of it. He could give no account of the works of his ancestor, which are wanting, and which are therefore in all probability, irrecoverably lost. The following stanzas are said to be those with which Sir Philip Sidney was first struck.

From him returning, sad and comfortless,
   As on the way together we did fare,
We met that villain (God from him me bless)
   That cursed wight, whom I escaped whylear,
A man of hell, that calls himself despair;
   Who first us greets, and after fair areeds
Of tidings strange, and of adventures rare,
   So creeping close, as snake in hidden weeds,
Inquireth of our states, and of our knightly deeds

Which when he knew, and felt our feeble hearts
  Embos'd with bole, and bitter biting grief,
Which love had lanced with his deadly darts,
  With wounding words, and terms of foul reprief,
  He pluck'd from us all hope of due relief;
That erſt us held in love of ling'ring life;
  Then hopeleſs, heartleſs, 'gan the cunning thief,
Perſuade us did, to ſtint all farther ſtrife:
To me he lent this rope, to him a ruſty knife.

> The following is the Picture of the CAVE of DESPAIR.

The darkſome cave they enter, where they find,
  That curſed man, low ſitting on the ground,
Muſing full ſadly in his ſullen mind;
  His greaſy locks, long growing, and unbound,
Diſorder'd hung about his ſhoulders round,
  And hid his face; thro' which his hollow eyne,
Look'd deadly dull, and ſtared as aſtound;
  His raw-bone cheeks thro' penury and pine,
Were ſhrunk into his jaws, as he did never dine.

His garments nought, but many ragged clouts,
  With thorns together pinn'd and patched was,
The which his naked ſides he wrapt abouts;
  And him beſide, there lay upon the graſs
A dreary corſe, whoſe life away did paſs,
  All wallowed in his own, yet lukewarm blood,
That from his wound yet welled freſh alas;
  In which a ruſty knife faſt fixed ſtood,
And made an open paſſage for the guſhing flood.

It would be an injury to Spenſer's memory to diſmiſs his life without a few remarks on that maſterly performance, which has placed him among the foremoſt of our poets. The work I mean is his allegorical poem of the Fairy Queen. Sir William

William Temple, in his Essay on Poetry, says, "That the religion of the Gentiles had been woven into the contexture of all the ancient poetry with an agreeable mixture, which made the moderns affect to give that of Christianity a place also in their poems; but the true religion was not found to become fictions so well as the false one had done, and all their attempts of this kind seemed rather to debase religion than heighten poetry. Spenser endeavoured to supply this with morality, and to make instruction, instead of story, the subject of an epic poem. His execution was excellent, and his flights of fancy very noble and high. But his design was poor; and his moral lay so bare, that it lost the effect. It is true, the pill was gilded, but so thin, that the colour and the taste were easily discovered."—Mr. Thomas Rhymer asserts, that Spenser may be reckoned the first of our heroic poets. "He had," says he, "a large spirit, a sharp judgment, and a genius for heroic poetry, perhaps above any that ever wrote since Virgil; but our misfortune is, he wanted a true idea, and lost himself by following an unfaithful guide. Though besides Homer and Virgil he had read Tasso, yet he rather suffered himself to be misled by Ariosto, with whom blindly rambling on marvels and adventures, he makes no conscience of probability; all is fanciful and chimerical, without any uniformity, or without any foundation in truth; in a word, his poem is perfect Fairy-land." Thus far Sir William Temple, and Mr. Rhymer; let us now attend to the opinion of a greater name, Mr. Dryden, who in his dedication of his translation of Juvenal, thus proceeds: "The English have only to boast of Spenser and Milton in heroic poetry, who neither of them wanted either genius or learning to have been perfect poets, and yet both of them are liable to many censures; for there is no uniformity

mity in the design of Spenser; he aims at the accomplishment of no one action; he raises up a hero f r every one of his adventures, and endows each of them with some particular moral virtue, which renders them all equal, without subordination, or preference: every one is valiant in his own legend; only we must do him the justice to observe, that magnanimity, which is the character of prince Arthur, shines throughout the whole poem, and succours the rest when they are in distress. The original of every knight was then living in the court of queen Elizabeth, and he attributed to each of them that virtue which he thought most conspicuous in them; an ingenious piece of flattery, though it turned not much to his account. Had he lived to have finished his poem in the remaining legends, it had certainly been more of a piece; but could not have been perfect, because the model was not true. But prince Arthur, or his chief patron, Sir Philip Sidney, dying before him, deprived the poet both of means and spirit to accomplish his design. For the rest, his obsolete language, and ill choice of his stanzas, are faults but of the second magnitude; for notwithstanding the first, he is still intelligible, at least after a little practice: and, for the last, he is more to be admired; that, labouring under such disadvantages, his verses are so numerous, so various, and so harmonious, that only Virgil, whom he has professedly imitated, hath surpassed him among the Romans; and only Waller among the English."

Mr. Hughes justly observes, that the chief merit of this poem consists in that surprising vein of fabulous invention which runs through it, and enriches it every where with imaginary descriptions, more than we meet with in any modern poem. The author seems to be possessed of a kind of poetical magic; and the figures he calls up to our view, rife up fo thick upon us, that we are at once pleafed and diftracted with the inexhauftible variety of them; fo that his faults may, in a manner, be imputed to his excellencies. His abundance betrays him into excefs; and his judgment is overborne by the torrent of his imagination.

Upon the whole, Mr. Warton feems to have given the moft accurate, candid criticifm on this celebrated poem, of all the writers on this delicate fubject.

"If the Fairy Queen be deftitute of that arrangement and œconomy which epic feverity requires, yet we fcarcely regret the lofs of thefe, while their place is fo amply fupplied by fomething which more powerfully attracts us; fomething which engages the affections, the feelings of the heart, rather than the cold approbation of the head. If there be any poem, whofe graces pleafe, becaufe they are fituated beyond the reach of art, and where the force and faculties of creative imagination delight, becaufe they are unaffifted and unreftrained by thofe of deliberate judgment, it is this. In reading Spenfer, if the critic is not fatisfied, yet the reader is tranfported.

Spenfer's works were publifhed in 6 vol. 12mo. by John Hughes, with an account of his life and a gloffary. Reprinted in 1750. Dr. Birch publifhed an edition of the Fairy Queen, 3 vol. in 4to. 1751. Three more editions of this poem were publifhed in 1758. In 1734, Dr. Jortin publifhed remarks on Spenfer's poems in 8vo. And laftly, Mr. Warton publifhed Obfervations on the Fairy Queen, which were fo well received, that a fecond edition was publifhed in 1762. Thefe being the feveral authorities from which our memoirs of this celebrated poet are taken, it is needlefs to add any other.

The

The Life of
WILLIAM SHAKESPEARE.

[A. D. 1564, to 1613.]

WILLIAM SHAKESPEARE, the immortal father of the British theatre; the glory of his age and of his country; whose dramatic works have stood the test of the severest criticisms, especially from foreigners, and, with all their imperfections on their heads, still remain unrivalled by any modern bard; was the son of Mr. John Shakespeare, and was born at Stratford upon Avon in Warwickshire, in April, 1564, as it appears by the public records of that town; and the family from which he was descended, are mentioned in the said records, as persons of good figure and fashion in that place, of the rank of gentry. His father, who was a considerable dealer in wool, being encumbered with a large family of ten children, could afford to give his eldest son but a slender education. He had bred him at a free-school, where he acquired what Latin he was master of; but how well he understood that language; or whether, after his leaving the school, he made a greater proficiency in it, has been disputed, and is a point very difficult to settle. However, it is certain, that Mr. John Shakespeare, our author's father, was obliged to withdraw him early from school, in order to have his assistance in his own employment, towards supporting the rest of the family.

"It

"It is without controversy," says Rowe, "that in his works we scarce find any traces that look like an imitation of the ancients. The delicacy of his taste, and the natural bent of his own genius, equal, if not superior, to some of the best of theirs, would certainly have led him to read and study them with so much pleasure, that some of their fine images would naturally have insinuated themselves into, and been mixed with, his own writings; so that his not copying at least something from them, may be an argument of his never having read them. Whether his ignorance of the ancients was disadvantageous to him or no, may admit of dispute; for, though the knowledge of them might have made him more correct, yet it is not improbable, but the regularity and deference for them which would have attended that correctness, might have restrained some of that fire, impetuosity, and even beautiful extravagance, which we cannot help admiring in Shakespeare."

As to his want of learning, Mr. Pope makes the following just observation: That there is certainly a vast difference between learning and languages. "How far he was ignorant of the latter, I cannot," says he, "determine; but it is plain he had much reading, at least, if they will not call it learning: nor is it any great matter if a man has knowledge, whether he has it from one language or from another. Nothing is more evident than, that he had a taste for natural philosophy, mechanics, ancient and modern history, poetical learning, and mythology. We find him very conversant in the customs, rites and manners of the Romans. In Coriolanus and Julius Cæsar, not only the spirit, but the manners, of the Romans, are exactly drawn; and still a nicer distinction is shewn between the manners of the Romans in the time of the former and the latter. His reading in the ancient historians is no
less

less conspicuous, in many references to particular passages; and the speeches copied from Plutarch in Coriolanus, may as well be made instances of his learning, as those copied from Cicero in the Cataline of Ben Jonson.

" The manners of other nations in general, the Ægyptians, Venetians, French, &c. are drawn with equal propriety. Whatever object of nature, or branch of science, he either speaks or describes, it is always with competent, if not extensive knowledge. His descriptions are still exact, and his metaphors appropriated, and remarkably drawn, from the nature and inherent qualities of each subject."

Warburton, bishop of Gloucester, has strongly contended for Shakespeare's learning, and has produced many imitations and parallel passages with ancient authors; in which I am inclined to think him right, and shall therefore produce a few instances of it. "He always," says Mr. Warburton, "makes an ancient speak the language of an ancient. So Julius Cæsar, act i. scene 2.

———Ye Gods! it doth amaze me
A man of such a feeble temper should
So get the start of the majestic world,
And bear the palm alone.

This noble image is taken from the Olympic games. " This majestic world," is a fine periphrasis of the Roman empire; majestic, because the Romans ranked themselves on a footing with kings; and a world, because they called their empire Orbis Romanus; but the whole story seems to allude to Cæsar's great exemplar, Alexander, who, when he was asked, Whether he would run the course of the Olympic games? replied, " Yes, if the racers were kings." So again, in Anthony and Cleopatra,

Cleopatra, act i. scene 1. Anthony says, with an astonishing sublimity,

Let Rome in Tyber melt, and the wide arch
Of the raz'd empire fall.

Taken from the Roman custom of raising triumphal arches to perpetuate their victories.

And again, act iii. scene 4. Octavia says to Anthony, of the difference between him and her brother,

———Wars 'twixt you twain would be
As if the world should cleave, and that slain men
Should solder up the rest.

This thought seems taken from the story of Curtius leaping into the chasm in the Forum, in order to close it; so that, as that was closed by one Roman, if the whole world were to cleave, Romans only could solder it up. The metaphor of soldering is extremely exact, according to Mr. Warburton; for, says he, " as metal is soldered up by metal that is more refined than that which it solders; so the earth was to be soldered by men, who are only a more refined earth."

But there are several places which one cannot forbear thinking a translation from classic writers. In the Tempest, act v. scene 11. Prospero says,

——— I have
Called forth the mutinous winds,
And, 'twixt the green sea, and the azur'd vault,
Set roaring war; to the dread rattling thunder
Have I given fire, and rifted Jove's stout oak
With his own bolt; the strong bas'd promontory
Have I made shake; and by the spurs pluckt up
The pine and cedar; graves, at my command,
Have

Have wak'd their sleepers, op'd and let them forth
By my so potent art.

So Medea, in Ovid's Metamorphoses.

Stantia concutio cantu freta; nubila pello,
Nubilaque induco, ventos abigoque, vocoque,
Vivaque saxa sua convulsaque robora terra
Et sylvas moveo; jubeoque emiscere montes,
Et mugire solum, manesque exire sepulchris.

The latest and most ingenious writer upon the the critical dispute respecting our author's learning, is Mr. Farmer of Emanuel college, Cambridge, who in his essay on this subject, has thrown out a presumptive proof that he was not so well acquainted with the learned languages as to read the Greek and Roman authors. Mr. Farmer mentions several English translations of classical writers extant in Shakespear's time, from which source he very naturally supposes he drew his imitations of particular passages in the antients, and he specifies particular references in his plays to some of these translations, from whence he concludes, that the studies of Shakespeare were confined to nature and his own language. Here we wish to rest the evidence on this undecided question; without drawing any conclusion of our own: that we may return to the more direct line of our duty; the narrative of the incidents of his life.

Upon his quitting the grammar school, he seems to have entirely devoted himself to that way of living which his father pursued; and, in order to settle in the world in a family manner, he thought fit to marry while he was yet very young. His wife was the daughter of one Hatchway, said to have been a substantial yeoman in the neighbourhood of Stratford.

In this kind of domestic obscurity he continued for some time, till, by an unhappy instance of misconduct, he was obliged to quit the place of his nativity, and take shelter in London; which fortunately proved the occasion of displaying his sublime genius for dramatic poetry. He had the misfortune to fall into ill company. Among these were some who made a frequent practice of deer-stealing, and who engaged him more than once in robbing a park that belonged to Sir Thomas Lucy, of Charlecot, near Stratford; for which he was prosecuted by that gentleman, as he thought, somewhat too severely; and, in order to revenge himself for this supposed ill usage, he made a ballad upon him; and, this, probably the first essay of his poetry, is lost; but it is said to have been so very bitter, that it redoubled the prosecution against him to that degree, that he was obliged to leave his business and family for some time, and to seek for employment in London.

This Sir Thomas Lucy was, it is said, afterwards ridiculed by Shakespeare, under the well known character of Justice Shallow. It was at this time, and upon this accident, that he is said to have made his first acquaintance in the playhouse.

Concerning Shakespeare's first mean occupation at the playhouse, we have the following curious particulars taken from unquestionable authorities: when he came to London he was without money and friends; and, being a stranger, he knew not to whom to apply, nor by what means to support himself. At that time, coaches not being in use, as gentlemen were accustomed to ride to the playhouse, Shakespeare, driven to the last necessity, attended at the door, and picked up a little money by taking care of the gentlemens horses who came to the play. He became eminent, even in that humble station, and was taken notice of for his diligence

diligence and skill in it. He had quickly more business than he himself could manage, and at last hired boys under him, who were known by the name of Shakespeare's boys. And though he soon found means of acting in his proper sphere, that of a dramatic writer, yet as long as the custom of going to the theatre on horseback continued, the waiters who held the horses retained the appellation of Shakespeare's boys.

Some of the players accidentally conversing with him, found him possessed of an admirable fund of wit, and talents adapted to the stage, and astonished at this unexpected discovery, they introduced and recommended him to the company, into whose society he was admitted, but in a very humble walk, and upon low terms; however, he did not long remain so, for he soon distinguished himself, if not as an extraordinary actor, at least as a fine writer. His name is printed, as the custom was in those times, amongst those of the other players, before some old plays, but without any particular account of what cast of characters he used to play; and after the most diligent researches, it appears, that the most considerable part he ever performed, was the Ghost, in his own historical tragedy of Hamlet.

It would undoubtedly afford great satisfaction to the curious to be able to ascertain from proper authorities, what was the first poetical essay of the immense genius of Shakespeare, that it might be traced through its gradual progressions to that summit of perfection it at length attained. But here likewise we are left in the dark.

The highest date which Rowe has been able to trace, is Romeo and Juliet, in 1597, when the author was thirty-three years old; and Richard II. and III. the next year.

Yet

Yet though the order of time in which his several pieces were written be generally uncertain, there are passages in some few of them, that seem to fix their dates. So the chorus at the end of the fourth act of Henry V. by a compliment very handsomely turned to the earl of Essex, shews the play to have been written when that nobleman was the queen's general in Ireland; and his eulogium upon queen Elizabeth, and her successor king James, in the latter end of Henry VIII. is a proof of that play's being written after the accession of the latter of these two princes to the throne of England.

Whatever the particular times of his writings were, the people of the age he lived in, who began to grow wonderfully fond of diversions of this kind, could not but be highly pleased to see a genius arise amongst them, of so pleasurable, so rich, and so abundant a vein, capable of furnishing variety of their favourite entertainments.

Besides the advantage which Shakespeare had over all men in the article of wit, he was of a sweet, gentle, amiable disposition, and was a most agreeable companion; by which he endeared himself to all who knew him, both as a friend and as a poet; so that he was introduced into the best company, and conversed with the finest characters of his time.

Queen Elizabeth had several of his plays acted before her; and she was too quick a discerner of merit, to suffer Shakespeare's to escape her notice. It is assuredly, that maiden princess, whom he thus describes

———A fair vestal, throned by the west.
     Midsummer Night Dream.

Queen Elizabeth was so well pleased with the admirable character of Falstaff, in the two parts of Henry IV. that she commanded him to continue it in one play more, and to make him in love. This is said to have been the occasion of his writing the Merry Wives of Windsor. And here I cannot help observing, That a poet seldom succeeds in any subject assigned him, so well as in that which is his own choice, and where he has the liberty of selecting.

Nothing is more certain, than that Shakespear has failed in the Merry Wives of Windsor: and, though that comedy is not without merit, yet it falls short of his other plays in which Falstaff is introduced; the knight not being half so witty in the Merry Wives of Windsor as in king Henry IV. nor the character so well sustained throughout.

It appears by the epilogue to Henry IV. that the part of Falstaff was written originally under the name of Oldcastle. Some of that family being then remaining, the queen was pleased to command him to alter it; upon which he made use of the name of Falstaff. The first offence was indeed avoided; but I am not sure whether the author might not be somewhat to blame in his second choice, since it is certain that Sir John Falstaff, who was a knight of the garter, and a lieutenant-general, was a person of distinguished merit in the wars against France, in the reigns of Henry V. and Henry VI.

Besides the royal patronage, Shakespeare received many great and uncommon favours from the generous earl of Southampton, so famous in history for his friendship to the unfortunate earl of Essex. It was to that nobleman he dedicated his poem of Venus and Adonis; and it is reported, that his lordship gave our author a thousand pounds to enable him to accomplish a purchase he heard he had a mind to make. A bounty, at that time, very
consider-

considerable, as money was then valued. There are few instances of such liberality in our times.

We have no clear account when Shakespeare quitted the stage for a private life. Some have thought that Spenser's Thalia, in the Tears of the Muses, where she laments the loss of her Willy, in the comic scene, relates to our poet's abandoning the stage: but it is well known that Spenser himself died in the year 1598; and five years after this, we find Shakespeare's name among the actors in Ben Johnson's Sejanus, which first made its appearance in 1603; nor could he then have any thoughts of retiring, since, that very year, a licence, by king James I. was granted to him, with Burbage, Philips, Hemmings, Condel, &c. to exercise the art of playing comedies, tragedies, &c. as well at their usual house, called the Globe, on the Bank-side, Southwark, as in any other part of the kingdom, during his majesty's pleasure. This licence is printed in Rymer's Fœdera. Besides, it is certain Shakespeare did not write Macbeth till after the accession of king James I. which he did as a compliment to him, as he there embraces the doctrine of witches; of which his majesty was so fond, that he wrote a book called Dæmonalogy, in defence of their existence; and likewise, at that time, began to touch for the evil; which Shakespeare has taken notice of, and paid him a fine-turned compliment upon it. So that the passage in Thalia, if it relates at all to Shakespeare, must hint at some occasional recess which he made for a time.

What particular friendships he contracted with private men, we cannot at this time know, more than that every one who had a true taste for merit, and could distinguish men, had generally a just value and esteem for him. His uncommon can-

dor

dor and good nature muſt certainly have inclined all the gentler part of the world to love him, as the power of his wit obliged the men of the moſt refined knowledge and polite learning, to admire him.

His acquaintance with Ben Jonſon began with a remarkable piece of humanity and good nature. Mr. Jonſon, who was, at that time, altogether unknown to the world, had offered one of his plays to the ſtage, in order to have it acted; and the perſon into whoſe hands it was put, after having turned it careleſly over, was juſt upon returning it to him, with an ill-natured anſwer; that it would be of no ſervice to their company; when Shakeſpeare luckily caſt his eye upon it, and found ſomething of ſuch merit in it, as to engage him firſt to read it through, and afterwards to recommend Mr. Jonſon, and his writings, to the public.

The latter part of our author's life was ſpent in eaſe and retirement; he had the good fortune to acquire a decent competency; and he reſided ſome years before his death at his native town, Stratford upon Avon, in a handſome houſe he had purchaſed, to which he gave the name of *New Place*; he had likewiſe the good fortune to ſave it from the flames, when a dreadful fire conſumed the greateſt part of the town in 1614. His pleaſant wit and good-nature engaged him the acquaintance, and intitled him to the friendſhip of the gentlemen of the neighbourhood. It is ſtill remembered in that country, that he had a particular intimacy with one Mr. Combe, an old gentleman, noted for his wealth, avarice, and uſury. It happened that, in a pleaſant converſation amongſt their common friends, Mr. Combe merrily told Shakeſpeare, that he fancied he intended to write his epitaph, if he happened to out-live him; and ſince he could not know what might be ſaid of him when dead, he
deſired

desired it might be done immediately; upon which Shakespeare gave him these lines:

Ten in the hundred lies here ingraved,
'Tis an hundred to ten he is not saved:
If any man asketh, who lies in this tomb?
Oh! oh! quoth the devil, 'tis my John-a-Combe.

But the sharpness of the satire is said to have stung the man so severely, that he never forgave it.

In the beginning of the year 1616, Shakespeare made his will, in which he left 150 l. to his eldest daughter, Judith, to be paid to her within twelve-months after his decease; and 150 l. more to be paid to her three years after the date of his will. But he appointed his youngest daughter, who was his favourite, and her husband Dr. John Hall, a physician of great repute in the county, joint-executors; bequeathing to them the best part of his estate. He also left legacies to his sister Joan, and her three sons; ten pounds to the poor of Stratford; his sword to Mr. Thomas Combe, and rings to his old associates in the play-house, Hemmings, Burbage, and Condel.

He died in April of the same year, and was interred on the north-side of the chancel, in the great church of Stratford, where a handsome monument was erected for him, on which the following distich is inscribed:

Judicio Pylium, genio Socratem, arte Maronem,
Terra tegit, populus mæret, Olympus habet.

And, on the grave-stone, in the pavement, underneath, are these lines:

Good

Good friend, for Jesus' sake forbear,
To dig the dust inclosed here.
Blest be the man that spares these stones,
And curs'd be he that moves my bones.

In the year 1740, a very noble monument was erected to the memory of our immortal bard, in Westminster-Abbey, at the public expence. For this purpose, his tragedy of Julius Cæsar was performed at the Theatre-Royal in Drury-Lane, on the 28th of April, 1738. The tickets for admission were fixed at an extraordinary price. The earl of Burlington, Dr. Mead, Mr. Pope, and Mr. Fleetwood, patentee of the theatre, were appointed trustees upon this occasion, and under their direction the monument was designed by Mr. Kent, and executed by Scheemakers, an eminent statuary.

The figure of Shakespeare is a whole length, in white marble, dressed in the habits of his time; reclining on the right arm, which is supported by a pedestal, from the top of which issues a scroll, having the following lines of his TEMPEST inscribed thereon:

The cloud-capt towers, the gorgeous palaces,
The solemn temples, the great globe itself;
Yea, all which it inhabit shall dissolve,
And, like the baseless fabric of a vision,
Leave not a wreck behind.

It is to be lamented, that so few incidents of the life of Shakespeare have been handed down to posterity; but this may easily be accounted for, from the little vicissitude to which it was subject. A single accident carried him to London; and here the constant exertion of his great abilities, conducted him by an easy regular transition, from indigence and obscurity to competency and fame: his found judgment, suggested to him the felicity of retirement, as soon as he had accomplished his moderate wishes; and here the scene of active life closing, no extraordinary occurrences happened to swell the annals of his peaceful days.

But his immortal works have afforded employment for some of the ablest writers of the present century. Of whose labours we shall give a concise account, referring the reader for better satisfaction to the several editors of his dramatic works, whose voluminous annotations, criticisms, and various readings, cannot be brought within the compass of this work.

It is generally agreed, that only eleven of his plays were printed while the author was living, and that these were neither revised by him, nor published under his inspection. It is likewise observed, by Dr. Samuel Johnson, " that he has suffered more than any other writer since the use of types, from his own negligence of fame, or perhaps by that superiority of mind, which despised its own performances, when it compared them with its powers; and judged those works unworthy to be preserved, which the critics of following ages were to contend for the fame of restoring and explaining."

The folio edition, in which all the plays we now receive as Shakespeare's, were first collected, was published by the two players, Hemmings and Condel, in 1623, seven years after the death of their author. From this period to 1714, no critic of superior genius attempted " to restore and explain:" in that year, the celebrated Mr. Rowe published an edition, but by more modern critics, it is said, that this is a very defective one, the plays being left exactly in the same incorrect state in which the editor found them; all he has done therefore, is to add notes, not much esteemed by the judicious.

In

In 1721, Mr. Pope printed a new edition, with several corrections and emendations; but he gained little or no reputation, for this very reason, that he pointed out his defects, at a time, when a false zeal for Shakespeare first began to shew itself: Pope unluckily, but with great truth observed, that as he had written better, so he had perhaps written worse than any other English dramatic writer. This from a brother poet was then ascribed to envy, but now, when prejudice and the idle vanity of one man, have taught the present generation to idolize Shakespeare, it is downright profanation.

'In 1733, Mr. Theobald published another edition in 8vo, which is one of the best; it was reprinted in 12mo in 1757, and again very lately. In 1744, Sir Thomas Hanmer, Bart. published a pompous edition in 4to, at Oxford, with emendations. In 1747, Warburton, bishop of Gloucester, published another edition in 8vo, with Pope's and his own notes. In 1765, a learned, critical edition, replete with typographical errors, because the editor is too great a man to attend to such minutiæ, was published by Dr. Samuel Johnson. In 1768, a correct edition in small 8vo was published by Edward Capell, Esq; and to close the list, Dr. Johnson, having found out an indefatigable coadjutor, in Mr. Steevens, a gentleman blessed with affluence and leisure, an adorer of Shakespeare, and a judicious, candid writer; they have jointly produced a very correct edition indeed, with respect to typography, but Mr. Steevens has been prevented by his idolatrous reverence for Shakespeare, and his unlimited veneration for Johnson, from doing the greatest honour to Shakespeare's genius, by expunging what could not be, what certainly never was his.

Yet, if any regard ought to be paid to the censures past on our immortal bard, by learned foreigners, and even by such of his countrymen, who have not been blind to his defects, while they admired all his real excellencies; it should seem, that the hint thrown out by Pope, might have been made the ground of a chaste edition of Shakespeare, freed from all the low ribaldry and obscenity, which we have reason to believe was foisted in by the players, his cotemporaries, to suit the humour of the times. That great critic very sensibly observes, "that the folio edition of Hemmings and Condel, contains additions of trifling and bombast passages, not to be found in the edition published in his life-time: that Shakespeare himself complains of the players, adding to their parts in the delivery," which custom prevails shamefully to this hour. And it must be remembered, that when Shakespeare first made his appearance as an author, dramatic writing was at a very low ebb; good players held a higher rank in the public estimation, than writers for the stage, and our bard was under the pressure of indigent circumstances.

Let us suppose this to be the case at present with any modern dramatic writer (the very reverse of the truth) and should not we be pestered in print, with the low puns, witticisms, and additional oaths of Messrs. Shuter and Weston, ambitious to circulate amongst the public, and to transmit to posterity their precious *addenda*, which might hereafter be incorporated with the moral drama of the chaste and sentimental Cumberland.

Pope pursues this idea, by remarking, "that in the old editions of Romeo and Juliet, there is no hint of a great number of the mean conceits and ribaldries now to be found there. In others, the low scenes of mobs, plebeians, and clowns, are vastly shorter than at present;" and he illustrates his just criticism by a variety of circumstances, which plainly demonstrate, that the folio edition was printed

printed from play-houfe printed copies, one of which he fays he faw, with additions to the parts in writing.

Why then fhould we be angry with Voltaire or David Hume, for pointing out the irregularities, abfurdities, and deformities which leffen the reputation of Shakefpeare, by being fuffered to remain, even in the lateft editions of his works?

" Had the author," adds Mr. Pope, " publifhed his own works, after his retreat from the ftage, we fhould not only have been certain which plays were genuine, but we fhould have found in thofe that are, the errors leffened by fome thoufands. And how many low and vicious parts and paffages might no longer reflect on this great genius, but appear unworthily charged upon him."

I want no better authority to countenance an affertion, for which I fhould otherwife be charged with arrogance and prefumption by that haughty dictator in the regions of literature, Dr. Samuel Johnfon; who, having eftablifhed a name, now infults the public with political trafh that would difgrace the pen of a fchool-boy.

I boldly maintain then, that the time and expence beftowed by Warburton, Johnfon and others, on furcharging our author's works with puerile, erroneous notes and criticifms, under the idle pretext of reftoring and explaining, would have been much better employed in compofing and publifhing fuch a chafte edition of Shakefpeare, as prudent profeffors in univerfities and academies at home and abroad fhould not be afhamed to put into the hands, and recommend to the ftudy of their pupils.

It will be faid, that fuch an edition muft proceed upon conjecture and prefumption of what is, and what is not Shakefpeare's. My reply is, that moft of the ufelefs notes and criticifms of Warburton and Johnson, are founded on wild, improbable conjectures, and arbitrary determinations.

Now let me ask any rational admirer, not a senseless adorer of Shakespeare, if better service would not be done to the cause of British literature and to the memory of Shakespeare, should some able critic proceed upon probable conjecture, to expunge, abridge, correct and purify Shakespeare's works, than by printing volumes upon volumes of such puerile notes.

It is confessed, that many of our author's plays now extended to five, originally consisted of only three acts; why not reduce them for the sake of banishing scenes and passages hardly fit to be represented or repeated in a booth at a village fair? Why not put the text into the language of the times, and the obsolete expressions into notes, to be preserved only as the relics of antiquity?

I will assign, what I fear is the true cause; his late editors; and the great, the inimitable personifier of his principal characters on the stage, have been more solicitous to erect trophies to their own vanity, than to increase and preserve the reputation of their great master, by enabling him to stand the test of an enlightened age, in which, sound learning, unclogged with scholastic pedantry, and true taste refined from the dross of low ribaldry, puns, jests and obscenities, enable us not only to judge when the drama is noble, chaste, and elegant; but to distinguish between the glaring defects, and the astonishing beauties of even the immortal Shakespeare.

Shakespeare's widow survived him seven years, and his family became extinct in the third generation after him; for his eldest daughter married Mr. Thomas Quincey, by whom she had three sons, but they died without issue.

As

WILLIAM SHAKESPEARE.

As for Mrs. Hall, she left one child, a daughter, who was married to Thomas Nash, Esq; and afterwards to Sir John Bernard, of Abingdon, but she likewise died without issue.

We have only to add the following list of the dramatic works published under our author's name, distinguishing with an asterism those which the critics, with great reason, reject, as pieces improperly ascribed to him.

1. The Tempest, a Comedy, acted in the Black Fryars, with applause.
2. The two Gentlemen of Verona, a Comedy, written at the command of queen Elizabeth.
3. The First and Second Parts of king Henry IV. The character of Falstaff in these plays is justly esteemed a master-piece; in the second part is the coronation of king Henry V. These are founded upon English history.
4. The Merry Wives of Windsor, a Comedy, written at the command of queen Elizabeth.
5. Measure for Measure, a Comedy; the plot of this play is taken from a novel of Cynthio Giraldi.
6. The Comedy of Errors, founded upon the Mænechmi of Plautus.
7. Much-a-do About Nothing, a Comedy; for the plot see Ariosto's Orlando Furioso.
8. Love's Labour Lost, a Comedy.
9. Midsummer Night's Dream, a Comedy.
10. The Merchant of Venice, a Tragi-Comedy.
11. As You Like it, a Comedy.
12. The Taming of a Shrew, a Comedy.
13. All's Well that Ends Well. The story, from one of the novels of Boccace.
14. The Twelfth Night; or, What you will, a Comedy.

15. The Winter's Tale, a Tragi-Comedy; the plot of this play, is borrowed from Robert Green's novel of Doraftus and Faunia.

16. The Life and Death of King John, an hiftorical play.

17. The Life and Death of King Richard II. an hiftorical play.

18. The Life of King Henry V. an hiftorical play.

19. The Firft Part of King Henry VI. an hiftorical play.

20. The Second Part of King Henry VI. with the death of the good Duke Humphrey.

21. The Third Part of Henry VI. with the death of the Duke of York. Thefe three plays contain the whole reign of that unhappy monarch.

22. The Life and Death of Richard III. with the Landing of the Earl of Richmond, and the Battle of Bofworth-field.

23. The Hiftory of the Life of King Henry VIII. This piece clofes the hiftorical drama of our author with refpect to his native country.

24. Troilus and Creffida, a Tragedy; the plot from Chaucer.

25. Coriolanus, a Tragedy; the ftory from the Roman hiftory.

26. Titus Andronicus, a Tragedy.

27. Romeo and Juliet, founded on a real Tragedy, that happened about the beginning of the fourteenth century. The ftory, with all its circumftances, is related by Girolame Corte, in his hiftory of Verona. And our author has varied very little either in his names, characters, or other circumftances, from truth and matter of fact; indeed this was his general rule, with refpect to his hiftorical plays, which makes them the more valuable.

28. Timon of Athens, a Tragedy; the plot from Lucian's Dialogues.

29. Julius

29. Julius Cæsar, a Tragedy.

30. The Tragedy of Macbeth; the plot from Buchanan, and other Scotch historians.

31. Hamlet, Prince of Denmark, a Tragedy.

32. King Lear, a Tragedy; the plot from Geoffrey of Monmouth.

33. Othello, the Moor of Venice, a Tragedy; the plot from Cynthio's Novels.

34. Anthony and Cleopatra; the story from Plutarch.

35. Cymbeline, a Tragedy; the plot partly from the Decameron of Boccace's novels; and partly from the ancient traditions of British history.

* 36. Pericles, Prince of Tyre; an historical play.

* 37. The London Prodigal, a Comedy.

* 38. The Life and Death of Thomas Lord Cromwell, the favourite of King Henry VIII.

* 39. The History of Sir John Oldcastle, the good Lord Cobham, a Tragedy. See Fox's Book of Martyrs.

* 40. The Puritan; or, the Widow of Watling-street, a Comedy.

* 41. A Yorkshire Tragedy; this is rather an Interlude, than a Tragedy, being very short, and not divided into acts.

* 42. The Tragedy of Locrine, the eldest Son of King Bruins. See the story in Milton's history of England.

The LIFE of
WILLIAM CAMDEN.

[A. D. 1551, to 1623.]

Including Memoirs of Sir THOMAS BODLEY, Founder of the Bodleian Library.

THE celebrated antiquary and hiftorian, Mr. William Camden, was the fon of Sampfon Camden of Litchfield, who fettled in London, where our author was born in 1551; the rudiments of education he received at Chrift's-hofpital; but at twelve years of age, having been greatly injured in his health by the plague, he was fent to Iflington for the benefit of the air, where he remained for fome time in fo languid a condition, that he was unable to purfue his ftudies. But upon his recovery, he went to St. Paul's-fchool, till he was fifteen years of age, and was then fent to Oxford, and admitted a fervitor in Magdalen college: here he finifhed his claffical learning in the fchool belonging to the college, under the care of Dr. Thomas Cooper, afterwards bifhop of Lincoln. Being difappointed of a demy's place in this college, he removed to Broadgate-hall, now Pembroke college,

lege, and continued his academical studies upwards of two years, under that able preceptor Dr. Thomas Thornton, who, entertaining sentiments of esteem and friendship for young Camden, became his first patron; and when the doctor was promoted to a canonry of Christ-church, he took his pupil with him, made him his companion, and lodged him in his own apartments.

The number of Camden's friends soon increased, by whose persuasion, he stood candidate for a fellowship in All-Soul's college; but the influence of the popish party prevailing in that society, the election was carried against him. In 1570, he met with a more severe mortification, being refused the degree of bachelor of arts, but no reason is assigned for this extraordinary circumstance.

About this time, he formed a close friendship with Richard and George Carew, gentlemen of respectable families and considerable fortunes in Devonshire, the latter of whom was created earl of Totness by James I. His new friends were antiquarians, and conversing with them, gave Camden an inclination to study this branch of history; with which he was at length so charmed, that he says, " he could never hear any thing mentioned relating to that subject, without more than ordinary attention." The antiquities of his own country were the objects of his laudable researches; and both before and after he left the university, he made frequent excursions, sometimes in company with the Carews, and at others alone, to the different counties of England, to procure informations and materials towards forming those collections from which he afterwards composed his celebrated work, intitled, BRITANNIA.

In 1571, he accepted a pressing invitation from two worthy divines, Dr. Gabriel Goodman, dean
of

of Westminster, and Dr. Godfrey Goodman, his brother, to settle near them in Westminster; and they undertook to supply him with books, and every accommodation of life at their expence, till he should meet with preferment suitable to his merit. In 1573, he went to Oxford, and staid there near two years; during which time, he took up his degree of bachelor of arts, without opposition; and in 1575, by the interest of his friend the dean, he was appointed second master of Westminster school; in which station he greatly distinguished himself, and strengthened his connections in life. He could now only devote his leisure hours to his favourite study, yet he had already made such a progress in it, that his reputation, as an antiquary, daily increased, and procured him the esteem and friendship of men of the first eminence in the learned world, both at home and abroad. Hotman, the celebrated French civilian and antiquarian; Justus Lipsius of Brussels, a most learned critic; James Dousa, or Vander-Doos, the younger, of the Hague, eminent for his Latin poetry; and Gruter of Antwerp, a famous critic and antiquarian, were all admirers of our author's talents for history and antiquities, and kept up a constant correspondence with him. But the chief promoters of his BRITANNIA were Sir Philip Sidney, who furnished him with some valuable materials, and made him many considerable presents; and Abraham Ortellius of Antwerp, the most celebrated geographer of the age, who visited England, and being introduced to Camden, was so struck with some specimens of his learned criticisms on historical subjects, that he importuned him by all means to complete and publish an history of the ancient state of Britain. Accordingly, in compliance with the solicitations of such respectable friends, with unwearied

wearied affiduity and clofe application he collated every hiftorical or curious anecdote to be found, difperfed in the works of the ancients refpecting the Britifh ifles: with the fame attention he examined all the hiftories of Britain then extant in our language, or written in Latin by our own countrymen: he likewife purchafed feveral valuable manufcripts, and he fearched all old records in the public offices; in fine, he vifited all the repofitories of learning in the kingdom, for information concerning the ancient hiftory of his country; and he infpected on the fpot, every monument of antiquity, which could ferve to illuftrate his work.

In 1581, the learned Jurifconfult, Barnaby Briffon, prefident of the parliament of Paris, who was affaffinated by the Leaguers in 1591, came to England on public affairs, and formed an intimacy with Camden, to whom he communicated fome material informations from ancient manufcrips in the French libraries; and this learned critic always fpoke in the higheft terms of veneration and refpect, for the great abilities of Camden.

At length, after ten years of indefatigable induftry, the firft edition of his BRITANNIA, in Latin, appeared in 1586, and in one volume, 8vo. The title in Englifh is, " Britain, or a Chorographical Defcription of the flourifhing Kingdoms of England, Scotland, and Ireland, with the adjacent Iflands, from the moft remote antiquity."

This elaborate work was dedicated to lord Burleigh, and the author gratefully acknowledges the kind patronage of that celebrated ftatefman, who, we may obferve by this inftance, was an encourager of every ufeful branch of literature, though he did not fmile upon the mufes. Camden's reputation was now raifed fo high, that he was ftyled by fome foreign writers the Varro, by others, the Strabo, and

and Pausanias of Britain; and these encomiums had a happy effect on the generous mind of our author, inciting him to add every improvement to his performance, the subject would admit of. With this view, he resided, during the year 1589, in Devonshire, and passed part of the time at Harcomb, a village which gives title to a prebendary of the cathedral of Salisbury, and to which Camden had been presented this year, by his friend Dr. John Piers, bishop of the diocese. After having visited every part of the west of England, where any vestiges of antiquity were to be found, he proceeded to Wales, in company with the learned Dr. Godwin, afterwards bishop of Hereford; by whose assistance he made many valuable discoveries of the antiquities of this celebrated country, and inserted them in the fourth edition of his *Britannia*, which was published in 4to, in the course of the year 1590.

Dr. Graunt, the head master of Westminster school, dying in 1592, Camden was appointed to succeed him; and being at this time afflicted with an ague, he did not make any excursions in pursuit of his favourite plan till the summer vacation in 1593; he then visited Oxford, and carefully copied the heraldry and inscriptions of all the curious monuments in the churches and chapels of this famous city.

Our learned antiquary's next performance was, a Greek grammar for the use of Westminster school, which was the only grammar in use in all the public schools for above a century after his death; and so constant was the demand for it both at home and abroad, that a new edition was printed every year. His friends however, thought the office of a school-master rather too fatiguing for his constitution; and the confinement not well adapted

to

to his active genius. To relieve him therefore from a station which prevented the exertion of his admired talents for history and antiquities, they procured him a more suitable employment, through the interest of Sir Fulke Greville, who obtained him the honourable office of clarencieux the second king at arms, an appointment which excited the envy of Ralph Brooke, the York-herald, who had a claim from long service to the promotion Camden had obtained by superior interest. Mr. Brooke determined to gratify his spleen, by attacking his succesful rival in the tendereſt part, published a tract, intitled, " A discovery of certain errors published in print, in the much-commended Britannia." The errors detected were very trifling, chiefly respecting pedigrees, in which branch it might well be imagined the herald, after many years practice, was more critically exact, than our celebrated historian; and in the fifth edition of the Britannia, proper notice is taken of Mr. Brooke's attack, which in part is refuted; at the same time the candid author acknowledges, that it was not possible to compile a work of that nature, without some errors. In the end therefore, his reputation was not injured by this piece of ill-natured criticism. In 1600, our indefatigable author undertook a journey to the North of England, accompanied by Sir Robert Cotton, the founder of the Cottonian library: they spent some time at Carlisle, and having surveyed every remarkable curiosity in that part of our island, they returned to London; and Camden, before the year closed, published, in small quarto, " A description of all the monuments of the kings, queens, nobles, and others in Westminster-Abbey, with their inscriptions; together with an historical account of the foundation of that church."

Mr.

Mr. Camden had long formed a plan for writing a civil history of England; but it is probable, that the change of affairs, upon the death of queen Elizabeth, prevented his carrying it into execution; for soon after that event, he sent his valuable manuscripts and printed copies, of the ancient historians of Britain, to Frankfort, where a new edition of the remains of these authors was printed and published under his correction, with the following title: " Anglica, Normannica, Hibernica, Cambrica, a veteribus descripta; ex quibus Asser Menevensis, Anonymus de vita Gulielmi Conquæstoris, Thomas Walsingham, Thomas de la More, Gulielmus Genuticensis, Giraldus Cambrensis. Plerique nunc in lucem editi ex bibliotheca Gulielmi Camdeni." This judicious restoration of such valuable authors, he dedicated to his constant friend Sir Fulke Greville. In 1605, he published, " Remains of a greater work concerning Britain, the inhabitants thereof, their languages, names, surnames, empreses, wife speeches, poesies and epitaphs." This curious tract chiefly relates to the habits, manners and customs of the ancient Britons and Saxons; and it is dedicated to Sir Robert Cotton, founder of the Cottonian library, but for what reason is not known; it is subscribed only with the final letters of our author's name E. N.

In 1606, we find Mr. Camden, for the first time, employed in the service of a royal patron, James I. who being desirous to expose to the eyes of all Europe the machinations of his popish enemies, and at the same time to justify the rigorous measures which were necessarily taken to secure the three kingdoms against future attempts of the same horrid nature as the gunpowder-plot then lately discovered; thought proper to cause a kind of manifesto

to

to be drawn up in Latin, in order to be sent abroad and dispersed by the British ministers at foreign courts, so as to be circulated to all parts of Europe; and our historian having at this time the reputation of being the most elegant and correct Latin writer in England, he was ordered to draw up this manifesto, in which likewise the foreign protestant churches were assured of his Majesty's protection, in case the designs of the popish party to extirpate the reformed religion, should be manifested by any act of open violence. This piece was published in 1607, and does great honour to Camden, not only with respect to the style, but to the masterly manner in which he has treated the subject of the memorial. The same year, he published the last perfect edition of his Britannia in folio, considerably enlarged and improved, and illustrated with maps; from which edition, all the translations in English, of any repute, have been made.

From this time to the year 1612, we have no account of this great man's literary labours, nor any anecdote concerning him, except that he had a fall from his horse, by which he hurt his leg so much, that he was confined for several months; and it is probable this accident might require a total remission of his studies for a time. But at the above-mentioned period, he was obliged to visit Oxford on a mournful occasion; to shew the last solemn token of respect to the manes of his deceased friend Sir Thomas Bodley.

This gentleman, who has endeared his name to latest posterity, by founding the noble library at Oxford, called after him, "*The Bodleian Library*," was the son of an eminent merchant at Exeter, who having early embraced the reformed religion, and being menaced with persecution on that account, fled with his son to Geneva, and remained there, during the turbulent reign of queen Mary.

Upon the accession of queen Elizabeth, they returned home, with the other protestant exiles; and young Bodley, having made a considerable progress at Geneva in divinity and the learned languages, was sent by his father to Magdalen college, Oxford; in 1563, he took his degree of master of arts; in 1565, he obtained a fellowship in Merton college; in 1569, he was elected one of the proctors of the university; and for a considerable time, during a vacancy, he supplied the place of university orator. His friends now having in view some preferment for him about the court, in 1576, he went abroad to make the tour of Europe, and perfect himself in the modern languages: he continued about four years on the continent, and upon his return, he applied himself to the study of history and politics to qualify himself for public employments; and he was very soon called upon to exert his talents in stations of great dignity and importance. From gentleman-usher to queen Elizabeth, he rose to be her Majesty's ambassador to the courts of Denmark and France; and her representative in the council of state of the United Provinces in 1588, where he managed the queen's affair so much to the satisfaction of the ministry at home, that he was continued in this high office till 1597, when all the public negociations with the states being successfully terminated, he was recalled. But instead of meeting with that reward for his eminent services he had a right to expect, he found his own interest declining with that of his patron the earl of Essex, and in a fit of disgust he retired from court and all public business; and though afterwards solicited, he never would accept of any new office under the government; but king James, on his

his accession, conferred on him the honour of knighthood.

To this retirement from the bustle of public life, the university of Oxford most probably stands indebted for the Bodleian library, justly esteemed one of the noblest in the world. The first step Sir Thomas Bodley took in this affair, was to write a letter to Dr. Ravis, vice-chancellor of the university, offering to rebuild the decayed fabric of the public library, to improve and augment the scanty collection of books contained in it; and to vest an annual income in the hands of the heads of the university for the purchase of books, and for the salaries of such officers as they should think it necessary to appoint. A suitable answer being returned, and this generous offer gratefully accepted, Sir Thomas Bodley immediately ordered the old building to be pulled down, and a new one erected, at his own expence; which being completed in about two years, he added to the old, a new collection of the most valuable books then extant, which he had ordered to be purchased in foreign countries; and having thus set the example, the nobility, the bishops, and several private gentlemen, made such considerable benefactions in books, that the room was not large enough to contain them. Upon which, Sir Thomas offered to make considerable additions to the building; and on the 19th of July, 1610, he laid the first stone of the new foundation, being accompanied by the vice-chancellor, and the heads of houses, with the usual solemnities upon such occasions; amongst which was a Latin oration in praise of the founder, pronounced by the university orator; which tribute of gratitude is still annually paid to his memory. Sir Thomas Bodley did not live to see this additional building completed, but he had the satisfaction t.on to know that it was intended, as soon as that was finished, to enlarge the plan of the whole edifice, and in the end to form a regular quadrangle; and as he knew his own fortune was inadequate to this great work, he made use of his interest with several persons of rank and fortune, and engaged them to make large presents to the university to forward this undertaking; to which he bequeathed his whole estate; he likewise drew up some excellent statutes for the regulation of the library, which seems to have been the last act of his life: he died on the 28th of January, 1612, and was buried in the chapel of Merton college, where a handsome monument was erected to his memory; and a 'statue was likewise put up in the library, at the expence of the earl of Dorset, when chancellor of the university.

Camden was so highly esteemed by Sir Thomas Bodley, that the university, upon the occasion of his attending the funeral of their benefactor, offered him the honorary degree of master of arts, but he refused it; probably resenting the affront that had formerly been put upon him, when he solicited and could not obtain his degree of bachelor of arts. In 1615, Camden made amends for the long suspension of his literary talents, by publishing his " Annals of the reign of queen Elizabeth to the year 1589, in Latin." He had begun this admired work in the year 1597, by the desire of lord Burleigh, who supplied him with many valuable materials. But, after the death of that minister, being desirous to complete his Britannia, he laid it aside, till he had finished his favourite work; and then receiving fresh materials from his friend Sir Thomas Bodley, who was possessed of a great number of state-papers, he published the Annals as far as he had proceeded. In the year 1617, he
completed

completed them by bringing the history down to the death of Elizabeth; but imagining there were some passages in this continuation which might not be well received by king James's court, he would not suffer it to appear while he lived. The first edition of the continuation was published at Leyden in 1625, in octavo. And the first edition of the annals complete in folio, at London, in 1627. But modern historians having made very valuable discoveries, and thrown new lights upon the history of England, at the æra comprised in these annals, they have now lost their original merit.

Camden, now grown old and infirm, laid aside his pen, and following the steps of his late worthy friend Sir Thomas Bodley, he resolved to devote part of the fortune he had acquired, to the encouragement of that branch of literature for which he himself was so eminent. In this view he founded a professorship of history at the university of Oxford, and settled a salary of 140 *l. per annum* on the professor, who reads public lectures on history in Term-time; and having nominated Mr. Degory Wheare, a gentleman who had been educated at the university, and had distinguished himself by his accurate knowledge of history, to be his first professor; it seemed as if the business of his life had ended with this institution, for in the same year, on the 18th of August, 1623, as he was sitting in his chair in his study, he suddenly lost the use of his hands and feet, and fell down upon the floor; he received no apparent hurt from this accident, and he even recovered the use of his limbs; but the disorder terminated in a fever, with which he languished till the 9th of November, when he died, at his house at Chislehurst in Kent.

His

His remains were depofited in Weftminfter-Abbey, in the fouth-ifle, near the learned Ifaac Cafaubon, of Geneva, a moft eminent critic on the works of the ancients, who died at London in 1614. Camden's funeral was conducted with great pomp; the college of heralds attending in their proper habits; feveral of the nobility and other perfons of diftinction walked in the proceffion, and a funeral fermon in Latin was preached by Dr. Sutton, the fub-dean. A handfome monument was likewife erected to his memory, which was defaced, as it is faid, by a young gentleman, who in refentment of fome reflection thrown out by Camden againft the reputation of his mother, broke off the nofe from his effigies, but it has been lately repaired at the expence of the univerfity of Oxford.

Mr. Camden's character, as a writer and as a man, acquired him the higheft degree of reputation, both at home and abroad; and every man of eminence for any branch of learning, cultivated his correfpondence and friendfhip. To have travelled into England, and not to have vifited him, would have been deemed fuch an omiffion in foreigners of note, that to avoid the imputation of it, he ufed to write his name, in their diaries or pocket-books, in teftimony of having feen them. And as to his own countrymen, the greateft ornaments of human learning, his cotemporaries, mention their veneration for him, and account it an honour to rank themfelves in the number of his friends. Befides, the works already mentioned, a large collection of his Latin letters, with fome fmall tracts, have been publifhed by Hearne, from the collations of Dr. Smith.

As to his capital performance the BRITANNIA, the beft Englifh edition is that publifhed by Edmund Gibfon,

Gibson, bishop of London, in 1695, which contains considerable alterations, improvements, and additions. It has been reprinted since the editor's death, with other corrections and additions, of which a work of this nature will always admit.

⁎ *Authorities.* Biog. Britan. Life of Camden, by Gibson, prefixed to his Britannia.

END of VOL. II.

www.ingramcontent.com/pod-product-compliance
Lightning Source LLC
Chambersburg PA
CBHW022045230426
43672CB00008B/1070